Interventionist Management Accounting Research

Interventionist research has been proposed as one way of increasing societal impact of management accounting (MA) research. However, there are no guidelines regarding what sort of phenomena would be the most suitable ones to be studied using research interventions. This book builds on the methodological literature of interventionist management accounting research, as well as the published studies applying it.

Through selected case studies, *Interventionist Management Accounting Research* shows how societal impact of MA research can be increased by not only applying the interventionist research (IVR) approach, but also looking into how MA is used in the borderlines between MA and other organizational functions. In many cases, MA research can provide tools and concepts helping to understand contemporary trends within the business environment, thereby naturally providing potential for increasing the societal impact of scholarly work. In particular, this book discusses how to position empirical research endeavors with interventionist elements in a way to ensure important theory contributions with outcomes interesting also outside the MA academia, whether that means MA practitioners, managers in general, or scholars in other fields of management.

Aimed at primarily researchers, academics, and students in the fields of research methodology, management accounting, and interventionist research, this book provides methodological guidance on how to execute research projects with interventionist elements, aiming at strong theory contribution with broader societal impacts. Focusing on research in accounting and management, this book also provides interesting insights to scholars and doctoral students in other fields of management research.

Jouni Lyly-Yrjänäinen is a University Lecturer in Industrial Management at Tampere University of Technology, Finland.

Petri Suomala is Vice President of Teaching and Learning Services at Tampere University of Technology, Finland.

Teemu Laine is Associate Professor at Tampere University of Technology, Finland.

Falconer Mitchell is Professor Emeritus of Management Accounting at the University of Edinburgh, UK.

Routledge Studies in Accounting

For a full list of titles in this series, please visit www.routledge.com/Routledge-Studies-in-Accounting/book-series/SE0715

Interventionist Management Accounting Research

Theory Contributions with Societal Impact

Jouni Lyly-Yrjänäinen,
Petri Suomala, Teemu Laine,
and Falconer Mitchell

LONDON AND NEW YORK

First published 2018 by Routledge

2 Park Square, Milton Park, Abingdon, Oxfordshire OX14 4RN

52 Vanderbilt Avenue, New York, NY 10017

Routledge is an imprint of the Taylor & Francis Group, an informa business

First issued in paperback 2019

Library of Congress Cataloging-in-Publication Data
A catalog record for this book has been requested

ISBN: 978-1-138-23104-7 (hbk)
ISBN: 978-0-367-88490-1 (pbk)

Typeset in Sabon
by Apex CoVantage, LLC

Contents

Figures and Tables

Figures

Tables

Preface

Interventionist research processes, in essence, are about making difference. Interventionist researchers acknowledge their role as active participants in events in practice, and seek to take advantage of such a role to better understand antecedents and impacts of changing the status quo. In this book, we focus especially on the interventionist research processes and their societal and theoretical impacts.

Unveiling the potential of the interventionist research processes has required support from and collaboration with several stakeholders, which is here gratefully acknowledged. The authors working at Tampere University of Technology (TUT) acknowledge the support of two projects. First, the book presents cases taking advantage of the project "Managing Service Impact, Engaging Facts and Feelings," funded by the Finnish Funding Agency for Technology and Innovation (TEKES), TUT, and participating companies. Second, one of the cases is based on the DIMECC: S4Fleet research project, and the authors greatly acknowledge the financial support of the Finnish Funding Agency for Innovation, TUT, and the companies, also in this project. Besides, the authors wish to thank all the colleagues at Cost Management Center for cooperation and effort in the projects underlying this book. Especially, we acknowledge the help of Mr. Vesa Tiitola in designing several pictures and tables of this book. Professor Falconer Mitchell wishes to thank University of Edinburgh and Royal Botanic Gardens Edinburgh for support during the research process as well as Dr. Alasdair Macnab for collaboration with the case work and write up.

Altogether, the authors want to thank the case companies' extremely valuable input, both in terms of research cooperation, and offering access to the interventionist research processes in the very core of this book.

Last but not least, the support of Routledge in various ways throughout the publication process of this book is gratefully acknowledged.

Finally, we do not see interventionist research necessarily as a special case in management accounting research. Instead, within management accounting research, there is an overall need for results with theoretical and societal impacts and implications. This ambitious aim is related to practically all management accounting research. Interventionist research is not a shortcut towards those impacts. We have to pay careful attention to designing and executing the research processes, and when needed taking the opportunities for creativity and iterations.

Tampere, March 20th, 2017
The Authors

Part I

Intervention as a Vehicle for Enhanced Societal Impact

1 Improving Societal Impact of Management Accounting Research

Management accounting (MA) is a discipline that helps refine data into knowledge, understanding, and wisdom for decision-makers both in profit and non-profit organizations. Management accounting, therefore, is an applied science (Kasanen et al. 1993), deeply rooted in real-life problems and decision-making contexts. Thus, an interesting question is why managers and other MA practitioners often see academia as not providing interlocutors they would prefer to interact with. For some reason these two worlds seldom seem to find a connection; academics prefer to talk about their theories, whereas practitioners would like to have solutions to their more pragmatic problems. And, when academics seek for collaboration with companies, these companies are merely seen as research subjects or some sort of guinea pigs for theory development without much attempt for mutual collaboration. However, deep and intense collaboration with real-life companies and other organizations may (and often does) provide access to the most fascinating empirical data, unthinkable of at the initial stages of the collaboration, an opportunity neglected by the academics. When practitioners and academics work together on problems relevant to companies, based on our experience, such projects often tend to lead us researchers to questions that provide a starting point for some very interesting theoretical work, considered relevant not only by the managers in the company but also amongst a broader practitioner audience. At the same time, such cases provide interesting theory contributions, too. Altogether, there are so many interesting problems within the MA practice that such work should not be left only for consultants and business people.

The role of MA researchers within the evolution of the discipline is nothing new. In the 1980s some scholars were in the opinion that management accounting research had failed in providing theories of practical relevance (Hopwood 1983; Kaplan 1984; Kaplan 1986; Johnson and Kaplan 1987). Although field research gained popularity among management accounting researchers in the 1980s (Ferreira and Merchant 1992), it did not end the discussion regarding the pragmatic relevance of management accounting research. Another important academic debate on what management accounting research is or should be took place in the early 2000s (Zimmerman 2001;

Hopwood 2002; Ittner and Larker 2002; Luft and Shields 2002; Lukka and Mouritsen 2002). In those days, Mitchell (2002) pointed out the need for improved integration between MA researchers and practitioners. In addition, some later studies have also approached the issue of how to increase pragmatic relevance of MA research (e.g., Inaga and Schneider 2005; Malmi and Granlund 2009; Malmi 2016).

One methodological research stream introduced in the 1990s attempted to increase pragmatic relevance of MA research. Constructive research introduced by Kasanen et al. (1993) emphasized development of MA constructs solving problems identified in case companies participating in such collaborative research venues. The truth-value of these constructs was argued based on managers willing to implement such tools (i.e., commit resources to them), called a weak market test. In the best scenarios, the researchers were to argue how such MA constructs helped the organization improve its financial performance, fulfilling the prerequisites of a strong market test. In constructive research, the MA-related tool, model, or framework developed by the researcher was argued as the theory contribution of the study.

Constructive research, however, has not gained much foothold in the MA academia. One likely challenge has been to convince academic peers on whether the tool, model, or framework developed by the researcher is truly valid and can be generalized in a larger population. The idea of pragmatic truth—if it works it is true—faces the issue that an organization can prosper regardless of a framework developed by the researcher. Convincingly arguing ceteris-paribus in such a context becomes overwhelmingly difficult; there simply are too many variables impacting the financial success (or non-success) that pointing out the impact of one construct becomes practically impossible. In the worst-case scenario, the construct works and provides good financial outcomes (as expected) for the company, yet is cancelled out by some other factors the researcher had no influence over. In other words, such constructs often not only have intended but also unintended outcomes, and some of the outcomes that erode the utility value of the construct may be totally unrelated to the construct itself nor influenced by the researcher.

Interventionist Research for Pragmatic Relevance

Despite the difficulties in fulfilling the criteria set for the theory contributions (e.g., the idea of market test and the challenges in creating such a ceteris-paribus setup for the studies), constructive research was an important initiative in the attempt to find better connection between academics and practitioners. Later one of the authors behind the idea of constructivist MA research, Professor Kari Lukka from Turku School of Economics, together with Professor Sten Jönsson from University of Gothenburg, broadened the interest on connecting practitioners and academics by introducing the concept interventionist research (IVR). In IVR, the researcher still actively collaborates with the case organization, but her role is now seen more broadly both in terms of what to offer to the case organization and also regarding how to position the theory contribution (see Jönsson and Lukka 2007). Unlike constructivist research, interventionist MA research has gained some visibility in academia, though still remaining at the outskirts of the MA domain.

In 2006, Chartered Institute of Management Accountants (CIMA) announced their Interventionist Research Initiative, providing funding for projects using an interventionist research approach. As part of their interventionist research initiative, CIMA provided funding for a book focusing on practical experiences in conducting interventionist MA research (Suomala and Lyly-Yrjänäinen 2012). The book wrapped up the lessons learnt during the ten years of interventionist research collaboration with industry partners. In that book, the focus was on the interventionist research process, strength of intervention, and its focal point in the process of contributing to the MA domain, to be more precise.

Soon after the CIMA research initiative, *Qualitative Research in Accounting and Management* (QRAM) dedicated a special issue on the topic with the focus on (1) how to construct an interventionist study, (2) justify and position it methodologically, (3) execute such studies, and (4) how to theorize on what is going on in the field (Westin and Roberts 2010). In that special issue, Baard (2010) developed the epistemological foundations of IVR by linking the discussion to the intervention theory used in social sciences. In addition to the methodological discussion, empirical studies using IVR were provided by Dumay (2010), Sunding and Odenrick (2010), and Suomala et al. (2010). Finally, the special issue was concluded with a paper written by one of the architects of the IVR approach (Jönsson 2010).

A few years ago, in his final editorial, Professor Robert Scapens reflected back to his experience as an editor-in-chief of *Management Accounting Research* (Scapens 2014). In his editorial, he pointed out the concerns on how MA research contributes to the MA practices and acknowledged the calls for IVR. However, he also pointed out the challenges in combining theory with practice, a fact noticeable as an editor subjected to manuscripts following the IVR approach. He proposed to overcome this problem by exploring how the theoretical knowledge of the researcher can be combined with the 'craft knowledge' of the practitioners and, in that way, create theory contributions with pragmatic relevance.

Most recently, a stream of literature has emerged that seeks to examine the potential of combining an IVR approach with certain theoretical lenses, in order to increase the theoretical impact and relevance of the accounting research (see, e.g., Laine et al. 2016a; Lukka and Vinnari 2017; Rautiainen et al. 2017). Lukka and Vinnari (2017) and Laine et al. (2016a) have examined the IVR approach in use with different theoretical lenses (actor network theory in Lukka and Vinnari 2017, and pragmatic constructivism in Laine et al. 2016a) and concluded that the IVR approach holds potential when used together with approaches that feature different actors and their interplay. Quite essentially, in line with Suomala et al. (2014), the recent studies highlight that the interventionist researcher should be interpreted as one actor, with a multifaceted, yet active role that evolves over time (Laine et al. 2016a; Lukka and Vinnari 2017). Theoretical underpinnings related to such a role of the interventionist researcher represent interesting avenues for further studies (see, e.g., Laine et al. 2016 for the interventionist researcher as a boundary subject in organizational interfaces). Besides, as Rautiainen et al. (2017) recently pointed out, the relevance of IVR approach and its applications requires comprehensive examination from different perspectives, such as societal and theoretical perspectives, in addition to narrow 'market tests' adopted from a constructive research approach.

In sum, the debate around interventionist research has emphasized the importance of ensuring theory contributions, not only practically relevant constructs (Jönsson and Lukka 2007; Suomala and Lyly-Yrjänäinen 2012; Scapens 2014; Lukka and Vinnari 2017). In other words, descriptions of the cases (though supported with deep involvement in the field) alone do not make IVR research. Nevertheless, despite the published studies applying interventionist elements in them, hence providing theory contributions (see, e.g., Cullen et al. 2013; Suomala et al. 2014; Laine et al. 2016), the practical outputs developed by the researchers tend to remain only in very local contexts. In other words, while such projects enable theorizing, the new practices developed and also published are not diffusing into the business environment, not to speak of society more in general.

This brings us to the main topic of this book; can IVR be seen as a tool for not only contributing to the theory and practice but also impacting the society more generally? As pointed out by Flyvbjerg (2001), social science should not focus on providing a theoretical mirror for the society but rather provide a society with knowledge that can be used as input to the dialogue on topical social challenges and solutions. In the same spirit, instead of a theoretical mirror on MA practices, MA research should aim to provide the society with knowledge that could be used as input to the dialogue on topical social challenges and solutions. As Scapens pointed out in his final editorial (2014), research in most countries is funded from various government sources and, as a result, the questions concerning the societal impact of research work may become more relevant in the future.

Towards Improving the Societal Impact of MA Research

Interestingly, the discussion on pragmatic relevance seems to have focused (at least implicitly) on how interventionist MA research can contribute to the (1) MA practices in companies participating in these case studies or (2) MA practices in contexts similar to the published studies (see, e.g., Jönsson and Lukka 2007). The role of MA research can, however, be seen more broadly.

In this book, we wish to continue the discussion on pragmatic relevance by not only discussing how MA research can produce theories with relevance to MA practitioners or managers. On the contrary, we wish to set the target one step higher and discuss how empirical MA research can help to make an impact on the society more broadly, not just within the companies participating in these empirical inquiries or managers who find themselves in similar decision-making situations to published studies. We see interventionist research opening up interesting venues that enable theorizing with not only pragmatic relevance but also potential to impact the society more broadly. The book will be based on five case studies showing how interventionist MA research not only benefits the case companies and provides potential for theory contributions but also enables participation in contemporary societal discussions, hence providing a voice in the society. In doing so, the book acknowledges recent calls for impactful interventionist research in MA literature (Scapens 2014; Lukka and Vinnari 2017), and provides an encouraging, yet critical examination on the potential of IVR in producing relevant theoretical, practical, and societal contributions.

One case of the book comes from University of Edinburgh Business School. In that case, IVR is applied to find a practical solution to a problem posed by an external agency, hence making it a classic implementation of IVR. Professor Falconer Mitchell, also as a past Chairman of the CIMA Research Board, is among the active scholars who have brought up the need for improving integration and communication between management accounting research and practice (see, e.g., Mitchell 2002). He has been continuously involved in challenging, re-thinking, and refining the paradigmatic foundations of MA research, towards increased relevance in practice (see, e.g., Baldvinsdottir et al. 2010; Nørreklit et al. 2010), in line with the idea of the IVR.

Four cases of the book take advantage of research projects conducted by Cost Management Center (CMC), a research group in Tampere University of Technology employing about ten full-time researchers focusing on cost management and MA research projects. The research group was established in 1998 and has completed more than 50 long-term research projects. Since day one, research projects have involved some industrial partners, with the fieldwork typically focusing on development of cost management or management accounting and control practices more broadly. Uniquely, the research projects have focused on timely management challenges that could potentially be supported by management accounting, and the focus of the projects has been on managerial work outside the financial department. At the same time, importantly, all the projects have focused on accounting development, at least in a broad sense. Therefore, the research projects can be labeled as management accounting research, with versatile research, practical, and societal implications. Based on these research projects, dozens of refereed articles and in total more than 200 research papers have been published.

This development work carried out with companies has led into opportunities to deepen the researchers' access to interesting events taking place inside these organizations as well as mutual learning opportunities. In other words, the development work itself is not the main outcome of interventionist research processes. The development work serves rather as a starting point for interesting dialogue with management, thus providing access to new problems, with significant potential for theory contribution and societal impacts. These potential impacts are essentially the starting point of this book as well. Besides, the longitudinal process underlying the impacts of the IVR process highlights the need for better understanding the antecedents of different kinds of impacts of the IVR research. Besides, the evolving role of the interventionist researcher within the IVR processes requires further attention.

Indeed, there are some unique characteristics with regards to the research funding in Finnish universities. Especially in the universities of technology, a significant amount of research funding is channeled through the Finnish Funding Agency for Technology and Innovation (TEKES). Also, other sources of funding, such as EU programs and Academy of Finland, play an increasingly important role in funding research in engineering. However, due to the peculiarities of the funding structure, engineering research in Finland has a long tradition in industry-university collaboration.

CMC, being a management-accounting-focused research group within a university of technology with most researchers having an industrial engineering background, has since its beginning conducted 'engineering-style' research, characterized with close industry-university collaboration. Thus, quite naturally, all the projects conducted by CMC have included at least some interventionist elements in them, though in some cases complemented with interview studies and even survey studies. Altogether, the scholars involved in (CMC's) research projects have further refined and utilized different kinds of methods, within the IVR approach, in order to take full advantage of the emerging opportunities of the research projects. In addition to these opportunities, the companies and other organizations involved in the projects have taken advantage of different opportunities stemming from the research projects, including ideas for new offerings, commercialization of new products, adopting new practices in networks or within single organizations, not to mention various ways of producing and utilizing financial information in decision-making and managerial work. Due to the successful mutual learning processes among researchers and industrial organizations, the number of participant organizations and university partners that have been involved in the projects has significantly increased over time.

Altogether, this book builds on and elaborates upon the rationale of IVR as presented in the MA literature during the past decades. The authors of the book and their teams have been active contributors in refining and utilizing IVR in management accounting. This book, in particular, takes advantage of numerous interventions undertaken in different business contexts, in connection with timely business phenomena. The analyses of the IVR processes and their outcomes, including examinations on the role of the interventionist researchers along with the process, thus enable novel discussions on interventionist research and its theoretical and societal impacts. Such discussion represents the contribution of this book.

References

Baard, V., 2010. A critical review on interventionist research. *Qualitative Research in Accounting and Management*, 7(1), pp. 13–45.

Baldvinsdottir, G., Mitchell, F. and Nørreklit, H., 2010. Issues in the relationship between theory and practice in management accounting. *Management Accounting Research*, 21(2), pp. 79–82.

Cullen, J., Tsamenyi, M., Bernon, M. and Gorst, J., 2013. Reverse logistics in the UK retail sector: A case study of the role of management accounting in driving organisational change. *Management Accounting Research*, 24(3), pp. 195–276.

Dumay, J., 2010. A critical reflective discourse of an interventionist research project. *Qualitative Research in Accounting and Management*, 7(1), pp. 46–70.

Ferreira, L. and Merchant, K., 1992. Field research in management accounting and control: A review and evaluation. *Accounting, Auditing & Accountability Journal*, 5(4), pp. 3–34.

Flyvbjerg, B., 2001. *Making social science matter: Why social inquiry fails and how it can succeed again*. Cambridge University Press, Cambridge.

Hopwood, A., 1983. On trying to study accounting in the context in which it operates. *Accounting, Organizations and Society*, 8(2/3), pp. 287–305.

Hopwood, A., 2002. If only there were simple solutions, but here aren't: Some reflections on Zimmerman's critique of empirical management accounting research. *The European Accounting Review*, 11(4), pp. 777–785.

Inaga, E. and Schneider, B., 2005. The failure of accounting research to improve accounting practice: A problem of theory and lack of communication. *Critical Perspectives on Accounting*, 16(3), pp. 227–248.

Ittner, C. and Larker, D., 2002. Empirical managerial accounting research: Are we just describing management consulting practice? *The European Accounting Review*, 11(4), pp. 787–794.

Johnson, T. and Kaplan, R., 1987. *Relevance lost: The rise and fall of management accounting*. Harvard Business School Press, Boston.

Jönsson, S., 2010. Interventionism—an approach for the future. *Qualitative Research in Accounting and Management*, 7(1), pp. 124–134.

Jönsson, S. and Lukka, K., 2007. There and back again: Doing IVR in management accounting, in: Chapman, C., Hopwood, A. and Shields, M. (Eds.), *Handbook of management accounting research*, Vol. 1. Elsevier, Amsterdam, pp. 373–397.

Kaplan, R., 1984. The evolution of management accounting. *The Accounting Review*, 59(3), pp. 390–418.

Kaplan, R., 1986. The role of empirical research in management accounting. *Accounting, Organizations and Society*, 11(4/5), pp. 429–452.

Kasanen, E., Lukka, K. and Siitonen, A., 1993. The constructive approach in management accounting research. *Journal of Management Accounting Research*, 5(Fall), pp. 241–264.

Laine, T., Korhonen, T., Suomala, P. and Rantamaa, A., 2016. Boundary subjects and boundary objects in accounting fact construction and communication. *Qualitative Research in Accounting and Management*, 13(3), pp. 303–329.

Luft, J. and Shields, M., 2002. Zimmerman's contentious conjectures: Describing the present and prescribing the future of empirical management accounting research. *European Accounting Review*, 11(4), pp. 795–805.

Lukka, K. and Mouritsen, J., 2002. Homogeneity or heterogeneity of research in management accounting? *European Accounting Review*, 11(4), pp. 805–811.

Lukka, K. and Vinnari, E. 2017. Combining actor-network theory with interventionist research: Present state and future potential. *Accounting, Auditing & Accountability Journal*, 30(3), pp. 720–753.

Malmi, T., 2016. Managerial studies in management accounting: 1990–2014. *Management Accounting Research*, 31, pp. 31–44.

Malmi, T. and Granlund, M., 2009. In search for management accounting theory. *European Accounting Review*, 18(3), pp. 597–620.

Mitchell, F., 2002. Research and practice in management accounting: Improving integration and communication. *European Accounting Review*, 11(2), pp. 277–289.

Nørreklit, H., Nørreklit, L. and Mitchell, F., 2010. Towards a paradigmatic foundation for accounting practice. *Accounting, Auditing & Accountability Journal*, 23(6), pp. 733–758.

Rautiainen, A., Sippola, K. and Mättö, T. 2017. Perspectives on relevance: The relevance test in the constructive research approach. *Management Accounting Research*, 34, pp. 19–29.

Scapens, R., 2014. My final editorial. *Management Accounting Review*, 24(4), pp. 245–250.

Sunding, L. and Odenrick, P., 2010. A method for action research interventions to improve joint problem solving in operational teams in the Swedish construction industry. *Qualitative Research in Accounting and Management*, 7(1), pp. 97–123.

Suomala, P., Lahikainen, T., Lyly-Yrjänäinen, J. and Paranko, J., 2010. Open book accounting in practice—exploring the faces of openness. *Qualitative Research in Accounting and Management*, 7(1), pp. 71–96.

Suomala, P. and Lyly-Yrjänäinen, J., 2012. *Management accounting research in practice. Lessons learned from an interventionist approach*. Routledge, New York.

Suomala, P., Lyly-Yrjänäinen, J. and Lukka, K., 2014. Battlefield around interventions: A reflective analysis of conducting interventionist research in management accounting. *Management Accounting Research*, 25(4), pp. 304–314.

Westin, O. and Roberts, H., 2010. Interventionist research—the puberty years: And introduction to the special issue. *Qualitative Research in Accounting and Management*, 7(1), pp. 5–12.

Zimmerman, J., 2001. Conjectures regarding empirical managerial accounting research. *Journal of Accounting and Economics*, 32(1–3), pp. 411–427.

2   Intervention in Teasing out Theory Contributions

IVR is a longitudinal case study approach in which active participant observation is used deliberately as a research asset (Suomala and Lyly-Yrjänäinen
2012; Lukka and Suomala 2014). As mentioned by Lukka (2005), it is often
assumed—at least implicitly—that a case study researcher tries to (or at
least should) avoid or minimize intervening with the course of action within
the organization under study. Thus, unobtrusive methods have been considered a natural aim for researchers, though difficult to achieve in a case study
because, as elegantly phrased by Jönsson and Lukka (2007), hmming in the
wrong place may already change the course of action in an organization.
In interventionist research, the 'inescapable feature of case studies,' i.e., the
unavoidable immersion, is translated to its strength (Jönsson and Lukka
2007). Thus, instead of ensuring the role as a neutral third party, or at least
minimizing the possible influence on the organization under examination,
the interventionist researcher actively and deliberately changes the course of
action in the organization, one way or another, to set in motion a change
process, providing then an opportunity to gather empirical data related to
that change process. Although IVR does not have to be based on case studies, considering the published interventionist studies, that seems to be the
case, at least thus far.

This chapter begins with a brief look at the various methodological alternatives discussed in management accounting literature with interventionist
elements in them, with the main emphasis on some of the latest venues in
the literature. We will then discuss the process of IVR, grounded with the
empirical experiences in applying the idea in practice and, based on these
experiences, emphasizing its iterative nature, contradicting the traditional
hypothesis-testing research. Furthermore, we will then analyze the core act
of intervention and how to look at these interventions in a more analytical
way, leading finally to the discussion on its role in the quest towards interesting theory contributions.

Interventionist Research

Interventionist research should be viewed as a form of case study in which
the researcher is deeply and actively involved with the organization under

study (Jönsson and Lukka 2007). Interventionist research forms a cluster of research approaches and is considered to include the following research traditions (Jönsson and Lukka 2007):

- Action research (originating from the work of Lewin 1946 in the field of social sciences)
- Action science (a stream of interventionist research proposed by Argyris et al. 1985)
- Clinical research (Normann 1976, in Finnish)
- Design science (introduced by van Aken 2004)
- Constructive research (Kasanen et al. 1993; Lukka 2000; Labro and Tuomela 2003; Rautiainen et al. 2017)
- Innovation action research (Kaplan 1998)
- Conditional-normative research approach (Mattessich 1995)

The research traditions listed above all see the researcher as an active, intervening participant in the research process in collaboration with an organization in which the research is conducted, hence constituting a family resemblance. These different traditions, however, differ in importance of practical work and theoretical views as well as the nature of the intervention itself. For a more detailed analysis, we recommend Jönsson and Lukka (2007).

Whereas the different variants of the interventionist research approach emphasize the intervening role of the researcher as a means to produce theoretical knowledge also relevant for practice, one additional, recent debate contributing to the discussion was provided by Van de Ven and Johnson (2006). In order to facilitate creation of theory with pragmatic relevance, they propose an approach called engaged scholarship. Engaged scholarship emphasizes active interaction between researchers and practitioners in defining and executing research projects. As mentioned by Van de Ven and Johnson:

> "Learning the nature of the question or phenomenon in such ambiguous settings is facilitated by obtaining divergent perspectives of numerous stakeholders."

Van de Ven and Johnson (2006) criticize the 'isolated role' of a researcher as a virtue in order to ensure high quality research. They point out the critique provided by Caswill and Shove (2000) on the assumption that theoretical advances require academic detachment and that collaborative research merely implements and exploits, but does not advance, social theory. Van de Ven and Johnson (2006) stress (1) the importance of asking big questions, (2) divergent compositions of research teams, (3) long duration of research collaboration in order to build mutual trust, (4) critical attitude to both theory and practice and, to some extent, (5) intertwined scholarly and clinical roles. As a result, both theory and practice may be enhanced, without certain restrictions on the nature of the theory contributions. Even though the intervening role of the researcher is not emphasized in the work of Van de Ven and Johnson, the clinical role taken by the researcher, nevertheless, creates a clear family resemblance to the interventionist research approach. As Lukka and Suomala (2014) point out, the flexibility to take advantage of interesting events in the field is one of the core virtues in interventionist research, in line with the intertwined scholarly and clinical roles.

In their article, Van de Ven and Johnson were emphasizing collaboration between researchers and practitioners as a way to do research with both theoretical and practical contributions. However, engaged scholarship can result in outcomes highly rewarding for practitioners even without direct practical application to the participating organizations, that is practically relevant (social) theory contributions. As pointed out by Van de Ven and Johnson, the practical relevance often is a result of a set of research projects after which the broader scope of the findings is realized. Whereas Suomala and Lyly-Yrjänäinen (2012) introduced the concept of a research stream, meaning a set of research projects carried out within the team focusing on the same phenomenon in different contexts and with differing viewpoints as a tool to result in theory contributions, Van de Ven and Johnson emphasize it as a way to enhance pragmatic relevance of the outputs.

Whereas engaged scholarship emphasizes the focus on topics/questions of managerial interest, Malmi (2016) introduces the idea of managerialist research. According to him, managerialist research refers to studies in which at least one of the aims is to directly support or help organizational decision-making and control. These studies he then divides into interventionist studies and non-interventionist ones. However, what is interesting in his analysis is the fact that he divides interventionist studies into those using action research and those applying a constructive research approach. With regards to the former, he then divides them into one aiming at (1) learning during the intervention, (2) demonstrating the value of existing concepts, (3) construct development without proof, and (4) field experiments. The field experiments, on the other hand, focused on studies developing a theoretically novel construct and demonstrating its practical applicability, in the spirit of a constructive research approach.

IVR literature has its roots in a constructive research approach (see, e.g., Kasanen et al. 1993) and perhaps that link is still implicitly connected to the discussion on the role of a research intervention in providing theory contribution. Despite the point raised by the spokesmen of IVR (Jönsson and Lukka 2007) that hmming in the right moment may influence the course of an organization and, hence, be considered an intervention, the focus in IVR literature has been (at least implicitly) on the intervention itself being in the core of the theory contribution. In this chapter we wish to focus the discussion more on the role intervention can play in 'teasing out' interesting results with theory contribution. Thus, the intervention must not be in the center regarding the theory contribution and, therefore, the role of the intervention in that process can be more multifaceted than yet pointed out in the IVR literature. We hope it will be considered fair to say that we wish to position IVR research perhaps one step backwards from the CRA towards action research (AR), though still emphasizing the importance of an active (i.e., intervening) participant observation. In such cases, the study does not necessarily purposefully focus on explicating any solution concept, but IVR is, as phrased by Jönsson and Lukka, "geared to certain ideas of teasing out change in the studied organization" and, through that process, contributing to the body of knowledge. This type of IVR Jönsson and Lukka (2007) refer to as a more process-oriented interventionist approach.

There and Back Again—IVR Process

The process for interventionist research was discussed in Jönsson and Lukka (2007). In their original work, they identify five stages in an interventionist venue. However, later the process was complemented with a pre-understanding stage, emphasizing the importance of having at least some ideas how the intervention is expected to provide theory contributions before engaging in the interventionist fieldwork.

0. Pre-understanding: what seems to be of interest in the case, where there may be need for improved knowledge and understanding
1. Starting the research collaboration: capturing and analyzing the situation in the case company
2. Pre-intervention: outlining the ideas for change or a design of a solution concept
3. Intervention: testing the ideas for a change or the designed solution concept by participating in its implementation
4. Post-intervention: reflection of the nature, elements, implementation, and effects of the change ideas
5. Reporting

The process above is discussed briefly using Lyly-Yrjänäinen (2008) as an example illustrating each step (for more profound discussion on the sample case study, see Suomala et al. 2014 and Lukka and Suomala 2014).

When doing research in collaboration with companies, the partner selection provides some challenges. Typically research funding in IVR projects is based on a group of companies brought together under a public-sector-funded (or other external funding agency) project. However, typically the participating companies need to share part of the costs and, therefore, they typically have expectations on the practical utility of the outcomes, too. When setting up IVR projects, researchers typically have to balance between finding suitable organizations from the theoretical point of view and organizations interested in participating in such a venue. Despite these uncertainties, it is important that the researchers have some idea regarding how the practice-oriented fieldwork will contribute to theory development; in business profits come with risks and, similarly, interesting theory contributions also do surface through processes with uncertainties in them. Nevertheless, well-executed research projects typically yield some interesting findings—it is again the skill of the researcher to, when in the field, position the interesting observations in the right theoretical context. Despite the fact that sometimes the interventionist fieldwork results in unanticipated discoveries, they nevertheless often have some links to the original themes defined/recognized at the beginning of the research collaboration.

> In his study, Lyly-Yrjänäinen (2008) was asked to help the company in developing a new modular/mass customized product family of hydraulic power units. His two previous patents on modular material handling systems provided a nice value-added input to the case company. Since the case seemed to provide potential to contribute to the MA literature on modularization/mass customization, a research project was set up, partially funded by the case company.

In early 2000, modularization was a hot topic in R&D literature and, therefore, MA researchers also were keen on providing their perspectives on the topic (e.g., Davila and Wouters 2004). Thus, there was, already from the beginning, an idea to which stream of literature the research project would attempt to contribute. The example above also shows how one important input provided by the researcher was the technical expertise related to modularization, a significant 'sales argument' motivating the company to fund their share of the project.

The first stage in IVR focuses is to gain understanding of the situation at hand (Jönsson and Lukka 2007). As emphasized by Jönsson and Lukka (2007), good understanding of the case context is needed for thorough understanding on problem that needs improvement efforts.

> In his study, Lyly-Yrjänäinen (2008) started to participate in monthly meetings of the development team. In addition, he spent three days assembling the power units, enabling informal discussions on the shop floor. Thus, instead of the case company allocating resources for training, the researcher learned about the products and processes while working with the assembly workers. In addition, the personnel related to the power unit business were interviewed at the outset of the project. Managers emphasized the need for simple cost drivers to capture the cost-reduction potential of the mass-customized power units credibly.

In their framework, Jönsson and Lukka (2007) emphasize the importance of this stage to ensure that the intervention eventually hits the bull's eye: "In order to design an intervention that promises to work in practice as well as to add to our theoretical knowledge, a good understanding of the situation is essential." This statement seems (at least implicitly) to emphasize the idea that the intervention plays a key role in the theory contribution itself. In this book, however, we will take a bit softer view on the intervention; the intervention itself must not always be in the core of the theory contribution. Nevertheless, planning of the researcher's role in the field is very essential; careful consideration regarding 'what' the researcher wants to gain access to in the case organization impacts the initial ideas on 'where' the researcher should intervene in. In order to be able to proceed with the focal company, as phrased by Jönsson and Lukka (2007), there needs to be a collectively constructed action project, attractive enough for the management to initiate the 'action' to realize the possibilities in the collaboration, based on good understanding of the situation.

During the second stage in the process (called pre-intervention), the researcher needs to identify where and how to intervene, based on the understanding of the situation at hand. Whereas the first stage is primarily data gathering about the context, hence resulting in rich 'thick' description (as phrased by Geertz 1973), the planning of the intervention now is a process more difficult to document; there is now plenty of heuristics involved since the researcher is, together with the case company, trying to find out the best way to help the organization while, at the same time, trying to gain access to processes/information providing potential for theory contribution. Even though at this stage the researcher may be tempted to focus on solving the problems of the case company, it is important to note that the process needs to be documented in a way that, should some theoretically interesting outcomes surface, the researcher is able to provide the chain of evidence through the rich description of the process. This, however, results in a dilemma; the researcher cannot document all the activities or conversations and some selection has to be made, at this stage, guided by the initial research agenda and, to some extent, the gut feeling.

> During the interview round (Lyly-Yrjänäinen 2008), most employees pointed out that the tanks of the power units seemed to delay the start of the assembly process. Whenever one component of the power unit was changed, there was likely some change in the tank; yet at the same time, the tanks can be considered as the physical platforms of power units and, hence, needed in the assembly first. Development of mass customized, common tanks would eliminate this bottleneck and reduce white-collar work related to the project management, hence likely to result in significant cost savings. Thus, at this point, the theoretical perspective of the case was repositioned to cost implications of component commonality. However, to be able to have some ex-post cost information, such common tanks had to be invented. Furthermore, in order to capture the potential cost implications, the cost reporting systems needed some improvement, too.

As illustrated above, based on the information gathered during the first stage, the interventions were focused on the development of a new product architecture and improvement of the cost reporting system. At the same time, the case was repositioned as a theory-testing case of cost implications of component commonality; there were calls for empirical papers on cost implications of component commonality (Labro 2004). The example shows how the initial area of theoretical interest was slightly repositioned thanks to the case itself and work published by Labro (2003). This sort of flexibility is (and should be) an integral part of interventionist research. A comprehensive (or growing) awareness of relevant theories and related contribution potentials is a remarkable asset for the interventionist researcher (or researcher team). Although the initially recognized contribution potential was not realized, the overall process could yield theory contribution in an alternative/refined area of theoretical interest. As discussed further in a specific section, the theory contribution of the IVR may be unveiled or enabled by the IVR process and serve various purposes ranging from theory building to theory testing/refinements.

In their study, Jönsson and Lukka (2007) emphasize that the design of intervention must be honestly expected to work in practice and provide potential for theory contribution, again highlighting (at least implicitly) the idea that it is the intervention that provides the theory contribution in the spirit of the constructive research approach. However, as illustrated with the example above, the intervention can be considered more like action enabling access to interesting events, not providing theory contribution per se. As shown in the example above, the interventions were needed to set the stage for (1) having common components the cost implications of which to study (and learn about the process for developing such components in practice) and (2) improving the cost reporting systems to ensure that the cost implications can be traced reliably. These interventions, though not providing theory contribution per se, were key enablers for the final theory contribution of the project, as will be discussed later.

In addition to the focus of the intervention (whether that is in the heart of the theory contribution or not), there is another aspect worth more detailed analysis. The idea that an intervention must honestly be expected to work is a very strong statement for an IVR project and gives the impression that intervention is something that is 'launched' at the focal company. In many cases the identification of the need (during the pre-intervention stage) then sets the stage for the intervention that is more like the development work itself, eventually resulting in something that the organization considers useful. The idea that there should be a shared understanding that the idea will work is a very strong expectation, since all development projects tend to include at least some uncertainties in them. Business people accept that profits come only with some risk; perhaps interventionist research should allow some risk regarding the functionality/feasibility of the interventions—especially if there are some 'radical' elements built in to these interventions.

In the end, even failed interventions may tease out unpredicted and even better theory contributions than the successful ones.

Medical research is based, for example, on testing how different molecules impact the pathogens; and even if some molecule turns out not to have a favorable outcome, the reported test can be considered an important contribution—at least no-one else should attempt to test those molecules for those pathogens, in that way increasing our body of knowledge though not resulting in a medical breakthrough. Naturally there has to be some arguments (i.e., hypothesis) why a certain molecule should have favorable results on the pathogen. However, in IVR MA research, we are not looking at such simple correlations; in-depth cases with close management collaboration typical of IVR research, based on our experience, often lead to new areas and findings, a research setup very different from hypothesis testing. Thus, this is an uncertainty IVR must tolerate, perhaps favoring more experienced researchers who are not under direct pressure to produce a dissertation in three or four years.

The third stage—intervention—then means that the researchers roll up their sleeves and start working together with the organization. In the framework of Jönsson and Lukka (2007), the intervention was seen more as an implementation of a solution developed by the researcher. Thus, in their framework the main emphasis was on pre-intervention; the researcher needs to work on the development of a solution to some organizational problem and the solution should not only be honestly expected to work but also provide potential for contribution. However, in this book we emphasize the development work as the intervention; the researcher works together with the management team to solve some problem identified with or by the case organization.

> In his study, Lyly-Yrjänäinen (2008) started to analyze the power units delivered during the past years in order to understand the different variables that needed to be taken into account when building common tanks. Since the power units typically were engineered to order, the researcher was capturing the emergent product architecture in a company that did not have systematic product architecture. That analysis gave good understanding of the impacts different component options had on the tanks, eventually leading into a solution that enabled an almost unlimited amount of product variants to be assembled with a limited number of common tanks. The discovery of this then enabled access to more detailed discussions with managers about the cost implications (ex-ante) of such common components. When the first power units with the common tanks were delivered to customer, the improved cost reporting systems then enabled some real-life (ex-post) cost data to be gathered and analyzed together with the management.

Whether the intervention is positioned as an implementation of a solution developed by the researcher or more collaboration to develop some solution together with the case company, one key issue is to ensure proper documentation of the process. As emphasized by Jönsson and Lukka (2007), the intervention plan usually includes a plan for systematic collection of data. This, however, provides an interesting dilemma for the researcher. Since the researcher plays a role in the development of the solution to the organizational problem, the development work consumes more time and 'brain capacity' compared to simply doing participant observation. In the latter, the key focus of the researcher is to 'play along' with the team and the key responsibility is to gather data through documentation. The former, however, requires that despite playing often a key role in developing issues of practical interest, the researcher must ensure proper documentation of the process and key events in it. However, to avoid information overload, it is important to have some ideas about the expected/planned theory contribution to help the researcher select the most useful information. This again emphasizes that the researcher is not a consultant helping the organization; instead this 'helping' is considered as the provider of access to 'be there' when interesting organizational processes are emerging or unfolding.

When the intervention has come to the end and the documentation has been done, the fourth stage (post-intervention) begins (Jönssön and Lukka 2007). According to Jönsson and Lukka (2007), this post-intervention analysis typically includes two elements: reverse engineering of the change process and re-contextualization of the findings through the lens of the chosen theoretical discourse.

First, this reverse engineering of the change process can be seen to have some clear connections to the CRA mind-set. In their work, Jönsson and Lukka (2007) emphasize that the researcher should now compare how the developed solution (i.e., intervention) was supposed to work (and based on what arguments) and then trace back the causalities explaining why an intervention worked or did not work as planned or expected. This sort of analysis will be based on the field diary, documents, interviews, and other data collected during and after the intervention (Jönsson and Lukka 2007). Thus, the post-intervention does not automatically mean that the researcher now withdraws herself in a chamber to reconstruct the intervention process but, on the contrary, the researcher can (and perhaps should) reflect on the process also with the management team. As a matter of fact, such reflection processes are likely to provide interesting material for the study itself.

Second, while reflecting on the intervention process with the management team, the researcher should start re-contextualizing the findings in order to position it in the appropriate stream of literature, i.e., reflect on the findings also to interesting streams of literature to (1) position the study in a best possible way and (2) explicate the theory contributions. If the solution developed by the researcher is to provide the theory contribution (as is the case in CRA), the reflection is based on the feedback on the solution and its link to the theory. However, in this book we emphasize more the intervention as an enabler of interesting reflections with the case company management.

> In his study, Lyly-Yrjänäinen (2008) was able to help the company develop common tanks enabling customized power units to be manufactured without the need for mechanical engineering and also capture related cost implications thanks to the improved cost reporting systems. Neither of these two interventions, however, was positioned as the key theory contribution; inventions in product architecture and some improvements in cost reporting systems hardly make interesting theory contributions in the MA field. Instead, the key theory contribution came through the reflection on this development process. There were many contradictions in the case compared to the existing theory on cost implications of component commonality waiting for explanations. During the reflection stage, it was noticed that existing literature on component commonality focused mainly on standard-product or assembly-to-order environments whereas the power units of the case company were engineered to order. This engineering-to-order (ETO) context turned out to have some characteristics explaining why the existing theory on component commonality did not seem to explain the cost behavior in that particular type of business environment. Interestingly, these outcomes could have been deduced by studying key characteristics of an ETO environment and viewing component commonality literature through that lens. Nevertheless, the exposure to the real context, in this case, guided the researcher to ask this question in the first place, later supported by theoretical triangulation.

The final stage in the interventionist research process is reporting. Typical of research projects, there are reporting needs for the case companies (auditors, for example, often require a written report of a research project to approve the costs) and the funding agencies. However, most interesting reporting (at least from the researcher's point of view) is targeted to fellow researchers in academic books and journals. Jönsson and Lukka (2007) mention that since interventionist research is likely to end up with very rich description with a large data set, it may be worth trying to split the case into several papers with different focuses.

> The dissertation of Lyly-Yrjänäinen (2008) provided an empirical case for a paper discussing the role of research intervention in interventionist MA research. The paper (Suomala et al. 2014) was published in *Management Accounting Research* as a retrospective analysis of an interventionist project similar to the paper written by Labro and Tuomela (2003) on practical experiences of the constructive research approach. Instead of management accounting journals favoring case study research, the literature on component commonality is found primarily in operations

research journals or R&D-related books, hence justifying the positioning of the paper.

The framework of Jönsson and Lukka (2007) poetically reminds the reader that successful IVR requires the researcher to dive deep into the practical world (i.e., 'go there') to gain understanding of the complex forces present in a real-life managerial case. However, in addition to that they also emphasize that the researcher must remember to reflect on the case through the theory (i.e., 'come back again') in order to argue for the theory contribution. Thus, interventionist research is not an excuse to link consulting work to the academic community but, on the contrary, a demanding way to tease out interesting empirical findings with theoretical relevance.

. . . And Again—Iterative Nature of the Research Process

An important question for—and key advantage of—IVR is how to gain deep practical understanding of the phenomenon under investigation. The process with six steps discussed above is certainly a helpful framework helping the researcher in the venue to gain interesting theory contribution through intervening participation in the field. However, based on our experience, the process perhaps is more complex in real life; very seldom the most interesting findings surface through such a linear process.

To help understand the transition to there and back in IVR, Jönsson and Lukka (2007) employ the dichotomy originally developed by Pike (1954). In IVR, according to them, the researcher is an active actor in the real-time flow of the events in the field and, hence, must adopt the *emic* perspective to the issues at hand. *Emic* perspective refers to the idea that the researcher has become a trustworthy member (i.e., insider) in the organization under examination; the researcher not only understands the meanings and actions of the members of the organization but also is able to communicate and act with them. Without such a position within the minds of the members of the organization, the researcher will be regarded as a 'tourist' and will be communicated with via 'child talk,' as elegantly paraphrased by Jönsson and Lukka. Thus, the intervention helps the researcher to become 'one of us' in the eyes of the actors in the field.

However, to contribute to the theory, the researcher must be able to link the findings to a theoretical frame (Jönsson and Lukka 2007). Thus, at some point of the research process, the researcher has to be able to distance him/herself from the apprehending flow of interesting events taking place in the field. Whereas the *emic* viewpoint results from studying human behavior from the inside, the *etic* viewpoint refers to studying it from the outside. As mentioned by Jönsson and Lukka, the *etic* viewpoint is unavoidable for any researcher at the initial stages of examining a new organization (i.e., an 'alien system').

In their study, Suomala and Lyly-Yrjänäinen (2012) pointed out that there is no such thing as an absolute insider or outsider, but the reality may rather be understood as layers (see Burrell and Morgan 1979; Tomkins and Groves 1983); some phenomena may be visible to everyone whereas some phenomena may be observed only by rare individuals. As concluded by Suomala and Lyly-Yrjänäinen (2012), instead of being an outsider or insider, the researcher may be regarded more as 'some sort of insider' depending on the depth of access. As shown in Figure 2.1, the lower the line goes, the deeper the access and, therefore, through more layers of reality the researcher is able to penetrate with the intervention.

In their study, Suomala and Lyly-Yrjänäinen also speculate how the penetration through the ontological layers may advance as a function of time. As shown at the top in Figure 2.1, the more time the researcher spends in the field, the deeper the access often gets. Furthermore, the more expert role the researcher is able to build, the faster this penetration may take place; Jönsson and Lukka (2007), for example, identify different roles (comrade, team member, and expert) an intervening researcher can choose to play while in the field. Whereas comrade and team member might be seen more as roles typical to studies focusing on the participant observation, the interventions often tend to call for some sort of expert role, or at least an attempt to evolve into one. Thus, as shown in the middle, the researcher may bring some 'expertise' to the organization but, nevertheless, be considered as

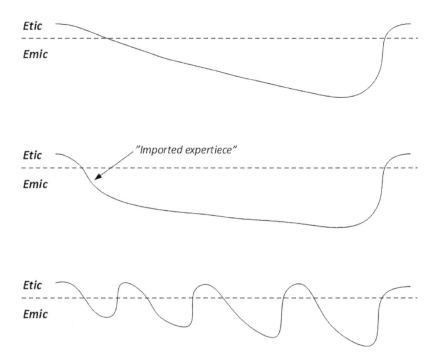

Figure 2.1 Different Ways of Moving Between the *Etic* and *Emic* Perspectives.

a 'tourist' regarding that particular context. However, as the intervening researcher studies the environment and starts to work on some solutions to a present managerial problem, the researcher may develop externalized knowledge on the context no-one else yet possessed. After some time, the researcher may be considered a specialist, not with everything related to the context, but a specialist in some novel, special areas within that context— and have visibility to, for example, some very interesting events, beliefs, and behavioral patterns present in the field. The visibility to these interesting elements, then, typically provides the most interesting potential for a theory contribution.

The example above emphasizes the idea that the expertise of the researcher evolves over the time spent in the field. However, the ultimate goal of the researcher is not to evolve into an expert in a certain practical area but contribute to the theory. Thus, it seems that in reality the *emic-etic* transition tends to have a more iterative nature. When the researcher enters the field, she has some ideas about the potential theory contribution. However, it is often the first interesting observations in the field or statements of the practitioners that arouse the researcher's interest. In many cases, such interesting clues fall slightly outside the intended scope and, hence, the researcher may have to switch to the *etic* mode in order to check whether that first finding might be a 'weak signal' of a potential theory contribution. If yes, the researcher now has to fine tune the research agenda in terms of where and how the case might provide theory contribution. When the researcher goes deeper into the *emic* mode, she may be able to tease out more profound findings about this novel area, again calling for the need to go back to the literature to guide the further inquiries. Thus, it seems that it is the interplay between the theory and practice that, in many cases, seems to provide the most fruitful venue to results of both practical and theoretical relevance, as illustrated at the bottom in Figure 2.1.

To penetrate through the layers of reality, the researcher may have to invest time in working with the members of the organization under study, with the ultimate goal to be accepted 'as one of us' in the eyes of the members of the organization. As mentioned by Jönsson and Lukka (2007), by acting accordingly, people can signal their will to be a member of a group. This is something an interventionist researcher will have to do in order to start the journey towards the *emic* role. Jönsson and Lukka use the concept 'membership work' (see Munro 2001) to describe what interventionist researchers do by aligning their acts with the group they wish to be members of. However, it is not enough to 'talk the talk' for a person to be a member of the group, they also need to 'walk the walk,' i.e., be able to contribute to the mission of that group (Jönsson and Lukka 2007), and here is where the intervention plays a key role.

A researcher doing participant observation may be able to penetrate deep into, for example, a recently discovered new culture simply by spending time with the people, but that is not the same with a business organization;

the access to a business organization needs to be more justified. Thus, the intervention provides the researcher the reason to be allowed access to that organization. Working together with the organization and providing the skills and knowledge to the use of the organization helps to earn the 'one of us' status in the organization. Interestingly, the expert role is really important to sell the role to the decision-makers allowing the access, yet at the same time the membership work has to be done in other organizational levels. As was pointed out by one of the interviewees in their study (Suomala and Lyly-Yrjänäinen 2012):

> "Getting real access and acceptance inside the organization is rather challenging. It is like in sales, you first have to sell yourself as a person. It requires quite a lot of social skills because, in many cases, the researcher is considered as a threat by many people inside the organization. People do not understand why young guys come and start asking questions. The employees feel that they know these things since they have been doing things for a long time already. The researchers need to be able to ask things in a way that it does not irritate the employees and managers too much. It is really challenging for an outsider to create a status of an insider and the only way to do this is to be present and work together with the people inside the organization."

With regards to the membership work, one interesting way seems to be to ensure that the researcher is indeed providing valuable inputs to the organization. In other words, the researcher has to be able to show her usefulness to the organization—otherwise the employees or managers find it difficult to accept an outsider present in various situations. Thus, as pointed out by one of the interviewees in their study (Suomala and Lyly-Yrjänäinen 2012), the organization is more likely to accept the researcher as 'one of us' only after they start to see the first results provided by the researcher:

> "The first results! Only after the first results is it possible to ensure that the damn fellow is right. That is how you break the organizational resistance. However, it is also important to communicate the results in a way that this was done together!"

The statement above highlights the main argument of this book, positioning IVR between action research and constructive research. Thus, in order to first gain access to the case organization and then peel through the different layers of reality to gain access to interesting empirical data, the researcher has to do something beneficial to the organization (like in constructive research) while, at the same time, the empirical data for the theory contribution is more likely based on the participant observation (similar to the action research). However, to earn the right to be present and see/experience some interesting flow of events in the field, the researcher may have to spend some time. As yet another interviewee pointed out regarding the penetration to the *emic* level (Suomala and Lyly-Yrjänäinen 2012):

> "Definitely this process needs time, one year is not enough for that (reaching the status as 'one of us')."

Thus, regarding the time frame of IVR, the processes tend to be rather long. Thus, in addition to the skills and capabilities needed to access organizations, the researcher faces many uncertainties. One may not know what the project will eventually reveal and what the final theoretical outcome will be. Interventionist research, therefore, is more similar to the product development project—there are uncertainties involved.

Intervention for Theory Contribution—Depth and Focal Point

Jönsson and Lukka (2007) emphasize that all research should seek increased theoretical understanding. Therefore, we also emphasize the importance of using the research intervention as a tool for contributing to the theory. However, before going deeper into how such research interventions help contribute, let us analyze a bit more about the intervention itself. The section above emphasized the role of the intervention not as the contribution, but rather a tool helping the researcher gain access to interesting empirical data, providing potential for theory contribution. The discussion pointed out some different ways in which a researcher gains the role as 'one of us' in an organization under examination. However, there is perhaps a need to discuss a bit further how to intervene in order to contribute to the theory.

In their study, Jönsson and Lukka (2007) analyze the impact the research intervention may have on the organization. Though theoretically speaking hmming in the right (or wrong) place or moment may have an impact on the organization, Jönsson and Lukka distinguish two types of intervention: modest and strong. On one hand, modest intervention focuses on initiation of an improvement process by 'manipulating the context' instead of re-engineering some of the processes or systems inside the company. Strong research intervention, on the other hand, is based on the idea that the researchers change the work processes of the case company either by modifying the information system (and that way impacting the flow of events) or then directly redesigning the work process. Again, strong intervention was considered to follow the spirit of constructive research approach, emphasizing the contribution potential of the intervention itself.

However, Suomala and Lyly-Yrjänäinen (2012) see the strength of an intervention more as a continuum with various levels:

- Intervention through presence, very limited participation in the process
- External expert, limited participation

- Rich participation within a limited domain
- Active and versatile participation ('almost family')
- Strong collaboration, native role ('one of us')

The first level would be researchers being involved in a development process, perhaps more as an expert bringing in some relevant knowledge to the company, but not getting their hands dirty on the practical development work—but certainly more than just being present and hmming. Presence of an accounting specialist in a development project may already remind the managers of the importance of the accounting perspective without much direct impact on the process. However, such a person is likely to be asked questions regarding the project at hand, hence making that person already a more intervening one. Sometimes rather informal discussions can impact organizations, as in the following case pointed out by one of the authors:

"Some years ago I discussed the meaning and methods of cost allocation with a large UK bank. This is an important issue for banks as different parts of them (for example current accounts) can be scrutinized by a government agency to assess whether excessive profits are being made. Cost allocation methods used have to be justifiable and following discussions they modified their approach to reflect an activity basis for as many of their common costs as possible. This gave them a more credible basis to justify their allocations to government."

The second level would be an external expert intervening in the flow of events in the area of expertise, though the presence in the field is, nevertheless, limited in time. A specialist can, for example, be involved in a certain part of a development project, meaning an intervention that is on one hand intensive yet on the other hand compact in terms of time spent in the field. Such an intervention may focus more on the thorough analysis of the starting point in order to help the organization change the course of action with a well-grounded plan (note that Jönsson and Lukka emphasized the importance of understanding the situation at the beginning) or then bringing the expertise for an already-planned course of action. In both cases, however, the researcher gains access to observe interesting organizational processes, possibly providing potential for theory contribution.

Such an interventionist research process can be illustrated with a research project focusing on life-cycle costing (Suomala and Lyly-Yrjänäinen 2012). The researcher team had experience on life-cycle costing from previous projects and got a project with Finnish Defense Forces to study the life-cycle costs of a weapons system. The interventionist role, however, was somewhat limited; researchers constructed a costing model and identified the key cost elements and assignment rules though the data gathering was mainly done by the organization itself. In other words, the researchers' input was related to the knowledge but no deep involvement in the flow of events in the organization was established.

The third level would be a research project of one to several years with good access to the case company. The researcher's role, however, remains focused on a narrow area in the case company. Perhaps the researcher is not even widely exposed to many people within the organization but focuses more on working within one function.

> An example of such an interventionist research process is based on a project focusing on costs of quality (Suomala and Lyly-Yrjänäinen 2012). The focus was on identifying the key factors that drive the quality costs in a project-based machine construction business and to derive possible measurement implications. In this case, the company had been collecting data on poor quality and had some ideas on how to utilize that. However, the company did not have the resources to develop a more detailed plan regarding how to crunch the existing data to provide meaningful metrics to help decision-making. Therefore, the management team asked for an MA specialist to do that for them, providing interesting access to rich data and rather free hands on how to utilize that in the best interest of the company. The work lasted about one year, with collaboration mainly with limited number of people, directly or indirectly connected to the cost of quality.

The fourth level would mean that the researcher is actively involved with the development work in the case company. At this level, the researcher is seen as 'almost family,' meaning that intensive and long-term presence in the field is needed. Typically such projects take two or more years, with some key stakeholders having some experience on collaboration with intervening researchers; otherwise the deep penetration into the *emic* level may take even more time. However, the researcher still is not quite part of the 'inner circle' of the case organization.

> One example of such research intervention is a study focusing on inter-organizational cost management (Suomala and Lyly-Yrjänäinen 2012). Researchers worked for about two years in a company supplying a large OEM to provide accurate product cost information for the manufacturer. The project team leader had worked with the OEM for many years in different research projects and, therefore, the key stakeholders were familiar with research collaboration; this relationship was used as a leverage to gain access to the supplier company. The intensive development work with the supplier's costing system resulted in a detailed cost analysis of about a dozen components supplied to that particular OEM. When that data was available, the researchers facilitated a meeting with the OEM and the supplier in which this cost information was

revealed to both parties. Based on this information, the pricing of some components was reconsidered to ensure acceptable, yet stable profits for the supplier. The second year, then, was used for replication of the study, with all 160 components that the supplier delivered to that particular OEM, providing a very comprehensive analysis for the top management of the company.

The fifth level in the framework categorizing the depth of the research interventions emphasizes the 'one of us' role the researcher attempts to gain through deep involvement in the flow of events. This level of access to the flow of events means, for example, that the researchers are granted free access to the premises (possibly even a key). The physical access, however, is not the key measure of the in-depth penetration; a more important measure is access to key information through formal or informal discussions with the key stakeholders. Managers can, for example, start sharing information they would never reveal to an outsider. The long-term collaboration with the research partner, therefore, is often times seen as a factor eventually, with the increasing mutual trust, placing the researcher in the middle of very interesting discussions with the managers, also providing insights guiding research work to areas with new, unforeseen theory contributions.

> The case used for illustrating the IVR project (Suomala et al. 2014) has been used as an example of this type of research intervention in Suomala and Lyly-Yrjänäinen (2012). The researcher had collaborated with the case company for about three years in two other projects, motivating the key stakeholders to continue the collaboration yet for another four years in the modularization of the power units. Thus, when exposed to the organization responsible for the power unit business, the researcher had a good relationship with the top management, providing access to the key pain points in this particular business. During the four-year collaboration, there were 100 visits with 400 hours spent on the site, in addition to the work related to intervening on the organization with analyses and development work done in the office. Though the researcher was not given a key to the organization, once inside the premises, the researcher could spend a day unattended, as if one of the employees. Despite the deep access, however, the main contribution was positioned more in the financial outcomes of the common tanks; not so much on the organizational aspects often revealed through long-term collaboration.

This discussion illustrated how an intervening researcher can peel the 'layers of reality' in an attempt to penetrate deeper and deeper into the organization. The deeper the access, the more interesting it becomes to compare the interviews and initial observations to the later findings; oftentimes providing interesting contradictions, then leading to fruitful in-depth discussions with the management. This, however, leads us to another important area regarding the research intervention, i.e., the focal point of the intervention and its relation to the positioning of the theory contribution. As one of the key messages of this book, the research intervention must not be in the heart of the theory contribution; in many cases the intervention is merely used as a tool to gain access to the organization and penetrate the above-discussed layers.

In their work, Suomala and Lyly-Yrjänäinen (2012) identified five scopes for the focal point of the research intervention:

- Solely focus on MA practices/tools
- Mainly focus on MA and partly other management fields
- Equally focus on MA and other management fields
- Mainly focus on other management disciplines with some MA elements
- Solely focus on other management disciplines

The first and last ones are somewhat problematic. It is difficult to argue an intervention that focuses only on MA practices or other management disciplines; the boundaries in the field are simply too vague for that. However, what is more important is the idea that the intervening MA researcher does not automatically have to be engaged in the development work in MA. In other words, the distance between the focal point of the intervention and the research question may vary, sometimes even rather significantly. Instead of showing examples of all the five ways to characterize the focal point as identified by Suomala and Lyly-Yrjänäinen (2012), let us discuss the focal point more as a continuum.

First, when looking at a study representing an interventionist project with core emphasis on the MA field, the intervening MA researcher rolls up her sleeves and works with the financial department on developing practices related to MA. This approach may have similarities with constructive research, yet in many cases the practical development work on MA tools is not considered the theory contribution; instead, the practical development of MA tools or practices oftentimes opens up venues for MA-related theory contribution outside the scope of the mere tools or practices.

An example coming from Suomala and Lyly-Yrjänäinen (2012) would be a case in which product profitability was analyzed using an ABC model built by the researchers. When the profitability of various products was discussed with the sales department, in order to impact the product portfolio in the spirit of the cases shown in Turney (1991), the sales people pointed out the importance of non-profitable products from the after-sales perspective. To respond to that, the cost model was expanded to take into account a life-cycle perspective of product profitability, still revealing unprofitable products that did not break even, even if all the wear and tear part were purchased from the OEM. Thus, here the financial department sat strongly in the driver's seat, yet at the same time some other organizational functions were penetrated too and the theory contribution positioned in integrating the life-cycle perspective on the profitability analyses.

Second, an intervention mainly on MA and partly on other management fields, perhaps, is a stereotype of actions taken by an intervening MA researcher. The main focus is on working in collaboration with the MA function (typical contact persons would be controllers or financial managers), yet the work tends to touch other functions as well, for example in the process of gathering data needed for cost analysis or when the costing systems are used for decision-making.

> The case focusing on OBA discussed above characterizes well this view on the focal point in the intervention (Suomala and Lyly-Yrjänäinen 2012). In that case, the most important work was done around building or fine-tuning the costing system of the supplier in order to provide accurate cost and profitability information for the open-book discussions. At the end of the process, however, the accounting information was used by the sourcing department, hence the pinch of a stronger non-accounting flavor.

Third, research interventions positioned in the middle of the spectrum are difficult borderline cases; it is hard to state exactly when non-MA overrides MA in an empirical case. The key perhaps is that even though accounting function may have the ownership of the research collaboration, the work on the research intervention rather equally engages other functions as well; or similarly, even though some other organizational function may have the driver's seat, the practical work around the research intervention strongly relates to the accounting or financial department.

> A borderline case provided by Suomala and Lyly-Yrjänäinen (2012) is a project focusing on an OEM evolving into a service and knowledge provider. The interventionist researchers were accepted as team members in a group that developed a business game concept to better understand the customers' business (as a basis for the service business), and the potential of the OEM in supporting the value creation in that business. Although the interventions were relatively strong and took place in the long-term, their impact remained somewhat limited due to the organizational restructuration during the research process. Altogether, the interventions helped to build a shared understanding about the central business phenomena among the parties involved, which paved the way for service business development—not as an immediate result of the interventions as such.

Fourth, one way to do interventionist MA research is by mainly intervening in areas other than MA. Whereas this may appear strange at first glance, this is very relevant, for example, when attempting to understand the role MA plays in many other functions or fields as well as setting the stage to study financial implications of various change processes. In a sense, the researcher may be mainly involved in helping an organization implement some new practices or drive through some other organizational change to study the financial implications or even study how to study the financial implications of such change processes or new practices.

> The case illustrating focal point of the intervention in an MA research project positioned as mainly "non-MA" is, again, the one focusing on component commonality and its cost implications. The research interventions were mainly related to the data crunching to reveal the emergent product family and, by using that understanding, to develop a family of common tanks enabling variations in the power units without impacting the physical platform. The theory contribution, however, was built around observations related how to try to capture the cost implications of such innovations in the engineering-to-order context, therefore with clear MA focus.

As illustrated in the discussion above, there are many areas where an intervening MA researcher may focus the fieldwork despite the intent to contribute to the MA literature. In the study of Suomala and Lyly-Yrjänäinen (2012), perhaps the focal point of the intervention—though an important aspect—was not yet conceptualized as well as the depth of intervention. Nevertheless, these two perspectives were used to create a matrix, then used for plotting all the discussed cases to provide an analytic framework positioning all the discussed cases. Important to keep in mind, however, is that in all the cases discussed above (as well as in Suomala and Lyly-Yrjänäinen 2012), regardless of the focal point of the intervention, the theory contribution was argued based on MA literature.

Intervention as a Tool for Contributing

The study of Suomala and Lyly-Yrjänäinen (2012) showed six cases plotted in the two above-discussed dimensions of intervention, i.e., strength and focal point of the intervention. There are many combinations with these two variables not discussed above. However, the key aspect is that the research intervention is not the end; it is merely a means to the end, i.e., theory contribution. Therefore, analyzing interventions is meaningless unless theory contribution is created.

One of the most important spokesmen of IVR, professor Kari Lukka, has pointed out in several occasions the weak theory connections of IVR studies published for example in conferences (see, e.g., Lukka and Suomala 2014). As phrased by Heller (1990, see Jönsson and Lukka 2007), action research is 'long on action and short on research' and that is why this chapter concludes with discussion on how research interventions are used for providing interesting theory contributions. As outlined above, the iterative process of IVR may serve several purposes of unveiling, enabling, and directing theory contribution. However, the locus and scope of the theory contribution require further examination.

Based on the analyses on the focal points and strengths of the actual interventions, there are versatile forms of conducting interventionist research in order to attain theory contribution. In all, IVR helps to understand the practices through active engagement of the researchers, with different level possibilities for contribution before, during, and after the research process. Besides, the actual domain of contribution may be regarding, connected to, or outside the subject of the intervention as such. In principle, operations management intervention may open avenues to formulate MA contribution, and MA interventions may result in contribution on strategy formulation as a practice. More particularly, IVR extends the idea of CRA in its nature of engaging with practice and finding unlimited possibilities to better understand and develop practices. Extending the idea of Jönsson and Lukka (2007), the IVR contribution in management accounting is not limited to the change (management), but the mechanisms of MA practice more broadly—regarding both theory building and theory testing depending on the particular IVR project and its implications.

Next, some different alternatives for theory contribution based on IVR are outlined and examined through examples. Regarding the locus of the theory contribution in the research process, first, the theory contribution may still be related to the intervention as such, somewhat similarly to constructive research; by examining and better understanding the processes before and after the intervention and the intervention as such, we may learn new things about the relevant theories.

Second, the process of interventionist research may contribute to the theory by revealing practices, procedures, or phenomena that otherwise would have remained unknown or impossible to study. That is, due to their interventionist role with embedded benefits to the studied organization, the researchers are granted access to the phenomena that are typically unreachable by the researchers. One example is the substantial access to the R&D project management granted to the interventionist researchers (Laine et al. 2016). In this case, the theory contribution was not based on the intervention as such, but more readily on unveiling the dynamics among the managers in overcoming challenges inherent in the ambiguous R&D portfolio management.

Third, the process of interventionist research may serve as a catalyst or enabler of new processes that lead to theory contribution. There are several cases (Laine et al. 2016; Tervala et al. 2017) where the interview data becomes much more valuable due to the earlier interventionist projects in the same (or similar) environments. Not only are the interview questions formulated in a more theoretically informed manner, but also the informants are more willing and capable of responding to such questions.

Regarding the scope of the theory contribution, we conclude that the earlier studies have well recognized the role of IVR in testing and implementing the theories. However, as pointed out by Van de Ven and Johnson (2006), the research that is engaged with practice could also pose better questions in terms of their connection to reality and find ways to address those questions from multiple perspectives in the collaborative research process. We share this idea and remind that IVR holds these collaborative characteristics, and that interventionist researchers benefit from the collaboration in identifying and addressing theoretically interesting questions. When conducted successfully, it is possible to create and refine theories with the help of the IVR, not just test the existing theories.

Provocatively, one may even propose that the engaged research, with the access to the reality and real-life business phenomena, will more probably enable major theoretical advancements compared to a research inquiry that is limited to the reflection of the researchers, within the scope of the research community of a particular field. Of course, at the same time, one needs to remember that a comprehensive, yet detailed understanding about the extant knowledge is a prerequisite for identifying and reporting a sound theory contribution.

Intervention is a concept that sometimes is considered to have some negative connotations in it. For example, social workers may do an 'intervention' to a family with domestic violence or guide an alcoholic to rehabilitation. Despite this unlucky choice of words, however, the concept captures well the core idea of interventionist research; it is more than just active participant observation. Active participant observation can mean a researcher that is active member of its group but even disguise her role as an observant. IVR, on the contrary, is more like a field experimentation. Like in the front line of social work, the intervening actors cannot have control over all the variables, also the interventionist researcher cannot have complete control over the setup; there are many other organizational forces pulling the organization in different other directions. However, despite this limitation, the intervening researcher, nevertheless, seeks to find/determine an experimental situation through her observations, acts on that situation together with the organization, observes the process and its outcomes, and connects the findings to a relevant theory framework (Jönsson and Lukka 2007).

References

Argyris, C., Putnam, R. and McLain Smith, D., 1985. *Action science.* Jossey Bass, San Francisco.

Burrell, G. and Morgan, G., 1979. *Sociological paradigms and organizational analysis.* Heinemann Educational Books, London, 432 p.

Caswill, C. and Shove, E., 2000. Postscript to special issue on interactive social science. *Science and Public Policy*, 27, pp. 220–222.

Davila, T. and Wouters, M., 2004. Designing cost competitive technology products through cost management. *Accounting Horizons*, 18(1), pp. 13–26.

Geertz, C., 1973. *The interpretation of cultures*. Basic Books, New York.

Heller, F., 1990. Some thoughts on the relation between research and action. Paper for the *3rd European Action Research Conference in Helsinki*, 25–27 August 1983.

Jönsson, S. and Lukka, K., 2007. There and back again: Doing IVR in management accounting, in: Chapman, C., Hopwood, A. and Shields, M. (Eds.), *Handbook of management accounting research*, Vol. 1. Elsevier, Amsterdam, pp. 373–397.

Kaplan, R., 1998. Innovation action research: Creating new management theory and practice. *Journal of Management Accounting Research*, 10, pp. 89–118.

Kasanen, E., Lukka, K. and Siitonen, A., 1993. The constructive approach in management accounting research. *Journal of Management Accounting Research*, 5(Fall), pp. 241–264.

Labro, E., 2003. The cost effects of component commonality: A literature review through a management accounting lens. *6th International Seminar on Manufacturing Accounting Research*, Twente, Netherlands.

Labro, E., 2004. The cost effects of component commonality: A literature review through a management accounting lens. *Manufacturing & Service Operations Management*, 6(4), pp. 358–367.

Labro, E. and Tuomela, T., 2003. On bringing more action into management accounting research: Process considerations based on two constructive case studies. *European Accounting Review*, 12(3), pp. 409–442.

Laine, T., Korhonen, T., Suomala, P. and Rantamaa, A., 2016. Boundary subjects and boundary objects in accounting fact construction and communication. *Qualitative Research in Accounting and Management*, 13(3), pp. 303–329.

Lewin, K., 1946. Action research and minority problems, reprinted in: Lewin, G. W. (Eds.), (1948), *Resolving social conflicts: Selected papers on group dynamics by Kurt Lewin*. Harper and Brothers, New York, pp. 201–216.

Lukka, K., 2000. The key issues of applying the constructive approach to field research, in: Reponen, T. (Ed.), *Management expertise for the new millennium, in commemoration of the 50th anniversary of the Turku School of Economics and Business Administration*. Publications of the Turku School of Economics and Business Administration, A-1, Turku, pp. 113–128.

Lukka, K., 2005. Approaches to case research in management accounting: The nature of empirical intervention and theory linkage, in: Jönsson, S. and Mouritsen, J. (Eds.), *Accounting in Scandinavia: The Northern lights*, Liber & Copenhagen Business School Press, Kristianstad, 404 p.

Lukka, K. and Suomala, P., 2014. Relevant interventionist research: Balancing three intellectual virtues. *Accounting and Business Research*, 44(2), pp. 1–17.

Lyly-Yrjänäinen, J., 2008. *Component commonality in engineering-to-order contexts: Contextual factors explaining cost management and management control implications* (Ph.D. thesis). Tampere University of Technology, Publication 766, 146 p.

Malmi, T., 2016. Managerial studies in management accounting: 1990–2014. *Management Accounting Research*, 31, pp. 31–44.

Mattessich, R., 1995. Conditional-normative accounting methodology: Incorporating value judgments and means-ends relations of an applied science. *Accounting, Organizations and Society*, 20(4), pp. 259–284.

Munro, R., 2001. Alignment and identity work: The study of accounts and accountability. In Munro, R. and Mouritsen, J. (Eds.), *Accountability—power, ethos & the technologies of managing*. Thomson, London.

Normann, R., 1976. *Luova yritysjohto (Creative leadership of the firm)*. Weilin & Göös, Helsinki, 258 p.

Pike, K. L., 1954. Emic and etic standpoints for the description of behaviour, in: Pike, K. L. (Ed.), *Language in relation to a unified theory of the structure of human behaviour*. Summer Institute of Linguistics, Glendale, pp. 8–28.

Rautiainen, A., Sippola, K. and Mättö, T., 2017. Perspectives on relevance: The relevance test in the constructive research approach. *Management Accounting Research*, 34, pp. 19–29.

Suomala, P. and Lyly-Yrjänäinen, J., 2012. *Management accounting research in practice: Lessons learned from an interventionist approach*. Routledge, New York, 139 p.

Suomala, P., Lyly-Yrjänäinen, J. and Lukka, K., 2014. Battlefield around interventions: A reflective analysis of conducting interventionist research in management accounting. *Management Accounting Research*, 25(4), pp. 304–314.

Tervala, E., Laine, T., Korhonen, T. and Suomala, P., 2017. The role of financial control in new product development: Empirical insights into project managers' experiences. *Journal of Management Control*, 28(1), pp. 81–106.

Tomkins, C. and Groves, R. 1983. The everyday accountant and researching his reality. *Accounting, Organizations and Society*, 8(4), pp. 361–374.

Turney, P., 1991. *Common cents—the ABC performance breakthrough*. Cost Technology, Hillsboro.

Van Aken, J., 2004. Management research based on the paradigm of the design sciences: The quest for field-tested and grounded technological rules. *Journal of Management Studies*, 41(2), 219–246.

Van de Ven, A. H. and Johnson, P. E., 2006. Knowledge for theory and practice. *Academy of Management Review*, 31(4), pp. 802–821.

3 Different Battlefields—Balancing Episteme, Techne, and Phronesis

The previous chapter focused on analyzing the different types of interventions a researcher can do when collaborating with an organization in order to contribute to the theory. The focus was on deeper understanding of the depth of the intervention as well as the focal point in the process of creating theory contributions. What was not discussed, however, was how such interventions are done in practice and what the different organizational forces pulling the intervening researcher simultaneously in various directions are.

This chapter will begin with the analysis of research interventions in the field and the organizational forces likely impacting the work of the researcher. The first section introduces the notion of battlefield (see Suomala et al. 2014) for illustrating these organizational forces. This discussion is then complemented with the ideas of engaged scholarship presented by Van de Ven and Johnson (2006). Whereas that discussion focuses mainly on forces coming either from within the case company or the research team (possibly funders), there is also a need for wider impact of the research efforts. This chapter, therefore, introduces the ideas of Flyvbjerg (2001) in helping case studies with interventionist elements contribute more to the societal discussion in the context of MA or bringing research-based MA knowledge to other societally relevant contexts. Finally, as a synthesis, the last section introduces the analysis framework used for discussing the cases in Part II, that is, the interplay between episteme, techne, and phronesis.

Balancing the Needs of Various Stakeholders—Intervention as a Battlefield

Although there seems to be something of a movement for IVR within management accounting academia accompanied with several calls for interventionist research (Labro and Tuomela 2003; Jönsson and Lukka 2007; Malmi and Granlund 2009; Quattrone 2009; Suomala and Lyly-Yrjänäinen 2012), it is noteworthy that the justification of IVR is articulated quite differently between these specific calls. Particularly regarding the notion of 'relevance,' we can recognize almost opposite schools of thought amongst the proponents of interventionist research in management accounting.

For Malmi and Granlund (2009), IVR is about solving practical (and accounting-related) problems with practitioners, the process also including a phase during which the presented local solutions for identified problems are brought to a more global level by 'synthesizing' them 'to a more general form.' Furthermore, it becomes clear that Malmi and Granlund (2009) recognize the role of theory in IVR, but rather than underscoring it as an outcome, they highlight it as an input or a resource one should draw from during the course of research:

> "Our position is favorable to interventionist approaches, as in our view the potential of generating directly applicable yet theoretically informed solutions to practitioners is important to pursue."

In his commentary, Quattrone (2009)—although criticizing some of the assumptions and definitions made by Malmi and Granlund (2009)—fundamentally shares the positive stance towards IVR. It is particularly interesting that while engaging a debate on management accounting theories and theorizing, Quattrone (2009) demonstrates explicit support for interventionist research not due to its potential related to theoretical development but for its capability to affect the non-academic world:

> "The paper [by Malmi and Granlund 2009] also makes an important point when it calls for interventionist research given that across the two sides of Atlantic and elsewhere, there is a widespread feeling that some accounting publications lack relevance for, and produce very limited effect on the non-academic world."

In contrast to these examples, some authors have put higher emphasis on the role of theory development when building justification to IVR as an approach. Jönsson and Lukka (2007) underscore that theoretical contributions are a 'must' in all types of research—and no less in interventionist research. However, they point out that the evidence from the existing examples of IVR studies shows that theory development is in many cases underplayed at the expense of promoting somewhat anecdotal empirical findings. In other words, while theoretical relevance should be an elemental virtue in IVR, making a theoretical contribution while simultaneously working meaningfully within a flow of real-life events is a true challenge for a researcher and success in this venture cannot be assumed—not least because the logics of practice and theory can significantly and fundamentally differ from each other (Van de Ven and Johnson 2006; Jönsson and Lukka 2007). Similarly, Suomala and Lyly-Yrjänäinen (2012) share the view that IVR should not be seen merely as a pragmatic exercise but that theoretical relevance is something to be pursued in parallel to providing value for the participating organizations.

Recently, Rautiainen et al. (2017) examined the different perspectives of relevance in IVR studies. They bring up the limitations of the market test approach of the constructive research approaches, with its focus on the benefits of the construct on the business as a determinant of the (also theoretical) relevance of the construct under examination. In line with the idea of this book, they base their argument on the work by Lukka and Suomala (2014) and Flyvbjerg (2001), and propose the relevance diamond diagram that takes into account practical value relevance, legitimative decision relevance, academic value relevance, and instrumental decision relevance. In this diagram, essentially, both short-term and long-term impacts of the interventions are taken into account. Besides, the relevance assessment includes considerations of the practical, theoretical, and societal impacts of the IVR approach (Rautiainen et al. 2017). In other words, to thoroughly understand the relevance and impact of the IVR approach, the three intellectual virtues (Flyvbjerg 2001; Lukka and Suomala 2014; Rautiainen et al. 2017) need to be sufficiently acknowledged and consciously balanced in the IVR process execution.

In practice, however, the IVR processes and the antecedents of different types of relevant impacts require careful examination prior to and during the research projects. Examining the relevance and impact of the IVR approach requires indeed several perspectives. Realizing such impacts and steering the IVR process towards higher impact potential is not, however, a straightforward process. This book, among other recent pieces of research (e.g., Suomala and Lyly-Yrjänäinen 2012; Suomala et al. 2014; Laine et al. 2016; Lukka and Vinnari 2017), highlights the need for considering the (potentially evolving) role of the researcher in the IVR processes, in identifying and realizing the impact potential. In this vein, based on an extensive account of conducted IVR studies, Suomala and Lyly-Yrjänäinen (2012) also identify a number of risks related to producing theoretical contributions through IVR, including the substantial length of research processes, incentive structures favoring practical results (possibly without a need for theoretical elaboration), the lack of visibility of the theoretical potential prior to committing oneself to working in the field, and finding a balance between individual capabilities needed for the different facets (practical/theoretical) of the IVR process.

In addition to the capabilities needed in the different facets of the IVR process, Suomala et al. (2014) pointed out the fact that there are, indeed, various forces pulling the research simultaneously in different directions. As phrased by Suomala et al. (2014):

"... the processes around the intervention constitute a battlefield of numerous and often conflicting agendas and interests of the organizations, the researcher and the academe, apt to render the researcher's task a true challenge."

As stated by Suomala et al. (2014), intervening in the flow of events in a real-life organization represents a true challenge for any researcher. It is not easy to find a match between the company's interests and the theoretical pursuit of the researcher in the first place. However, to make things even more complicated, these interests tend to change throughout the duration of the interventionist field study. For example, managers may not pay much attention to the empirical work until something interesting surfaces, after which the very same managers may place significant pressure to push forward further inquiries. To secure the benefits of all the key stakeholders in the IVR project, Suomala et al. (2014) recommend taking balancing acts, not only within the *emic* and *etic* domains but also between them, since choices made in one domain are likely to affect the other. To maneuver successfully in this battlefield, Suomala et al. recommend balancing acts within four different domains:

- within the *emic* domain
- within the *etic* domain
- between the *emic* and *etic* domains
- dynamic processes of developing the theory contribution.

First, when looking at the challenges within the *emic* domain, one key aspect for the researcher is to keep the research process flowing. One core aspect regarding this, emphasized by Suomala et al. (2014), is to maintain consensus between the key stakeholders. Even though there may be organizational forces pulling the researcher in different directions, it is important to resolve these with open dialogue and active negotiations driven by the researcher. In some cases, it may benefit the researcher to, at least temporarily, emphasize elements not necessarily directly contributing to the main research questions simply to ensure collaboration in the field; such compromises may pay off in the later stages of the research process. Such collaboration in the areas of the organizational interest, according to Suomala et al., may serve as a valuable asset enabling empirical access and presence in interesting events and situations in the field. Even the expert role may not justify a rigid role in the flow of events, but rather the researcher would have to evaluate case by case whether there would be areas that need extra effort, even without a direct link to the research questions.

Second, most research approaches enable the researcher to choose rather freely the focus and scope of the study, with scholarly knowledge and judgment as phrased by Suomala et al. (2014). However, they consider this fundamentally critical in IVR, since the expectations of the case organization are oftentimes at stake. In other words, even though the case company management may not have direct interest in the theoretical positioning of the study, the positioning may affect the resources available for the interventionist work and, hence, the pragmatic outcomes. This, then, makes the management indirectly interested in the theoretical positioning of the work.

Thus, even though Suomala et al. emphasize the importance of having some clear ideas about the theoretical potential of the case, some flexibility may be justified in order to enable the positioning of the theoretical focus to be done in a way that ensures that the interests of key stakeholders are taken into consideration.

Third, as illustrated by the case of Suomala et al. (2014), the balancing acts between the *emic* and *etic* domains are likely to be motivated by stimuli external to the actual field research, emphasizing the importance of opportunities to disclose initial findings without the fear that these ideas are not yet well-developed. Sharing initial findings may open up new and interesting venues from the theoretical point of view, hence helping seize the theoretical potential of the case at hand. Suomala et al. explicitly warn researchers with expert status to not stick too much to the initial agenda falling in their comfort zone; precisely experienced researchers should possess the capabilities to take full advantage of such potential.

Finally, Suomala et al. (2014) point out how IVR uses extant theories to make sense of the empirical environment and, to some extent, push it forward. However, the empirics also help make sense of the theory and push it forward. The role of simultaneous fieldwork and exploration of literature for insightful theoretical underpinnings was highlighted. The latter, as discussed in the paragraph above, helps to position the research in a relevant academic discussion. They also suggest that identifying potential research questions in IVR benefits from connecting the extant literature with the practical interests of the target organization, with the emphasis on not compromising either one. The theory contribution is, eventually, the key responsibility of the researcher, but she should not merely focus only on it but also take into consideration, not only the needs/interests of the organization to ensure the continuous access to the field but rather see the management and their sometimes irrational requests/comments as an asset helping in polishing the key theoretical arguments.

It seems evident that there is no full consensus on the potential of IVR to produce theoretically relevant results. Only recently, Lukka and Vinnari (2017) as well as Laine et al. (2016) have examined the use of different theoretical lenses together with the IVR approach. More particularly, Lukka and Vinnari (2017) studied how actor-network theory (ANT) works together with the IVR approach, and thus how IVR projects could yield theory contributions. The recognized barriers hindering potential theory contributions through IVR were identified. As a result, there seem to be perceived differences between the different perspectives or 'academic tribes,' that is between IVR and ANT. At the same time, Lukka and Vinnari (2017) highlight the importance of actors in both perspectives, and the desired connection with innovation processes with respect to both IVR and ANT. Therefore, Lukka and Vinnari (2017) conclude that no major obstacles exist, but more readily there could be remarkable opportunities in applying ANT (similarly to many other theoretical lenses in social sciences) to yield theory contributions.

Similarly to Lukka and Vinnari (2017), who highlighted the importance of acknowledging interventionist researchers as actors in the actor network underlying theory contribution, Laine et al. (2016) employed pragmatic constructivism and IVR together to better understand the role of the interventionist researchers in the organizational boundaries (as 'boundary subjects'). In their study, pragmatic constructivism enabled detailed examination of the interventionist researchers in cooperation with other actors representing different business functions, and thus a rich account of accounting development in practice featuring knowledge integration and interaction.

So far, the empirical examinations of the relationship between IVR and theory contribution potentials have largely resulted in statements of the overall potential. At the same time, it is fair to say that such a potential has neither been thoroughly recognized nor sufficiently realized. Besides, it becomes clear from the debate on the theory contribution potential embedded in IVR that most authors interested in IVR, nevertheless, distinguish between the types of relevance—typically by referring to a dichotomy between theoretical relevance and practical relevance. It is interesting that authors seem to either explicitly or implicitly hint that placing an increasing effort for either one of the domains would somehow lead to sacrificing another. This juxtapositional view is analogously present also in the retrospective accounts on critical accounting research as articulated by Neu et al. (2001):

> "Indeed the cynical might argue that we have emphasized third-party theorizing instead of direct praxis, focusing on academic scholarship in 'learned' journals where the only contact with the 'real world' is mediated through the screen of the reviewers."

This observation leads us to ponder if and how it would be possible to respect both of these goals and to find a balance within the interventionist research process that leads not only to practically but also theoretically relevant results, which would facilitate IVR in management accounting and contribute to wider societal debates as well. Already, Lukka and Suomala (2014) suggested balancing the three intellectual virtues in (or through) interventionist research. A similar idea is embedded in the relevance diamond diagram proposed by Rautiainen et al. (2017). At the same time, it is fair to say that we do not know enough about how these goals could (or should) be set for interventionist research processes, and how the balance could be intentionally found or refined during the interventionist research processes. More particularly, not that much is known about the relationship between the desired societal impact and the other perspectives of relevance. In response, this book seeks to unveil such a relationship, also by carefully examining the interventionist research processes at hand in five different business environments.

Societal Impact of MA Research

Another interesting discussion on combining practical work in the field and theorizing based on it has been provided by Van de Ven and Johnson (2006). They stress the need to ensure that research, while producing theoretically relevant outcomes, also benefits the practitioners, and introduce the idea of 'engaged scholarship' as a solution. According to Van de Ven and Johnson (2006), engaged scholarship consists of:

- The importance of asking big questions
- Divergent compositions of research teams
- Long duration of research collaboration in order to build mutual trust
- Critical attitude to both theory and practice
- Intertwined scholarly and clinical roles.

First, in order to produce theory contributions raising interest also amongst the practitioners, researchers should focus on asking 'big questions' that are likely to touch people with differing interests. Such 'big questions' may not have easy answers, especially from the practitioner's point of view. Nevertheless, such questions raise the managerial interest, even though the actual theoretical contribution may not be in the core of the practical world. As Van de Ven and Johnson point out, even if a single research project may not provide solid answers to such big questions, a series of studies may already offer some. This is in line with the idea of research streams proposed by Suomala and Lyly-Yrjänäinen (2012), referring to a set of research projects (either parallel or in a sequence) with a certain managerial phenomenon as a common denominator. Thus, whereas the theory contributions of independent studies may not be considered of much use by managers, the wider picture portrayed through the argued theoretical contributions in the research stream may have wider implications also in practice.

Second, Van de Ven and Johnson (2006) highlight the importance of designing a research project as a collaborative learning community in which both the academics and practitioners sit at the same table discussing and debating issues relevant to the study. Through active dialogue between the members of the research team (containing practitioners and academics from various disciplines), after sharing different but complementary views on the case at hand over time, they learn to respect each other as team members providing valuable insights on the issue. Through such dialogues, practitioners learn to see the value of more academic debate and, similarly, the academics will have an improved view on practical, related matters occupying the practitioners. Van de Ven and Johnson also point out the possibility to use such heterogeneous compositions in the advisory boards or steering committees of research projects.

Third, Van de Ven and Johnson (2006) cite Minzberg (1979) and Pettigrew (2001) in pointing out that time is a critical factor when building relationships of trust. Thus, in order to accomplish research outcomes of practical interest, researchers must commit themselves to spend time to interact with the organizational participants. This is in line with the earlier statements of Suomala and Lyly-Yrjänäinen (2012) regarding the long duration of research projects playing a key role for gaining access to the 'real' ways of thinking and execution in the target organizations. Thus, as stated by Van de Ven and Johnson, such longitudinal processes promote deeper learning by enabling repeated exposure to the phenomenon under investigation. As phrased by Van de Ven and Johnson, gaining a 'world class competence' on a certain research topic is a "path dependent process of pursuing a coherent theme of research questions from project to project over an extended period of time."

Fourth, Van de Ven and Johnson (2006) recommend researchers to apply multiple models and methods because any given theory is an abstraction of the reality, incapable of describing all the aspects of a phenomenon. Using multiple models and methods simultaneously not only enables triangulation but also maximizes the learning related to the topic in question. However, in addition to the models and methods, again the sharing of the ideas and approaches with the research team members (whether academic or practitioners) is likely to result in more solid theoretical outputs. Thus, comparisons of alternative explanations, whether theoretical or practical, with a critical mindset are likely to result in outcomes that are not only of theoretical importance but also interesting for the practitioners.

Finally, in order to provide theory contributions that have value for practitioners, researchers not only must be able to possess competencies on both clinical and scholarly work but also be capable of analyzing which role he or she is playing at different points in time. Thus, while it is important to be able to credibly wear both hats, the researcher must be able to reflect which hat is (or was) used when and how that may or may not have impacted the findings. As commented in Suomala et al. (2014), having good skills in both domains is a rare combination and, therefore, the role of the research team is highlighted in ensuring this. Thus, even though one single researcher may not be able to master both clinical and scholarly roles alone, the team can provide assistance and, sometimes, the team can also play an important role in the reflection on when either one these two roles were dominating. It is noteworthy that in this book, with respect to the interventionist processes of the five cases, a broader perspective has been taken to examine the role of the interventionist researchers during the IVR processes. More particularly, in addition to examining the practical and theoretical perspectives, and the depth of the interventions (see, e.g., Suomala and Lyly-Yrjänäinen 2012), the evolving roles of the interventionist researchers during the IVR processes in connection to the impacts of the cases have been unveiled and examined.

By unveiling the IVR processes and the roles of the researchers in them in a broader sense, the analysis can be extended to the dynamics inherent to the cases under examination. Compared to the battlefield notion of Suomala et al. (2014), Van de Ven and Johnson emphasize the collaboration with the practitioners not only as a tool for gaining access but also as a tool for providing theory contributions with more pragmatic use and impact. As Suomala et al. (2014) pointed out in their study, academic peers can play a major role in helping the interventionist researcher find the right questions to ask (i.e., the right theoretical positioning for the study), having the practitioners also participate in that process brings one more variable in this setup already characterized as a battlefield. Nevertheless, especially when the objective is to do research with wider impact, this perhaps is worth noting.

However, thus far the focus has been on combining theory and practice in order to produce research outcomes of interest to the practitioners. Van de Ven and Johnson, when introducing the idea of 'engaged scholarship,' see that mainly as a tool to increase pragmatic relevance of research. Van de Ven and Johnson, however, do not emphasize that the practical utilities do not have to focus only on the participating organization but rather on practical impacts more in general, hence contributing to the discussion on societal impact of research. As Lukka and Suomala (2014) point out, an even broader perspective might be welcome for MA research to justify its role not only in academia but also within the society. They call for discussion on the dynamic processes of developing the theory contribution with societal impact.

In this book we wish to shed further light on how IVR research and the intervention in particular produces outcomes with both practical and theoretical interest. However, instead of focusing the practical relevance only on the case company and companies having similar issues with the case company, we wish to show that interventionist MA research has the potential to take part in the debate related to various contemporary phenomena present in the society. Thus, following the idea of Van de Ven and Johnson (2006), MA research should be looking at big questions and, as Lukka and Suomala (2014) suggest, there should be broader perspective on relevance. Lukka and Suomala apply the ideas of Flyvbjerg (2001) into the interventionist MA research genre, providing an interesting way to enhance the scope of research contributions.

In his book, Flyvbjerg (2001) introduces the idea of phronetic social science, social science that actively seeks ways to impact the society. As phrased by Lukka and Suomala (2014), the starting point of Flyvjberg's book are the three intellectual virtues that a researcher can pay attention to introduced by Aristotle (1955): episteme, techne, and phronesis. First, Flyvjberg views episteme as knowledge that is invariable in time and space, based on analytic rationality, and corresponding to the modern scientific ideas of natural sciences (see Lukka and Suomala 2014). Episteme, according to Flyvjberg, concerns 'know why' types of questions. Second, techne focuses on craft and art and, according to Lukka and Suomala, as an activity it is concrete, variable, and context-dependent. Techne is based on practical instrumental rationality and, therefore, responds to 'know-how' type of questions. Finally, phronesis, while closely connected to action and being context dependent, refers to ethically practical wisdom and knowledge on how to behave appropriately in particular circumstances (see Suomala and Lukka 2014). Phronesis in research, therefore, corresponds to questions like 'Where are we going?,' 'Is this desirable?,' or 'What should be done?' (Flyvbjerg 2001, p. 60). In addition to the above, Flyvjberg, as a social scientist, also emphasizes the question 'Who gains and who loses and by which mechanisms of power?' Thus, the phronetic social science proposed by Flyvbjerg (2001) can be defined as 'a social science that matters,' hence focusing on the societal impact of the research work.

For Flyvbjerg (2001), the primary objective for phronetic social science is not to provide a theoretical mirror for a society but to provide society with knowledge that can be used as input to the dialogue on topical social challenges and solutions:

> "Carry out analyses and interpretations of the status of values and interests in society aimed at social commentary and social action, i.e. praxis."

When seeking to fulfill this objective, according to Flyvbjerg, research has to address four wide questions, which are inherently value-rational: 'Where are we going?,' 'Is this desirable?,' 'What should be done?,' and finally 'Who gains and who loses and by which mechanisms of power?' (Flyvbjerg 2001). Flyvbjerg underscores the difficulty of these questions, and reminds that no single person—valid also for a social scientist—is capable of providing full answers for these. Instead, Flyvbjerg insists that partial answers ought to be pursued through which social science can engage with discourse in society.

Given that the full answers for the questions phrased by Flyvbjerg are impossible to produce and that even partial answers might be hard to formulate, what can then be done? To begin with, Flyvbjerg advises that the researcher must not settle with practicing 'science' in general, but she has to make it explicit whether she is practicing episteme, techne, or phronesis. Concerning the selection from or emphasis between these three virtues, Flyvbjerg advocates the potential of social sciences as phronesis and techne, whereas he is extremely doubtful when it regards the episteme qualities of social research. When talking about the possible roles social sciences can play within society, he goes on to formulate (Flyvbjerg 2001, p. 62, emphasis added):

> "In any event, this role of social science will be linked to **real** problems with **a material** foundation that one can fight for or against."

In terms of research setting and approach, this stance would lead the researcher towards context-specific inquiry and appreciating case-based research, which can draw from the power of examples and thus create depth that complements the breadth produced by large sample surveys.

Lukka and Suomala (2014) apply the ideas of Flyjvberg in the field of management accounting. Thus, at best, MA research can (and should) provide value to the organizations participating in these research venues, provide outcomes that are theoretically interesting (as emphasized by Lukka and Suomala), and, finally, provide inputs to societal debates on contemporary issues. Lukka and Suomala (2014) summarize the methodological guidance of Flyvbjerg for 'pragmatically governed interpretation of studied practices' which, in addition, is 'an analytic project, not a theoretical or methodological one.' To achieve this, Flyvbjerg (2001) proposes nine principles:

1. Focusing on values: the researcher must reject both the view that central values are universal and the view of relativism (that any set of values is as good as another); instead the researcher seeks to draw from the studied context and situation and tries to capture the common view among the group or setting under study.
2. Placing power at the core of analysis: in addition to values, power serves as another key element of context being analyzed. For the phronetic researcher, power is quite elusive and versatile; not negative or positive per se, but something that is exercised and produced within and between institutions and structures.
3. Getting close to reality: researchers try to anchor their studies in the contexts that are being studied (without necessarily going native in the ethnographic sense) and establish close relations with stakeholders in order to stimulate reactions and interest to the research, which is to test and evaluate the findings and their value.
4. Emphasizing little things: the researcher seeks to build as general findings as possible but through a procedure that takes off by putting effort towards understanding details and 'little things.'
5. Looking at practice before discourse: phronetic research sees actual daily practices and actual deeds more fundamental as the targets of analysis than discourse or theory. At the outset, each individual practice is documented in itself without taking positions regarding 'the truth-value and significance ascribed by participants to the practice studied.' At the second stage, the researcher seeks to establish the relations from the local practices to the wider context.
6. Studying cases and contexts: judgment is regarded as central to phronesis, and since judgment lies in specific contexts, the phronetic researcher draws from case-exemplars in order to understand judgment—be the cases experienced or narrated.
7. Asking "how?" and doing narrative: building an understanding and explanation of any given phenomenon is believed to start by asking 'how' questions. Narrative, for one, is regarded as a fundamental

vehicle for 'making sense of experience' but also for means to recognize future alternatives or scenarios before actually encountering them.

8. Joining agency and structure: practices, actors, and structures ought to be studied together, understanding that they are profoundly intertwined. Micro- and macro-level analyses should be combined not between separate studies but within individual studies in order to understand how structures shape individual choices and which are structural consequences of individual actions.

9. Dialoguing with a polyphonic voice: research is not regarded as the one voice of claiming authority. Instead, the interpretations provided by the phronetic research are understood as inputs for societal dialogue and praxis, which serve as an actual test for the interpretations produced. In this test, the strength of interpretation depends upon (the competition related to) the acceptance of validity claims underpinning the interpretation.

Flyvbjerg's (2001) view on phronetic social science has much in common with the typical characteristics of IVR. In IVR, the researcher is an active actor in the real-time flow of life in the field and, for coping with and for balancing between various interests present in cases, she has to adopt, or at least consider, the *emic* (insider's) perspective to the issues at hand. IVR is a problem-solving-oriented venture with explicit connections to challenges present in praxis. In IVR the researcher typically participates in an organizational change project and faces the practical challenges together with the representatives of the case organization, and it has an element of field experimentation, during which a novel or typically not yet fully diffused concept is put into an empirical test (Suomala and Lyly-Yrjänäinen 2012). IVR can be viewed as a process of bundling together things (in the design of the solution construction and its implementation test) and after that unbundling them in order to analyze the findings of the project and examine their theoretical contribution (Jönsson and Lukka 2007). However, to justify their societal role and reason for existence, MA researchers should also ponder how they benefit the society at large with the (typically) public sector funding received. Thus instead of MA research providing a theoretical mirror for accounting-related issues, following Flyvjberg's notion, MA research should provide society with MA-related knowledge that can be used as an input to the dialogue on topical social challenges and solutions.

Capturing the Interplay between Episteme, Techne, and Phronesis

As Flyvjberg mentions, "the primary objective for social science is not to provide a theoretical mirror for a society but to provide the society with knowledge that can be used as input to the dialogue on topical social challenges and solutions." This notion can be modified to MA research: the primary objective for MA research is not to provide a theoretical mirror for the management community, but to provide the community with knowledge that can be used as an input to the dialogue on topical management challenges and solutions. Thus, MA research should not only provide inputs to the MA challenges and solutions because MA oftentimes provides insights to broader managerial challenges and even societal issues, too.

Van de Ven and Johnson (2006) recommend trying to identify 'big questions' which then would motivate all stakeholders to participate in the research venue. While Lukka and Suomala (2014) appreciate the comment of Van de Ven, they also point out that coming up with such kinds of big questions might be a challenge. Thus, the question is how to then come up with even 'bigger' questions which do not only provide potential to theory contribution and attract interest of the stakeholders in the research venue, but also provide interest at the societal level. According to Van de Ven and Johnson, recognizing such 'big questions' requires interaction with the involved parties. Such interaction also enables improved understanding of the phenomenon at hand, making it possible to create new theories and not only test and implement existing theories/ideas.

The process of identifying such a 'big question' and responding to it by means of interventionist research requires further examination. In this book, the analyses of the cases include, in essence, detailed analyses of the three intellectual virtues at hand at different phases of the research processes. Besides, the reflections and analyses of the interventions include separate considerations on the roles of the interventionist researchers involved in the IVR processes. As the emphasis on 'phronesis,' 'episteme,' and 'techne' tend to evolve during the processes and vary from one case to another, so do the roles of the researchers enabling/supporting the realization of such impacts. Therefore, not only the width and depth of the interventions (see Suomala and Lyly-Yrjänäinen 2012), but also the peculiarities of the actual interventions and the roles of the researchers (and other parties involved in them) make a difference.

In this book, we will discuss the evolving roles of the researchers within a multidisciplinary research team, and more particularly an evolution of a researcher's role from a comrade to an expert. Besides, in line with the ideas presented in Laine et al. (2016), we examine the role of intervening researcher as an integrator and the role of the new cost information attained through interventions in facilitating product development. Finally, in line with the idea of extending the relevance of the IVR approach to include societal impacts, we examine the process of diffusing the ideas stemming from the interventionist process within the sector and beyond—representing wider societal impacts. As a whole, the cases help us better understand the nature of the mechanisms through which the impact potential and relevance of the IVR processes are identified, potentially refined along with the process, and eventually realized.

As this book argues, discoveries on little things provide new perceptions on big questions, though this may require repositioning of the empirical work and theory framework. Such an interplay takes places within the IVR processes among the researchers and other stakeholders. The divergent research teams, emphasized by both Flyvbjerg (2001) and Van de Ven and Johnson (2006), enable dialogue with a polyphonic voice, also paving a road to discoveries with societal implications. These two combined with long-term research projects facilitate interplay between *emic* and *etic* perspectives in an iterative manner, which is an important input for the theorizing process. As shown in the book, the societal implications may stem from the context and techne (though not downplaying the importance of theory contributions) or from the process of theorizing the discoveries of the case. For each case, the book describes the starting point at the beginning of each chapter followed by the description of the case, interventions, and key findings. Finally, we will 'reverse engineer' the iterative interplay between episteme, techne, and phronesis as well as how the societal relevance was achieved in each case.

References

Aristotle, 1955. *The ethics of Aristotle: The Nicomachean ethics*. Penguin, Baltimore.

Flyvbjerg, B., 2001. *Making social science matter: Why social inquiry fails and how it can succeed again*. Cambridge University Press, Cambridge.

Jönsson, S. and Lukka, K., 2007. There and back again: Doing IVR in management accounting, in: Chapman, C., Hopwood, A. and Shields, M. (Eds.), *Handbook of management accounting research*, Vol. 1. Elsevier, Amsterdam, pp. 373–397.

Labro, E. and Tuomela, T., 2003. On bringing more action into management accounting research: Process considerations based on two constructive case studies. *European Accounting Review*, 12(3), pp. 409–442.

Laine, T., Korhonen, T., Suomala, P. and Rantamaa, A., 2016. Boundary subjects and boundary objects in accounting fact construction and communication. *Qualitative Research in Accounting and Management*, 13(3), pp. 303–329.

Lukka, K. and Suomala, P. (2014). Relevant interventionist research: Balancing three intellectual virtues. *Accounting and Business Research*, 44(2), pp. 1–17.

Lukka, K. and Vinnari, E. 2017. Combining actor-network theory with interventionist research: Present state and future potential. *Accounting, Auditing & Accountability Journal*, 30(3), pp. 720–753.

Malmi, T. and Granlund, M., 2009. In search for management accounting theory. *European Accounting Review*, 18(3), pp. 597–620.

Minzberg, H., 1979. An emerging strategy of "direct" research. *Administrative Science Quarterly*, 24, pp. 582–589.

Neu, D., Cooper, D. J. and Everett, J., 2001. Critical accounting interventions. *Critical Perspectives on Accounting*, 12(6), pp. 735–762.

Pettigrew, A., 2001. Management research after modernism. *British Journal of Management*, 12(special issue), pp. 61–70.

Quattrone, P., 2009. 'We have never been post-modern': On the search of management accounting theory. *European Accounting Review*, 18(3), pp. 621–630.

Rautiainen, A., Sippola, K. and Mättö, T. 2017. Perspectives on relevance: The relevance test in the constructive research approach. *Management Accounting Research*, 34, pp. 19–29.

Suomala, P. and Lyly-Yrjänäinen, J., 2012. *Management accounting research in practice: Lessons learned from an interventionist approach.* Routledge, New York.

Suomala, P., Lyly-Yrjänäinen, J. and Lukka, K., 2014. Battlefield around interventions: A reflective analysis of conducting interventionist research in management accounting. *Management Accounting Research*, 25(4), pp. 304–314.

Van de Ven, A. H. and Johnson, P. E., 2006. Knowledge for theory and practice. *Academy of Management Review*, 31(4), pp. 802–821.

Part II

Theory Contribution with Societal Impact Through Research Interventions

4 Agile Experiments Facilitating Technology Diffusion in Healthcare

The case company is a startup providing a medicine dispensing service to help elderly people take care of their medication more independently. The customer base consists of home care service providers (mainly public organizations in Finland) and the service helps these organizations reduce the number of home care visits to the patients, hence reducing the resource consumption of these home care organizations. The service the case company offers provides potential for a significant productivity increase in the home care of elderly patients. Thus, the societal impact of this case is primarily argued based on the need of governments in welfare societies to find ways to 'do more with less' to be able to take care of their aging populations. In other words, the case company itself is focusing on such an interesting societal problem, thus also positioning the start of the case in that area (phronesis).

The collaboration with the case company was a part of a research project focusing on ergonomic management accounting. In that project, the idea was to find ways to make accounting information widely available and easier to use. To make accounting information accessible to various stakeholders not only within but also outside the companies, the project focuses on the interaction of facts and feelings in managing customer value and profitability. Unveiling such interaction represents a starting point for effective accounting development, and at the same time seeks to respond to the timely societal challenges with scarce resources. As the managing director mentioned regarding this particular case:

> "Population is aging and we cannot manage the costs of taking care of the elderly. We need tools that will convince managers in the health care sector as well as the city-level politicians about the cost savings and other benefits our new technology can provide to them. Our stakeholder group is very heterogeneous and emotions also play important role in the decision-making, yet we have to be able to reach them with our message."
>
> —Jyrki Niinistö, Managing Director, Evondos Oy

Introduction to the Case

In Finland, the aging of the population has been faster than in any other European county in the 2000s (Hartikainen et al. 2008). In 2007, 16% of the population was over 65 years old, and until 2016 it had climbed up to 19%. In 2030, the share of elderly people over 65 years of age is expected to reach 26% (statistics Finland 2007, 2015). Healthcare in Finland is mainly publicly funded, and the aging population requires new solutions to the care of the growing elderly population (Kröger and Leinonen 2012). At the same time, the current healthcare trend encourages elderly to stay in their own homes as long as possible (Kröger and Leinonen 2012); assisted living consumes fewer resources than placing the elderly people in old-age homes or hospitals. In addition, the elderly prefer independent living in their own homes (see, e.g., Andersson 2007), also supporting the trend. Consequently, public sector healthcare organizations have home care units with nurses committed only to serving patients living in their own homes. The responsibilities cover help in preparing meals, cleaning, and various nursing tasks such as blood pressure or blood sugar measurements. If the patients are no longer able to master their medications independently, nurses prepare pill dispensers for them. This is a time-consuming process, keeping in mind that home care patients often have multiple comorbidities and need a large variety of medicine. Despite the fact that home care nurses are well-trained professionals, manual preparation of the pill dispensers while interacting with the patients creates potential for human errors.

The process of preparing the pill dispenser can be made faster and more reliable through a prepacked multidose sachets service offered by pharmacies. The doctor in charge of a home care patient defines which medicines to take and how many times a day. The nursing staff then, in close cooperation with the pharmacist, prepares a more detailed daily schedule for the medication. When this information is sent to a pharmacy, the pharmacy packages all the medicines of one 'intake' into a small disposable pouch (i.e., sachet), resulting in a roll of sachets. Each sachet has the patient's name printed on it as well as the date and time when the pills in the sachet should be consumed. An example of such a roll of sachets and the printed text in one are shown in Figure 4.1.

However, if the home care patients suffer from a memory disorder, the pill dispenser or prepackaged medicine rolls no longer provide a reliable solution. When that is the case, the home care nurses have to visit the elderly whenever it is time for them to take their medicine, tying up resources. This is where the case company service provides a solution.

The core of the service is a medicine dispensing robot (shown left in Figure 4.1) placed at the patient's home. The prepacked multidose sachets already used by most home care organizations are compatible with the dispensing robot. The roll is inserted in the medicine dispenser by the nursing

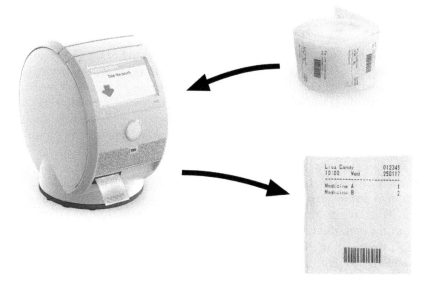

Figure 4.1 Evondos Medicine Dispensing Robot and a Roll of Prepackaged Medicine.

staff and the dispensing robot then uses machine vision to read the plain text on the sachets to check that (1) the sachets are for the right patient and (2) when the next dose is to be taken. When it is time to take the medicine, the dispenser notifies the patient and, when the patient pushes the button on the front panel, the sachet exits the machine. The dispensing robot has been designed for safe medicine intake and, therefore, will not simply push out the sachets at the right time; the patient needs to acknowledge the dispenser each time to gain access to the medicine. In case the patient does not acknowledge the dispensing robot, the alarm will continue until there is a risk that the time window between two different medicine intakes become too small. When that happens, this particular sachet is stored in a locked compartment and the Evondos Telecare System notifies the healthcare organization so that the nurses can then initiate the necessary action. The home care nurse on duty may visit the patient to check why the medicine was not taken on time or, in case the medication in that sachet is not critical (such as just some vitamins), the nurse may decide to let the patient simply skip that medicine without any further action. Thus, the service provides detailed control of the medicine intake of the patients, yet empowers the nurses to make decisions regarding what to do in each case. In case no immediate action is needed, the dispensing robot stands by until it is time to proceed with the next sachet.

To summarize, the medicine dispensing robot can be characterized as a locked medicine cabinet that reminds the patient when it is time to take the medicine and opens only at the right time for the right medicine. In addition, the robot notifies the healthcare organization if the medicine is not taken as planned. However, after the notification, the action to be taken is left for the nurses to decide, based on their professional opinion. Thus, the service provides valuable help for those patients who would like to take their medicine as prescribed yet no longer are able to do that independently. However, if a patient is not willing to take the medicine, the service is not a solution; the service only reminds the patient to take the medicine but does not monitor whether or not the medicine is consumed.

The fact that the operation of the medicine dispensing robot is based on machine vision is very important; there is no need for the healthcare organization to do any programming whatsoever regarding when to take the medicine. When the doctor defines the schedule for the medication, the pharmacy prints the date and time on each sachet and the robot uses that information. Thus, the sachet itself tells the dispensing robot when it wants to be handed out to the patient, making it an example of product-centric control (see Kärkkäinen and Holmström 2002). In other words, the sachets ask for service providers (nurses and robots) to take the needed action at the right time for the right patient (Kärkkäinen et al. 2003). In case of bad printing on the sachet, making the text unreadable by the machine, the support staff of the service provider can look at the sachet online to manually instruct the robot what to do—if the text is readable/interpretable with human eye—without the healthcare organization even noticing. In case the text is unreadable by the service operator, the dispensing robot will be stopped and the healthcare organization notified.

It would be easy to assume that the home care patients do not like the home care visits to be replaced by a machine. In fact, that usually is one of the first comments given on the service by people not directly involved with home care work. However, most home care patients appreciate the independence; many elderly people would prefer not to have the home care nurses visit their homes. As mentioned by one nurse:

> "Patients do not like us coming to their homes; they value independence very highly. They like Evondos because it gives them the feeling that they are in control of their daily medicine intake."

Elderly with memory disorder have problems in taking their medicine, resulting in the need to visit some patients several times a day just to hand out medicine. The average home care visit in Finland costs approximately 40 Euros. With the monthly fee of the service (165–300 Euros, depending on the healthcare organization's volume), reducing a half a dozen visits per month makes the service break even. That combined with the fact that many home care organizations already use prepacked multidose sachets with their elderly home care patients should make the diffusion rate of the service very high. However, the company has faced slower growth rates than expected. As mentioned by the Managing Director:

"Our value proposition is a no-brainer, yet it has not been easy to deliver our message to the public sector decision-makers."

Healthcare managers today are cost-conscious; however, many decisions regarding public sector healthcare are made in councils consisting of local politicians, many of whom may not be experienced in working with numbers and cost information in particular. As was stated by the Managing Director:

"Before our project I had not realized that there are many stakeholders in the healthcare decision-making process not necessarily accustomed in dealing with cost-benefit calculations in their daily work like the health-care managers and us business people. Thus, tools that can help such stakeholders understand our value proposition would be highly welcomed in our toolbox."

The initial plan of the research project was to study tools that would help clarify such cost analyses to the various stakeholders involved in the decision-making process. One emergent idea was to create an animation that the sales people could customize with the data of the customer organization and then the animation would walk the customer through the cost-benefit analysis. However, despite the close relationships with the healthcare organizations implementing the service, the case company had faced challenges to access data related to the benefits of their service. Information regarding the financial impact of the service had been provided only in bits and pieces, eroding visibility of the financial impacts and the big picture. For example, in one city purchasing the service for 50 elderly people, the average reduction in the number of visits was 17 per patient. However, the company was not able to access in more detail how the patients had been selected, not to speak of the health profiles of those patients, making it difficult for the company to learn from that implementation. This, then, made it very difficult to work on such sales tools.

As a result, when the research collaboration started, one of the ideas was to use researchers as additional resources helping home care organizations analyze the impacts the service would provide them. Thus, the case company would allocate the researchers at the disposal of the home care organizations. The idea was that the researchers intervening in the customer organization would simultaneously provide better visibility to the patient selection, and to the impacts the service had on the home care organizations, helping the company to learn about these customer cases.

The intervention, however, was easier said than done. Healthcare organizations continuously collaborate with research organizations and, therefore, they have very detailed procedures for granting researchers access to their organizations. Since the healthcare resources already struggle with high workloads, the management is very conscious regarding who is allowed access to burden them. Despite the idea that the researchers were positioned as an additional resource placed at the disposal of the healthcare organization, the MA researchers were automatically placed under the same category of various medical research organizations, mainly consuming the resources of the healthcare organizations without directly contributing to their operations.

City of Joensuu, however, saw the potential in collaboration. City of Joensuu, located in the eastern border of Finland, had made a decision to pilot the medicine dispensing service to learn who the service would benefit most. As mentioned by the Project Manager:

> "Our interest is to find the profiles for customers whom the service would benefit the most while also providing cost savings."

The Project Manager realized that she would anyway have to prepare the analyses on cost savings and it would only be to her benefit if the researchers were helping out. In addition, researchers were seen as neutral, third party actors interested in analyzing the impact of the service instead of company representatives trying to prove their value proposition. As a result, access to the home care organization was granted without any bureaucracy whatsoever.

Interventions

City of Joensuu had started an EU-funded project for piloting new technologies facilitating elderly people to stay home longer, and one of the technologies to be piloted was Evondos medicine dispensing service. To gain better access to the implications of their service, Evondos management offered researchers as additional, free resources for analyzing the financial implications of the medicine dispensing service during the pilot. Following the principles of IVR, the researchers were to work actively with the healthcare organization, providing access to the organization and interesting in-depth data on cost. The interventions were to pave the road for accessing valuable customer information regarding the benefits of the service needed for visualizing their cost-reduction potential to the various stakeholders and, in that way, gaining interesting empirics for theorizing. The interventions were as follows:

- Visiting patients with nurses
- Participating in the training sessions
- Interviews regarding expected outcomes
- Analysis of ERP data (e.g., visits, scheduling, travelling, and blood pressure)
- Nurse interviews on actual outcomes
- Experiments on the process implications of a new anticoagulant.

First, to get familiar with the home care organization and their daily processes, the researcher spent three shifts visiting the homes of home care patients with the nurses, some of whom were to take part in the Evondos pilot. As a management accounting researcher, visiting home care patients with the nurses was outside the personal comfort zone of the researcher. The interaction with home care patients differs to some extent from the discourse with business people and managers. In addition, the practicalities of the healthcare sector became very evident when, for example, one of the visited patients was carrying bacteria resistant to antibiotics, hence requiring safety procedures very different from manufacturing industries. The visits with the nurses gave a good, practical insight about the home care, and the nurses appreciated the effort to get exposed to the daily practice of home care work, as later mentioned by one of the nurses:

> "I wish our managers would also join us more often in the home care visits to see what our daily work really is."

Thus, spending time on the front line of home care work not only provided some insights into what was going on in the field but also set the stage for good, easy-going collaboration with the nurses. Interestingly, the case company policy requires that all executive board level managers spend time on the field with home care nurses to ensure first-hand understanding of the context they work in. However, it has not been easy for them to gain access to actual Evondos users and, therefore, the research collaboration with the Joensuu team was considered highly valuable.

Second, the researcher was invited to join the Evondos training sessions provided for the home care nurses. On one hand, there was no need for a special training/introduction session to be arranged for the researcher. On the other hand, that provided interesting opportunities to observe the training session and nurse feedback as well as get familiar with the nurses. The first training session was for the lead users and took all day, with the morning focusing on the back office software needed to manage the dispensing robot fleet. This was important because the lead users would take charge of setting up the medicine dispensers at the patients' homes and primarily manage the back office software. The training session was given by one of the R&D engineers, and it turned out rather technical, focusing on how to input data to the system. This, unfortunately, caused some of the nurses to lose the big picture, though the afternoon, focusing on the medicine dispenser itself, gave the nurses more pragmatic understanding of how the machines work and how the fleet is managed through the back office software:

> "It was not until in the afternoon when I realized that this is how this service must work. . . . There must be things in the background like this back office system."

The other two training sessions were organized for the nursing staff. Here the focus was no longer on the back office software but completely on how the dispensing robot works and what actions nurses will have to take in order to load it. After a short introductory lecture, the nurses started to practice inserting the roll of medicine into the dispenser, with a couple of lead users and the researcher acting as tutors. Nurses are used to working with their hands and, therefore, the practical training was appreciated in the feedback. However, the training was started with filling up the dispenser without a step-by-step introduction to what the medicine dispensing robot is and what it does. This caused unnecessary confusion within the nurses regarding the service, easily avoidable with a good demo. When introducing such a new technology to the nurses in the field, it is of utmost importance to ensure that everyone understands what the service is about and what it is not. For example, the service does not suit a patient hostile towards taking the medicine because, after taking the sachet, there is no way to ensure that the medicines will actually be consumed. When everyone understands the realities of the service, it is easier to concentrate on the training, as was mentioned by the project manager of the City of Joensuu:

> "At the beginning we often forgot to mention that this device actually is with the customer at home. When the nurses or patients first hear about the service, many of them think that the dispenser gives the medicine to the nurse at their office before the home care visit."

Third, at the beginning of the collaboration, the nurse teams were interviewed regarding the patient selection. The main interest was on the key arguments why the patients had been selected and what the expected outcomes would be; the idea was to gather the profiles of planned service users. As the Project Manager mentioned:

> "We have invested time on the customer selection with the attempt to find customers that would benefit the most."

Previously the company had identified two important patient groups: patients with memory loss not able to take care of their medication and, within that group, Parkinson patients who need to take their medicine very systematically throughout the day. The latter group was very interesting considering the potential reduction in daily visits. In some cases, four or five home care visits had been eliminated with the new service. The Joensuu team, however, had identified yet another interesting group of users: people addicted to painkillers or antidepressants. Thus, in that category the memory loss no longer was the common denominator; it was the need to keep the medicines locked up to be consumed in a controlled manner.

During these group interviews, nurses were interested in the service, though they were asking more transparency on what it costs, what it does, and how it is expected to give benefits to the patients. The nurses appeared to be agitated by the fact that the price to the patient or the healthcare organization was not discussed in the training. Somehow, the nurses had the impression that there was something secret in the pricing of the service, resulting in critical comments:

> "Why can't they openly tell as what this costs to us? Why is that kept like some sort of a secret?"

During these group interviews, the price of the service as well as the above-discussed payback analysis (a half a dozen visits less per month to cover the service fee) was openly shared with the nurses, who then seemed to calm down, again showing the importance of good tools for communicating the (cost) benefits of the service to different stakeholders. As was admitted by one of the skeptical nurses:

> "Knowing this, with one of my patients, already the traveling costs easily cover the service fee."

The openness in sharing the cost for the healthcare organization and possible fee paid by the patients themselves is something that the company is now seriously considering. On one hand, they feel that most nurses are not interested in the cost side of the service but prefer the focus on the well-being of the patients and improved care. On the other hand, the nurses are sometimes a bit hostile because the service provider is a private company, though when the value provided is shared openly with the nurses, the resistance may diminish. However, the company has no clear policy on that aspect yet, even though the intervening researcher believes in shared understanding and empowerment of the nurses in the front line.

Fourth, one interesting element in the collaboration with the City of Joensuu was the access to the home care ERP data on the selected Evondos patients. Whereas the researchers were not granted direct access to the ERP, the Project Manager provided the researchers with data pulled from the database. In that data, the names of the patients were taken out, yet the researchers were provided with actual data on medications, number of visits, times of the visits, and the duration of the visits. The graph in Figure 4.2 shows the number of home care visits for each patient before (light gray) and after (darker gray) the implementation of the service. Before the pilot, there were on average 640 home care visits per month within the selected patient group. However, there were some customers whose health collapsed during the pilot, causing the number of visits to increase by seven to 647. Thus, despite the reduction in the number of visits with some patients, the net impact of the service turned out to be slightly negative, as shown by the accumulated curve. However, it is important to note that the increase in the number of visits had nothing to do with the service. On one hand, the

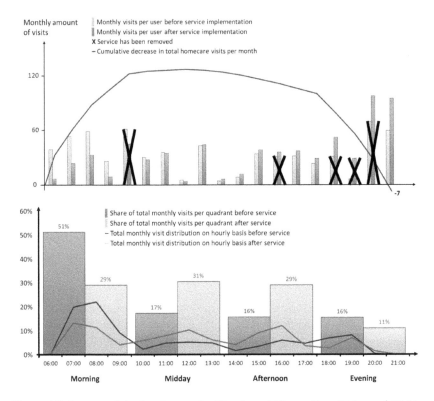

Figure 4.2 Impact of the Service on the Number of Home Care Visits and Visiting Hours.

pilot was used for experimenting with the medicine dispensing robot and, therefore, the home care team was not looking for the most optimal patients for the service. On the other hand, with some of the patients, their condition simply worsened, meaning that more personal home care visits were needed regardless of the service. As also shown in the figure, regarding the patients with increased number of visits, with most cases the use of the service was cancelled. Nevertheless, the data shown in the figure still includes those patients to give a systematic overview of the case.

One aspect burdening the home care resources is the fact that morning hours are very busy when the nurses have to visit many patients to help some of them get out of the bed, help some prepare breakfast, and give them all their morning medicine, preferably before noon. The service enabled the selected patients to take their morning medication independently, making it possible to distribute the home care visits more evenly during the day. The graph in Figure 4.2 shows how the visits during the morning hours were reduced. In other words, when the service woke the patients up in the morning and instructed them to take their morning medication, there was no longer such a hurry to visit all the patients in the morning hours.

Concerning the total costs of servicing the patients, also the duration of the visits as well as the travelling time and travelling costs had to be taken into account. The nurses were making a time stamp with their mobile phones pointing out the time they arrived in the patient's home and the time they left, providing reliable data on the duration of the visits. Though patients were only charged for the time spent on their premises, also the time needed to travel to the patients as well as the cost of using a car was added to the cost analysis. The main cost driver was, nevertheless, the number of visits.

Finally, to get better understanding on the real situation regarding the number of visits, the nurse teams were interviewed to get direct feedback from the service. First, despite some skepticism at the beginning, the nurses were very happy with the service concept. As one of the nurses pointed out frankly:

> "Here we would like to stress that our customers have been very happy with the service and we (nurses) would like to see this service used also in the future."

As mentioned above, solutions such as the one discussed in this case are easily criticized for the reduced human interaction with the elderly patients. However, as pointed out by the interviewees, there are elderly who would like to be more independent and would prefer to have fewer home care visits. As was mentioned by one of the nurses:

> "I have one patient that really would like to be more independent. Without the service, we would have to visit him every day. Now we visit him only once per week. And he likes when the dispenser talks to him with a female voice."

The key cost driver for the home care organization is the number of home care visits, and the same goes with the patients, too. As was mentioned by one of the nurses:

> "Many of our customers have a very small pension and the home care is rather expensive for them. Even if the service is subsidized by the government, the patients pay for the service. Some of them are happy to use the service if it brings down their home care fee."

Even though the study focused mainly on the financial benefits of the service, the safety and possibility for improved care process are worth pointing out. With some of the patients, even though neither the number of visits nor the time of the visits changed, the patient was able to take the medications on time, hence impacting the well-being. As mentioned by one of the nurses:

> "The urinating medicine of one of my patients to work requires that the drug is taken very systematically. That is now possible with the service without burdening our organization."

The nurses seemed very pleased with the new service being piloted, which had become evident to the Project Manager, too. The service clearly provided value added to the care processes, though the number of visits did not come down, as explained earlier. The positive feedback from the nurses raised the interest that perhaps all is not as it seems and worth more detailed considerations. When the reasons for the increased number of visits with some patients were investigated, the nurses pointed out that without the service the number of visits, with many of those patients, would have increased even more. Thus, the service seemed to smoothen the resource impact of the weakening patients on the home care organization. When pondering these findings, the Project Manager came up with an idea to ask the nurses the needed number of visits if the service was terminated.

Thus, as part of the interviews regarding the feedback on the service, the nurse teams were asked to estimate how many visits would be needed and why for each patient participating in the pilot without the service. The outcome is illustrated in Figure 4.3, with the darkest columns showing the estimates of the nurse teams for each patient. When the results were summed up, the nurses estimated the total number of visits needed without the service would go up to 1178 per month. This compared with the 640 monthly visits at the beginning and the 647 after the pilot shows how significantly the service had reduced the need to increase the resource use of the home care nurses, despite the worsening condition with some of the patients. The curve in the figure shows the net impact between the situation with the

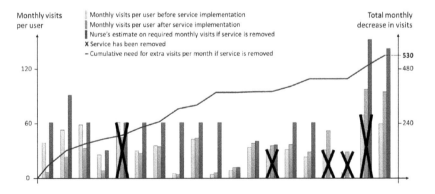

Figure 4.3 The Service Buffering the Need to Increase Nurse Capacity.

service and had the service been cancelled, resulting in net impact of negative 530 visits.

Thus, despite the slight increase in the total number of home care visits documented by the ERP data, the real need would still have been significantly higher without the service. As the Project Manager mentioned:

> "Now, whenever we analyze our customers using the Evondos service, we always ask the nurses to estimate the number of visits needed if the service was cancelled to provide understanding on how it has helped us reduce the workload or the need to place the patients under more intensive care."

The analysis provided convincing evidence to the healthcare organization; the pilot was extended and more medicine dispensers were ordered. The analytics provided the healthcare management a good understanding regarding the patients whose resource consumption had increased due to the unexpected collapse in health during the pilot. Usually, the business impact analyses are able to capture and show increases or decreases in volumes, costs, and revenues respectively. However, a more detailed examination of the context, here in the conditions of the patients under examination, enabled analyzing the potential consequences with and without Evondos service. An advanced business impact analysis (see, e.g., Laine et al. 2016) should be sensitive enough to examine the value of the new service or product, even if it represents 'maintaining the status prior to the change.' In practice, also outside the healthcare context, numerous investments are required in order to avoid cost increases or future losses. Understanding and realizing the value of such investments requires, however, cost consciousness and related communication from the overall organization.

Impact of the Case—'Ex-Post' Cost Information for Decision-Making

When the nurses were interviewed after the pilot, similar to the previous experience of the case company, the nurses provided very openly positive feedback about the service. However, the nurses also pointed out that several patients required one home care visit per day only to be given their daily doses of anticoagulant. In other words, even though all the other medicines could be handed out using the service, hence taking out the need for daily visits to the patients' homes, the home care still had to make one visit per day only to give this particular drug. This drug is important considering the well-being of the patients and, therefore, the home care simply could not leave it to the patients to administer the drug themselves.

One particular generic anticoagulant is widely used with the elderly to prevent vein thrombosis. The drug has a long history and it is very cheap, only a few Euros per month per patient. However, this medicine requires systematic monitoring with blood tests and, in case the blood values have changed, also the dose needs to be changed. This was mainly the reason why that particular drug could not be included in the service. When the 'pilot population' was analyzed in more detail, it turned out that one out of five had to be visited once a day only to administer this anticoagulant. Therefore, fixing this issue alone would reduce the number of actual home care visits by more than 100 (four patients out of 20 with the anticoagulant the only reason for a daily visit), making the case clearly break-even (less than 540 visits vs. 640 visits at the beginning), despite the deteriorating health of some of the patients. As a consequence, finding a solution to this had good potential.

When the researchers brought up the issue with an anticoagulation specialist working in a university hospital, she pointed out that there had just recently been indication for two new anticoagulation drugs against vein thrombosis for elderly people. These new drugs no longer required systematic blood testing, so the local pharmacy was visited the very next day. The pharmacist pointed out that an alternative had existed for some time; however, when further investigated, this drug was sensitive to humidity and had to be sealed in foil until consumed. The packaging, therefore, made it unsuitable for the prepacked multidose sachets service.

The issue was brought up again with the anticoagulation specialist and she said the pharmacist must have taken a look at the wrong drug. Thus, the pharmacists were approached again. Interestingly, these pharmacists did not find any other anticoagulants with indication to be used as an alternative with the elderly people. Consequently, the anticoagulation specialist was consulted once more to confirm the usability. According to her, the indication for the elderly people was so new that printed material (which the pharmacists had used when checking the indication) would not show it yet. Thus, the pharmacy had to be visited once more, now with the instructions to check the indications in the Ministry of Health Internet sources, in which they were eventually found. Now the pharmacists were convinced about the usability of the drug as a replacement for the widely used anticoagulant, but the problem was the suitability to the prepacked multidose sachets service. The pharmacists found no special sensitivities mentioned in the Internet nor in the packages; an indicator that they might be suitable for the service.

This information was then passed on to both Evondos management and Joensuu team. Evondos managers checked very quickly whether the drugs would already be available in the prepacked multidose sachets service while the Joensuu Project Manager checked the price rates. The drugs indeed were available in the prepacked multidose sachets service; hence no bottleneck there. However, one of the drugs cost about 50 Euros per month and the other about 100, thus significantly more compared to the widely used one. As mentioned above, one home care visit costs approximately 40 Euros. When the home care no longer has to do a daily visit but, instead, fill in the medicine dispensing robot twice a month, the amount of monthly visits is reduced by 28. With these assumptions, the medicine dispensing service costing 150–300 Euros per month combined with the 100 Euros per month more expensive anticoagulation drug together save about 600–800 Euros per patient.

When the Project Manager and the nurses inquired about a possibility to change the medication of these patients, one doctor refused to even negotiate the alternative medication. As stated by one of the nurses:

> "Our doctor said that there has to be a medical reason for him to change the anticoagulation medication of his patient."

This, in a sense, was an interesting claim since there were no medical reasons not to change the medicine; the indications for using these drugs to replace the old drug were well documented. Luckily, there was another doctor willing to consider the new anticoagulants in order to reduce the resource consumption of the home care organization. This particular doctor was willing to first prescribe it to one of the patients and, if the outcomes were positive, both in terms of the patient and home care organization, he would then also change the medication of the others. As stated by the nurses:

> "We nurses proposed the idea to our local physician. He then consulted the doctors at the hospital and was willing to change the medicine. We are lucky in our area that we have a doctor who listens to us and is willing to find ways that work the best for both the patient and us as well."

Interestingly, the patient in question was only happy to try the new medication; the old anticoagulant, despite being a widely used, well-known drug, has also some side effects. As the nurse team pointed out:

> "The old anticoagulant requires regular blood tests and our customers do not want that drug."

To notify the home care management, a small report was prepared showing the cost analysis and the fact that the first patient had already agreed to try the new drug. However, at this point, it is important to note that the new drugs had been approved for this use, though they were new to the geriatrists treating the elderly in the City of Joensuu. When the cost analysis was reported to the healthcare organization, the head of the home care organization immediately responded:

> "Is the cost analysis based on real numbers?"

To this question the Project Manager in charge of the Evondos pilot simply responded:

> "Yes it is."

As the Project Manager later mentioned, she could sense the Euro signs in the eyes of the manager in charge of the home care. A development manager in the healthcare organization, however, pointed out that 600–800 Euro monthly cost saving may sound small to many people. She recommended the team to prepare a more 'eye-catching' cost analysis. Thus, assuming there are 500 Evondos users, with the same 20% of the patients requiring one daily visit only because of the anticoagulant, the changing of the anticoagulation medicine will result in cost saving of almost 1 MEUR per month. Such an analysis on cost saving then is not only about facts anymore; the way the cost reduction potential is illustrated now involves the element of feelings, too.

A few months later the Project Manager pulled out the statistics of home care visits, and the number of visits had come down from 30 per month to 12–13 per month. As the Project Manager mentioned in her email:

> "Today I took a look at the data regarding the home care visits in our system. During the summer, the number of visits had dropped from 33–36 per month to 11–13 per month. I then checked from the medical records whether this was the customer or not. And it was. Nice indeed."

After the patient had had the new drug for about six months, the nurses involved in the 'experiment' were interviewed to get some feedback about the experiment. As one of them stated:

> "We simply defined the right doses and we have never had any problems after that. The patient has been taking the new drug without any further blood testing."
>
> "The patient, in addition to administering the medications also needs to be washed. That is why we still have to visit her two to three times per week."

This was very relieving news. Thus, this agile experiment showed that indeed the Evondos service could be used also with patients who need anticoagulants. Considering the case company, elimination of this bottleneck with the newly released medication can increase the value potential of the case company 20–30%, making this intervention very interesting from the company point of view, too.

Reflection on the Interventions—Evolving From a Comrade to an Expert

In this case, the interventions were executed in different levels. On one hand, the active role in the development of the case company's business practices, such as the training processes, provided one layer of interventions. This is perhaps what typically research intervention is considered to be; the researcher becomes involved in the development processes under investigation within the case company. On the other hand, in addition to the interventions in the company, the researchers also intervened in the customer organization by engaging in dialogue with the home care nurses, providing analyses for the home care management, and also working in close collaboration with the Project Manager in analyzing the financial implications. However, the focus in the research work was on analyzing the financial implications of the offered service and, thus the interventions aiming at the key theory contributions took place in the customer organization. The interventions on the case company practices can be seen more as 'byproducts' or direct implications of keeping the eyes open in the field, though considered valuable by the case company management. Based on our experience, for some reason many companies are hesitant in allowing researchers access to their customers; it seems that the communication with the customers is seen as something so sacred that outsiders should not be permitted to talk to them, at least not MA researchers possessing knowledge about cost structures of the company and its processes. Thus, this case was an interesting one exactly because of involvement with the customers.

When looking at how researchers positioned themselves in the field, researchers possessed long experience in the cost management field, though the home care was a new context. Despite the fact that ABC, for example, has a long history in the healthcare sector, the research team had not attempted to systematically build a reputation on that field, though some cost management projects had been conducted, for example, in the occupational healthcare and laboratory diagnostics. Nevertheless, both the case company management and the project management in the Joensuu home care organization appreciated the MA expertise imported in the case by the researchers. However, because the context was new to the researchers involved in the fieldwork, the researchers positioned themselves more as comrades (see Jönsson and Lukka 2007); the idea was that the researchers join the management teams in both organizations in the journey of finding out how the case company service impacts the customer organization without strong expert position. That, perhaps, was a good strategy. First, even though the case company was a startup, the management team consisted of experienced professionals from the ICT industry and had already gained significant knowledge on the healthcare practices and the role the service could play in it. Second, the healthcare organization naturally was more knowledgeable on the treatment and service processes. The comrade role enabled researchers to ponder current practices of both the case company and the home care organization openly. Whenever some doubts were raised, in both organizations, the employees and managers were sharing their knowledge with the researchers to fill in the gaps. The researchers would then ask for more clarifications and sometimes even express their doubts, leading into more profound dialogue with the organizations.

Since the beginning, it seemed that both organizations were appreciating the outside view—and to some extent management accounting view—on the home care processes. However, the more knowledge the research team was able to gather, also the role in the case started to change. Suomala and Lyly-Yrjänäinen (2012) pointed out the evolving role of the researcher; the researcher may through analytics or innovations quite rapidly increase the 'expert status' within the development team, an important element in order to facilitate deeper access within the organization. In other words, even though the researcher starts the collaboration with a low profile (i.e., as a comrade), the accumulated understanding of the phenomenon based on analytics repositions the researcher more in the expert role, though often within some narrow, novel area. The ideas regarding the anticoagulant and the agile experiment with it provided a new standing point for the researchers within both the Joensuu healthcare organization and the case company. The knowledge of new drugs available and the estimates of the potential implications provided the researchers a new role in the game and facilitated a new type of dialogue with both organizations. The researchers were no longer gathering knowledge from the case organizations and digesting it in a more representable form; instead, they were importing valuable information for both organizations in terms of the new drugs and a way to test the process implications using such agile experiments.

Joensuu case provided one interesting view on the process implications of the new service concept. Unfortunately, with regards to the number of visits (the key cost driver), the customer cases did not prove to be as favorable for the service as expected, though the new service was able to prevent the resource consumption from increasing and other benefits regarding the patients' well-being. Joensuu case, however, proved to be a valuable reference for the case company; since one home care organization had allowed the researchers access to study the financial implications of their service, it was easier to ask others the same. Thus, after a year of collaboration with the City of Joensuu, the case company asked the researchers to evaluate the implications of the service in the City of Vantaa. In this case, the organization did not have an ERP system tracking down the time spent on each patient and, therefore, such ex-post data was not available for an analysis. Because of this, the researchers simply interviewed the Evondos key users in each home care team to provide an analysis of the implication. The analysis shows the patient profile, the number of visits before and after, as well as some comments explaining the change in the number of visits and visiting hours. An example of the data is shown in Table 4.1, with the outcome of the analysis at the bottom.

The outstanding results in the Vantaa case showed that the service does provide significant potential for the home care organizations; as shown in Table 4.1, the number of home care visits came down 42% and some visits were rescheduled to ease the resource consumption during the peak hours. Sales Director asked the home care organization permission to use the above data in their sales/marketing material, which they were granted. Interestingly, when the researchers wished to see the material used in the sales process, Sales Director simply mentioned that it is the material provided by

Table 4.1 Impact of the New Service in Vantaa.

Patient ID	Before	After	Additional Remarks
Patient 1	60	30	Time of the visit more flexible, too
Patient 2	60	30	Visit now on the midday, previously morning and evening
Patient 3	30	4	Medicine control only
Patient 4	90	90	Eyedrops require three visits a day, at least for now
Patient 5	30	20	Visit delayed to outside the busy hours
...	...	...	...
Total	384	224	

the researchers. When some clarification was asked, for example, to see the visual appearance of the material, he pointed out the following:

"We certainly do not wish to edit the material into Evondos slideshow, it would only reduce its value at the eyes of the customers. The authentic table seems to work better because it even looks like a study done by researchers."

The comment above positions the researchers in a very interesting way; the data needs to have a not-so-attractive appearance for it to be credible. Otherwise it could be confused with the company's sales and marketing material without such 'objective' credibility.

In Joensuu case, the researchers had access to the organization before the patients for the Evondos pilot were selected. However, the researchers did not participate in the discussions regarding the patient selection—that was taken care of by the Project Manager and the home care organization. In Vantaa case, the researchers gained access only after the patients had already been selected and the service was in use because the bureaucracy needed for the access took some time. However, since the Vantaa case emphasized the importance of patient selection, this was something the research team was interested in observing. A nice opportunity was provided by the home care organization in the city of Harjavalta.

Motivated by the results in the city of Vantaa, the case company proposed to the home care organization in the city of Harjavalta that researchers could be placed under their disposal for analyzing the implications of the service in their organization. In this case, the researchers were provided access to observe the meeting during which the case company Project Manager was helping the nurse team select the patients for the service. The head of the home care organization provided some motivating comments for the team and then the Evondos service was discussed. At this point the researchers remained in the background. However, while the organization was getting acquainted with the service and the robot, the researchers showed Vantaa's results to the head of the home care organization to illustrate the potential the service can offer when the patients are selected properly. In addition, the

Joensuu analyses were also disclosed to show the analytics the researchers would be able to deliver if provided access to the data. The manager seemed impressed regarding both the outcome of the Vantaa case as well as the analytics based on the Joensuu ERP data and, during that discussion, access to spend some time with the home care organization was granted and access to ERP data was promised.

With regards to the patient selection, the case company had advised the nurse team to prepare a list of potential patients for whom the service would provide clear benefits. The nurse team had provided a long list with about 50 patients that were then discussed one by one to select the patients for the short list. The first patient provided potential to reduce two visits per month and the second four, yet both were shortlisted. At this point one of the researchers stood up and explained the prerequisites for the service to break even:

> "The monthly cost of the service is about 200–300 Euros. If an average home care visit in Finland costs roughly 40 Euros, 5–6 visits need to be eliminated per patient in order for the service to provide financial benefits for the home care organization. Thus, in my opinion, we really should be looking at patients where we have potential to reduce at least one visit per day. Would it be possible to go through the list first to identify the most potential customers for the short list?"

The Project Manager chairing the session seemed surprised about this 'outburst' sharing the prerequisites for the service to bring concrete financial benefits for the home care organization; the case company had never communicated this so openly to the nurses during the patient selection phase. The comment initiated a very interesting dialogue. Some nurses immediately emphasized the prioritization of the well-being over the cost aspects:

> "You are accounting researchers and, therefore, it is only natural that your interest is on the financial outcomes. Our main concern is the well-being of the patients."

The comment indicates that, perhaps, the first impression of the Project Manager indeed was correct; such financial 'realities' should not be openly discussed with the nurses. However, the nurse in charge of the scheduling of the home care work took another standing point:

> "In the end, we are managed by the numbers. If we start a pilot like this, we need to show our management that the new service provides concrete benefits."

This comment totally changed the tone of the discussion. The nurses started to exchange ideas in small groups regarding the patients with the most potential spontaneously. Then they started to point them out to the entire team for further evaluation, resulting in a short list with totally different outcomes. With the first 15 patients shortlisted, the number of home care visits came down from 500 to 200 (see Table 4.2). However, with some patients the nurses recognized the role of the service preventing the number of home care visits from increasing, similar to the analysis in Joensuu of estimated service need without the medicine dispensing robots. Finally, with some patients included in the short list, the nurses only identified an improved service for the patient without direct cost implications. For example, one patient had bad eyesight (Patient 4) and, therefore, the robot was to facilitate independent living without even an attempt to bring cost savings. Thus, despite the nice budgeted potential, with some of the patients shortlisted the benefits were related more to the quality of life and not at all to financial implications.

One interesting feature identified by the nurse team was that some patients would spend two weeks in a month in an elderly home. This enabled family members, for example, to get some rest. Some nurses saw this as a factor preventing the use of the service. However, as pointed out by one of the nurses:

> "With the elderly, the sequencing between the weeks 'in and out' is usually stable, meaning that it is possible to synchronize also the prepacked multidose sachets to contain the medication for one week from Tuesday to Tuesday and then a break for a week."

This comment again shows how the empowered nurses are able to find creative ways to overcome such obstacles. Interestingly, despite the 60% reduction in the number of visits, within the 15 patients shown in Table 4.2, five patients would spend every other week in the elderly home. This indicates that the service indeed provides nice cost reduction potential if the right patients are identified.

The observations regarding the patient selection process in Harjavalta were communicated to the case company management. The interesting finding was that actively pushing the nurses to select patients with cost reduction

Table 4.2 Sample of Budgeted Outcomes in Harjavalta Case.

	Before	After	Additional Remarks
Patient 1	56	26	Other side paralyzed, no second visit on Fridays
Patient 2	45	22	New anticoagulant, every second week in elderly home
Patient 3	8	2	Postponing the need to increase home care visits
Patient 4	30	30	Bad eyesight, the service helps in consuming the drugs
Patient 5	60	30	Evening visit was only about administering the drugs
...	...	...	...
Total	491	205	

potential seems to result in some nice cost savings. However, the challenge is how much the cost saving aspect should be emphasized in the early patient selection and what role the other benefits should be given. As commented by the Sales Director:

> "On one hand we have to show our customers that there is plenty of potential users for our services with different benefits but, especially in small-scale pilots we increasingly have to ensure that we find a nice set of customers also providing attractive cost savings."

Whereas most interventions had been focusing on the customer organizations, the company management now asked the research team to participate in the development of the patient selection process. This was the first time when the researchers were engaged in such internal development work. Thus, not only were the researchers taking a more active 'expert role' with the new home care organizations, but also the case company management started to see the researchers as 'experts' to be used more actively in their internal development work, too.

One challenge for capturing the potential within the service, however, was that the patients also have to accept the service. Eventually, once the actual patient selection in Harjavalta was done, only one out of four originally suggested patients ended up accepting the service, and the reduction in the number of visits was 'only' 50%. Some patients originally shortlisted were afraid that they would not be able to manage with the machine and others were afraid that the machine would replace the nurses. As a result, helping the nurses in the patient selection might not be enough to ensure that the most potential patients are selected, but the training and motivation of the nurses also has a large role in the success of the pilot project. The nurses, in the end, have to sell the new service to the patients and often to their family members, too. If a nurse happens to get a wrong impression about the service, it might reflect in the way they communicate the benefits to the potential patients, possibly resulting in unnecessary refusals. Thus, it was not enough to have good training material regarding the key cost drivers (and of course other benefits) to help the nurses in the patient selection; the nurses needed training material to sell the service also to the patients and their key stakeholders. This became also another area where the researchers were asked to provide their expertise for the case company.

The evolving expert role within the team was also demonstrated by the fact that the researcher was asked to verify the value potential of the service to the potential investors. In the middle of the negotiations with some venture capitalists, the Managing Director called the researcher:

> "We are in the middle of a funding round to gather more capital to finance our international growth. Our potential investors are willing to invest in us if our service provides the customer value we promise. Can

I tell to our potential investors that, if they want, they can contact you and you will share your views with them, too?"

The researcher pointed out that, based on Vantaa and Harjavalta cases, the service most certainly provides nice potential for cost reduction. However, as the researcher pointed out too, based on these cases, the patient selection seems to play a crucial role, yet it would be impossible to estimate how many patients benefitting from the service exist, for example in Finland. However, as Vantaa and Harjavalta cases clearly show, it is not so difficult to find groups of patients with almost 50% reduction in the number of visits. At the same time, what the Joensuu case well illustrated, the service provides potential to help keep the elderly home care patients within the home care instead of the need to place them on full-time care in, say, hospital or elderly home—an important element considering the national spending on elderly. In addition, the service not only provides improved quality-of-life (which is difficult to measure in Euros) but the steady medications also help prevent other medical conditions, yet even more difficult to quantify.

In this case, the role of the researcher has gradually changed from a 'comrade' to a 'specialist' in the narrow fields investigated as part of the interventions. Naturally, the researcher still does not possess all the knowledge to, for example, be considered as a competent manager in the case company. At the same time, the researcher has become an 'equal' partner in discussing and brainstorming about the development of the business, especially regarding the financial and process implications and how to communicate them to the home care organizations and decision-makers. This evolving role of the researcher within a case study is something worth keeping in mind when analyzing special characteristics of interventionist research.

Interplay Between Episteme, Techne, and Phronesis

At the beginning of the project, one of the key drivers was the societal importance of the case; aging population requires new approaches to healthcare processes and MA can play a role in helping new technologies diffuse in the field, especially when implications are communicated in the spirit of facts and feelings. Thus, this case started with the emphasis on the societal impact (phronesis), mainly explained by the industry at hand, as shown in Figure 4.4.

When the collaboration started, there was an idea of building a value calculator that would first ask either salesperson or customer input about the size of the fleet and estimated patient profiles, highlighting the importance to accessing the customer profiles and cost implication within each profile. Then the calculator would have created a simple sales animation to help visualize the cost reduction potential of the service offering (techne). The idea was that the logic of value creation could then be shown to the various stakeholder groups in an easy-to-grasp way, following the idea of ergonomic MA.

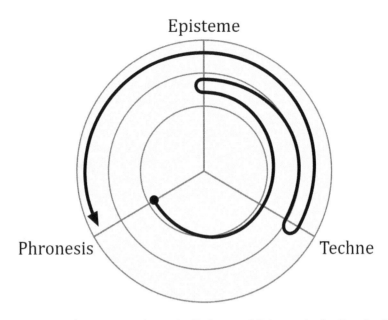

Figure 4.4 Interplay Between Phronesis, Techne, and Episteme in the Case Study.

This then led to the discussion on the visualization of financial information, especially for employees/stakeholders not dealing with numbers in their daily work (episteme). Soon after the first attempts, also the narrative rhetoric was needed to make the animations more powerful, again providing an interesting opportunity to position the study in terms of theory contribution. As concluded by Nyuppieva et al. (2016), management accounting narratives help clarify and understand experiences, viewpoints, and attitudes of different managers and other stakeholders (see also Seal and Mattimoe 2016). Besides, management accounting could create a cognitive connection between accounting information and the users of that information (Cardinaels 2008; Keim et al. 2008). Maybe, sometimes authentic figures taken from the operations, although less visually attractive, can be interpreted to be more credible than more carefully designed reports. One may argue that it depends on the case, how the figures and their visualization best support the relevant narrative underlying decision-making.

Despite the interesting potential of using visuals and narratives in communicating cost information to various stakeholders not accustomed to financial information, the case took a turn to yet another interesting area. The interviews revealed the widely used anticoagulant as a bottleneck preventing the service from reaching its full potential, raising the researchers' interest. The attempts to overcome this bottleneck iteratively positioned the work to the pragmatic flank (techne). Despite the initial challenges, the research team helped facilitate the agile experiment regarding the use of the newly released drug amongst the selected home care patients in collaboration with the doctors, nurses, case company managers, and healthcare management. Here the intervention was not so much about doing but looking at the well-known problem from outside the box with the willingness and commitment to see whether the issue could be tackled. Naturally, the commitment was deeply motivated by the bottleneck role identified when the cost implications of the Evondos service were analyzed.

In order to overcome the objection of some of the physicians, the idea of testing the new drug quickly with one of the patients was brought forward. This lead into yet another interesting discussion from the theoretical point of view—using such agile experiments to provide empirically tested, 'ex-post' cost information for the stakeholders, though only in the small scale (episteme). Nevertheless, such empirically tested 'ex-post' cost information can be a powerful tool to overcome organizational resistance. Similar to how the openness in pricing helped nurses to accept the new service, the first-hand experience of the organization itself on the potential (cost) implications of the new service can play an important role in helping a new technology or service penetrate/diffuse within that particular organization. The positive word-of-mouth gained with such experiments should not be understated. Interestingly, healthcare management literature does not talk about the use of such agile experiments in reducing the organizational resistance regarding new technologies or process models; thus, the potential of 'self-experienced ex-post cost information' acquired through such small-scale, agile experiments will provide an interesting, new approach to managing technology diffusion in healthcare organizations.

Interestingly, experiments and healthcare are two words difficult to link to each other; the first connotation can be related to something like Frankenstein. Thus, it is important to note that the new drugs used for the agile experiment were approved for that particular purpose and the agile experiment was only about how these newly approved drugs would work together with the service concept. Nevertheless, the oxymoron resulting in connecting these two concepts provides a very fruitful starting point for more conceptual analysis of this approach in the development of healthcare services, definitely worth some further investigation. Whereas the theory contribution of the study will be primarily positioned in this idea of providing 'self-experienced ex-post cost information' to support diffusion of a new technology or process model within an organization, the case can be seen to contribute to contemporary discussion at the societal level (phronesis) in at least two ways.

First, the demographic changes taking place in the Western societies create challenges these societies need to cope with. MA—when properly used—can play an important part in finding good solutions to these challenges and help these solutions diffuse within different organizations and society more in general. Such agile experiments used for providing ex-post cost information may work even in the healthcare sector for providing facts and, in that way, help reduce organizational resistance during a wider implementation. This is a very contradictory approach compared to large-scale implementation projects often linked to new technologies, especially in the healthcare sector.

Second, the case highlights the role of a multi-professional team consisting of nurses, supervisors, healthcare management, doctors, technology and service providers, and outside facilitators in finding a solution to the identified bottleneck and creating the setup for the agile experiment. This probably could be positioned as one of the prerequisites for a successful agile experiment also from the theory-development point of view. However, we wish to highlight it as an input to the societal discussion on development of the healthcare processes. Healthcare organizations still tend to be characterized by hierarchical management cultures and such multi-professional teams may be powerful tools to rethink existing practices and implement new ones.

References

Andersson, S. 2007. *Kahdestaan kotona: Tutkimus vanhoista pariskunnista* (Ph.D. thesis). University of Helsinki,.158 p. (in Finnish)

Cardinaels, E., 2008. The interplay between cost accounting knowledge and presentation formats in cost-based decision-making. *Accounting, Organizations and Society*, 33(6), pp. 582–602.

Hartikainen, S., Lönnroos, E. and Rusanen, S. 2008. *Geriatria: arvioinnista kuntoutukseen.* Edita, Helsinki, 352 s. (in Finnish)

Jönsson, S. and Lukka, K., 2007. There and back again: Doing IVR in management accounting, in: Chapman, C., Hopwood, A. and Shields, M. (Eds.), *Handbook of management accounting research*, Vol. 1. Elsevier, Amsterdam, pp. 373–397.

Kärkkäinen, M., Ala-Risku, T. and Främling, K. (2003). The product centric approach: A solution to supply network information management problems? *Computers in Industry*, 52(2), 147–159.

Kärkkäinen, M. and Holmström, J. (2002). Wireless product identification: Enabler for handling efficiency, customisation and information sharing. *Supply Chain Management: An International Journal*, 7(4), pp. 242–252.

Keim, D., Andrienko, G., Fekete, J.-D., Görg, C., Kohlhammer, J. and Melancon, G., 2008. *Visual analytics: Definition, process and challenges*, in Kerren, A., et al. (Eds.), *Information visualization*, LNCS 4950. Springer-Verlag, Berlin, Heidelberg, pp. 154–175.

Kröger, T. and Leinonen, A. 2012. Transformation by stealth: The retargeting of home care services in Finland. *Health & Social Care in the Community*, 20(3), pp. 319–327.

Laine, T., Korhonen, T., Suomala, P. and Rantamaa, A., 2016. Boundary subjects and boundary objects in accounting fact construction and communication. *Qualitative Research in Accounting and Management*, 13(3), pp. 303–329.

Nyuppieva, E., Laine, T. and Lyly-Yrjänäinen, J., 2016. Visual narratives in the value chain of new management accounting knowledge. *10th Conference on New Directions in Management Accounting: Brussels*, Belgium, 14–16 December 2016.

Seal, W. and Mattimoe, R., 2016. The role of narrative in developing management control knowledge from fieldwork. *Qualitative Research in Accounting and Management*, 13(3), pp. 330–349.

Suomala, P. and Lyly-Yrjänäinen, J., 2012. *Management accounting research in practice: Lessons learned from an interventionist approach*. Routledge, New York.

5 Management Accounting Research in National Research Policy

The case company is a spin-off of an Italian manufacturing company. The Italian parent manufactures fittings used in hydraulic hose assemblies. The company used to have a distributor in Finland who was making hose assemblies for OEMs using its fittings. The distributor was supplying one of the largest hose assembly customers in Finland, and this particular OEM was purchasing its hose assemblies in machine-specific kits. Manufacturing hose assemblies in machine-specific kits requires labor intensive, manual manufacturing processes and, hence, the distributor was not happy with the profitability of that customer relationship, resulting in pressure to increase the price. The OEM, however, was not pleased with such a plan; instead it started orchestrating a research project for bringing automated hose cutting technology to Europe with the attempt to build a new manufacturing concept around it. The pragmatic idea of the project was to help the supplier reach its target performance for the OEM to avoid the price increase. As Sourcing Manager of the OEM later replied (see Lyly-Yrjänäinen et al. 2016):

> "I have been asked by many other hose assembly manufacturers that why is such an OEM investing in the development of hose assembly manufacturing process. According to them, that should be the responsibility of the specialists in the field, in other words them. I always answer to them that it is in our best interest to help our suppliers reach their cost reduction targets."

The starting point of the research project, therefore, was mainly positioned in techne with the idea of developing a new way of manufacturing hose assemblies in machine-specific kits, with clear cost-reduction targets. The potential for a theory contribution was expected, initially, to lie in analyzing how cost information can be used for diffusing a new technology in a new market. Thus, the theory contribution was positioned in the interface between the technology diffusion and cost management literature, with the more detailed theory contribution to be argued later based on the empirics and reflection of the case.

The research project was to involve the OEM, its hose assembly supplier (the distributor), the representation of the US-based manufacturing technology provider, and the research team focusing on cost management. In addition to the above, the steering committee was complemented with professors in hydraulics and machine automation to bring in the special expertise needed for the development of the new manufacturing concept. In the background, the Italian fitting manufacturer was supporting the project by investing in the new hose cutting technology as one of the first adopters in Europe with the attempt to learn about the opportunities it provided. Thus, as a non-Finnish organization it could not play a formal role in the government-funded research project while, at the same time, it played a key role in development of the new manufacturing concept, though behind the scenes.

However, when the project proposal was being prepared, the distributor delayed the final decision on participating in the project, meaning the application for the project funding was delayed, too. At the same time, the research team was pushing the new production concept, resulting in a situation that most of the technology uncertainties related to the new production concept were solved. When, eventually, the project application was filed, the funding agency turned it down. According to the research funding agency, a sufficient degree of technology uncertainty would be required for such projects to be funded—it would be impossible to justify government support on the innovation process without sufficiently high risk and potentially high reward embedded in the project—which makes perfect sense. Interestingly, about at the same time the distributor also made a decision to not participate in the project and invest in the new production concept. Instead, it restarted the negotiations on the price increase, making the OEM dissatisfied. At this moment, the Italian fitting manufacturer stepped in and agreed to establish a hose assembly manufacturing unit in Finland based on the new technology in order not to lose the fitting business of that particular OEM. Six months later the factory was up and running and in charge of the hose assembly manufacturing for that OEM. Despite the fast ramp-up schedule, the case company has been breaking even starting from year one, making the case a successful cost management project.

Introduction to the Case

This case is based on a long-term collaboration with a company manufacturing hose assemblies. Hose assemblies are used in machines powered by hydraulics; a hose assembly consists of a piece of hose with fittings that are crimped (i.e., squeezed) at both ends, as shown in Figure 5.1.

Starting in the late 1990s, many OEMs began to order their hose assemblies in machine-specific kits in order to reduce the indirect costs of their internal logistics. To respond to this demand, some hose assembly manufacturers

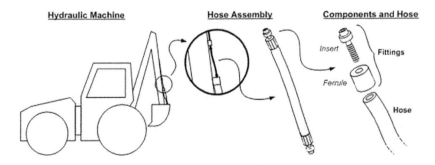

Figure 5.1 Example of a Mobile Machine, Hose Assembly, and Its Key Components (Lyly-Yrjänäinen et al. 2016).

make hose assemblies in batches, stock them, and prepare the kits in the storage facility right before shipping them. With this approach, simply reducing batch sizes will lead to wasteful handling and a greater amount of complexity in planning and order administration. Thus, hose assembly manufacturers with such processes struggle to effectively serve OEMs that customize machines. When machines are customized, the kits differ between machines, and may even contain some unique hose assemblies that have never been manufactured previously. As a result there is the need to produce hose assemblies in machine-specific kits.

The OEM customer of the case company manufactures mining machines. Such machines oftentimes have some customized elements in them, resulting in the need for some new hose assembly configurations, too. The hose assemblies specified for each machine were delivered straight to the assembly line in a wheel cage. Such an order typically contains three to six kits, with each kit placed in a different compartment within the wheel cage. Given that one kit contains 1–50 hose assemblies, one wheel cage (i.e., order) typically holds 100–200 hose assemblies.

When the main researcher got involved with the process of introducing the US-based automated hose cutting technology into the European markets, there were other machines made in Europe for automated hose cutting. These machines, however, were not very optimal for kit manufacturing. When these machines were originally introduced in the 1990s, most hose assembly manufacturing was based on batches. Thus, it was acceptable to cut one or two hoses to calibrate the machine for that particular hose type until running a batch of 100 or 200 hoses. Conversely, about ten years later most European OEMs started to prefer hose assembly deliveries in kits and, therefore, this need for calibration of the machine by first cutting one or two hoses was no longer acceptable. As a result, most factories in Europe shifted back to manual cutting machines.

When the US-based machine maker started to introduce their technology in European markets, the welcome was not very warm; most manufacturers had an old automated hose cutter that was no longer used due to the above-mentioned reason. The cutting machine of that US-based company did not require calibration so the idea was born to position this new technology as a superior technology for kit manufacturing. At this point the researcher set up a meeting with the key sourcing people at the OEM to discuss the potential this new hose cutting technology could provide. One of the sourcing managers at the OEM started to collaborate with the researcher and the technology provider in order to see if this new technology could indeed be used to push the hose assembly kit manufacturing to the next level. The sourcing manager at the OEM also introduced the other key players to the researcher.

Thus, a meeting was organized with the key stakeholders including the OEM, its hose assembly supplier, Sales Director of the US-based machine provider, professors in hydraulics and machine automation, as well as the public-sector research funders (Finnish Funding Agency for Technology and Innovation). All the key stakeholder groups showed interest and, hence, preparation for a research project was started with the aim to use the US-based hose cutting technology as a platform for a new, more productive way for manufacturing hose assembly kits.

Consequently, before the collaboration was started, the Italian fitting manufacturer had just invested in a small hose assembly manufacturing unit. Though the core competence of a fitting manufacturer would be more related to turning metal, the company had realized that its fittings were always connected with hose and, therefore, it would not be a bad idea to have also knowledge on how their customers used these fittings in the hose assembly manufacturing. As Managing Director pointed out:

> "Our strategy is to offer port-to-port solutions and, therefore, understanding how to use our fittings to make hose assemblies is an important element in that."

As a result, when Sourcing Manager suggested to contact him, the company had just had its first experience in making hose assemblies in house. The researcher met Managing Director in an exhibition in Las Vegas and he was interested in collaboration in the development of a new hose assembly manufacturing concept and was willing to take the first steps. While the other parties were still talking about possibilities for a research project, the Italian company decided to invest in the development of the concept. As Managing Director said:

> "Italy has at least 100 companies making hose assemblies and we did not simply want to be yet another company. When I was introduced

to the ideas that the OEM was pushing forward with the researchers, I saw something in it."

The collaboration of the development work went forward, mainly pushed by the Italian fitting manufacturer and OEM, though the Italian fitting manufacturer was not formally part of the project team. The negotiations regarding the collaboration in the research project, however, took time. During that time the key technological uncertainties around the implementation of the new hose cutting technology into the process of making customized hose assembly kits were solved, resulting in a situation that the project no longer involved technological uncertainties, a prerequisite for governmental research funding.

When the funding of the research project was turned down, the OEM started sensing that the distributor was not deeply committed to the investment in the new production technology. At the same time, the need for the price increase was lifted back on the table, making the OEM sourcing rather unhappy. Since that particular OEM counted for a significant business for the Italian fitting manufacturer, it agreed to finance the development of the new production system and, as a last resort to keep the business, invest in a production facility in Finland, if needed. When the final decision was made, the Italian fitting manufacturer and the OEM both wanted the researchers to be involved in the development process, hence providing the needed funding. About six months later, the case company was up and running and supplying the hose assemblies to the OEM. Furthermore, instead of the price increase, the company gave a small discount. Despite the discount, the case company has been breaking even from year one.

Interventions

The colorful events described above show some realities which interventionist researchers sometimes must cope with, especially when involved in inter-organizational research projects. However, the practical work on the interventions was carried out pretty much as if these inconsistencies never happened; despite the uncertainty considered painful at the time, retrospectively they are seen mainly as an extra pudding on top of the interesting case. Thus, the main interventions the researcher was involved with were as follows:

- Analysis of the new hose cutting technology and its cost reduction potential in kit manufacturing
- Analysis of the OEM's hose and fitting consumption
- Design of the one man cell concept for kit manufacturing
- Facilitating the demonstration in Italy
- Break-even analyses for the new factory.

The first action taken was to try to see how the new hose cutting technology would best be applied in European kit manufacturing. This work was done in collaboration with the US-based technology provider. Even though the machine had very high capacity, the key feature was the accuracy of cutting without any calibration; one could simply insert a new hose in the machine and it would always cut the right length according to the cut list. With such cutting speed and accuracy, the next challenge was to figure out how such machine capabilities could be utilized in the kit manufacturing process in the best possible way. As mentioned by Key Account Manager of the distributor in charge of the OEM's business (later Managing Director of the case company):

> "Such fast cutting technology alone is not enough. The other parts of the process must be developed to the level that they can process the output of the fast saw (i.e., cutting machine)."

In the hose assembly industry in Europe, the key measure for the productivity was 'hose assemblies per man per hour.' In a typical company manufacturing hose assemblies in kits, the performance was around 15 hose assemblies per man per hour. Considering that the automated cutting machine could cut easily 500 hoses per hour, there was a need to improve the assembly process, too.

First attempts were focusing on separating cutting and the other hose assembly process. Thus, the manufacturing would be organized more as a job shop with a specialized cutting cell feeding several assembly cells. One of the core features of the new cutting machine was the ability to print instructions for the operator directly onto the hose (Figure 5.2). The cutting machine is integrated with an inkjet printer, and while the cutting machine is measuring the hose to be cut, it also prints on the hose all the relevant work-order information needed. As illustrated in the figure below, the hose is travelling through the cutting machine, and the end that is coming out of the machine has already been printed with the work-order information needed

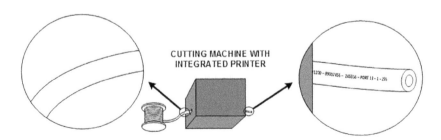

CUTTING MACHINE WITH
INTEGRATED PRINTER

Figure 5.2 Integrated Cutting and Printing Enable Work-Order Information to Be Printed on the Hose (Lyly-Yrjänäinen et al. 2016).

for making the hose assembly. This then would have abled the machine to cut hoses in fast speed, yet the operators would have been able to identify which components to assemble on each hose and which kit each hose assembly belongs to. This integrated printing would also enable the manufacturer to combine kits for the cutting process, hence reducing the setup times needed for inserting a hose in the cutting machine because the print on the hoses would enable a fast kitting process after the assembly work.

Thus, the first intervention was related to the analysis of various alternative approaches for implementing the new hose cutting technology into European kit manufacturing. The large variety of hoses used by OEMs presented still a problem on how to utilize the new solutions in the best possible way. However, when this new hose cutting technology got introduced to the OEM, they immediately provided the researcher access to their annual hose and fitting consumption. The analysis of the actual hose and fitting use, therefore, was the second intervention the researchers did.

The analysis of the actual hose and fitting use of the OEM provided a major breakthrough. Eighty percent of the hose assemblies were made using three hose types and six fittings. Thus, using the new cutting technology only with these three hoses would enable fast processes for 80% of the hose assemblies. The remaining 20%, then, could be manufactured with the traditional process. In other words, the new state-of-the-art automation would be used to streamline the manufacturing of the high-volume, low-variety production, whereas the low-volume high-variety production would remain manual. It is important to note that all the hose lengths would be different, but from the machine setup point of view, these hoses would be similar; the automated cutting machine simply considers the hose length as a variable managed digitally. If it were possible to manage this low-variety segment efficiently, the remaining 20% would not even play such an important role when considering the productivity in the factory level, especially when considering how much the reduced variety would ease the development work. This discovery became a major breakthrough and enabled a totally new way of looking at the production system for hose assembly kits.

While the project was being planned, the third intervention was to be involved in the development of the production cell taking full advantage of the new cutting technology. With the emphasis on the kit cutting and the focus on the high-volume hoses, the development work took yet another interesting turn. It was decided that, despite the capacity of the new cutting technology, the most convenient way to manufacture kits would be to let the automated cutting machine feed an assembly cell one hose at the time. The print on each hose would then help the operator to assemble the hose and place it in the right compartment in the wheel cage. Once the hose was finished and placed in the wheel cage, there would be a new piece of hose waiting for the operator. Thus, the automated cutting machine would work simultaneously with the operator in the cell, though always one hose ahead.

With the team, this idea caused some contradictory comments. Many managers faced trouble accepting that a machine with such capacity would be used to feed one manual cell, one hose at a time. The problem was that trying to increase the usage rate of the saw would have created need for complex factory logistics or conveyor systems and, in case the machine was down, there would be many assembly cells idling. The OEM, however, appreciated the approach; the company had been one of the first European manufacturers to adopt Lean philosophies in their operations and understood the benefits of such a single piece flow system. Even though one saw with an integrated printer cost 100,000 Euros, the worker was still the most expensive resource in the cell. In other words, when the machine cost is divided over the ten-year period, it makes only 10,000 per year (no time value of money concerned). However, when running the machine in two shifts, the labor cost of one cell can easily be around 60,000–70,000 Euros annually. Thus, the machine would be used as a 'production supervisor' systematically managing the workflow in each cell.

Another problem in kit manufacturing would have been the sequencing of materials and production queue. This, however, was to be avoided, too. The manufacturing of hose assembly kits is based on knowing the range of hoses and fittings that the OEM customers use in their active products, as later pointed out by Managing Director of the case company (see Lyly-Yrjänäinen et al. 2016):

> "With regards to our current OEM customers, we know the hoses they use, approximately 100 different ones, and the fittings they use, approximately 200 different ones, but we do not know the individual hose assemblies nor their combinations in each kit and the combinations of the kits in each order."

Thus, the idea was that an automated cell would contain always enough high-volume hose in it as well as compatible fittings; the cell would be able to produce any type of hose assembly using the active components of that OEM. The manual cell, on the other hand, would contain all the other active hoses and fittings of that particular OEM. In both cells, the materials would be replenished with visual inventory control. With this materials management solution, any active hose assembly configuration could be completed, leaving no need for material requirement planning. In other words, the necessary materials would always be available in the production cells so no back-office material planning and preparation activities would be necessary and thus no sequencing on the shop floor, either.

Fourth, while the research project was still being negotiated with the different parties, the Italian fitting manufacturer deiced to take the initiative and purchased one of these new cutting machines. The idea was to build a test manufacturing cell and invite all the key players for a visit to have a look at how the new hose cutting technology would work in the kit manufacturing. To support the test, the OEM had provided some EDI order data that could be used for making some assemblies to be sent to Finland, hence simulating a real OEM customer order. Later the Managing Director admitted that he took some risks in taking the initiative in the development work:

> "I must say that the decision to purchase the first machine in Europe was more based on the gut feeling. However, that started a very interesting journey that has provided us plenty of knowledge on how our products are used by the customers. In the end, if our customers are not competitive in the market, we are out of the business."

A cell layout was built with a new saw and a crimping machine, and the OEM provided some test orders with the three high-volume hoses. The Finnish distributor would make the missing hose assemblies using the low-volume hoses. The planned factory concept was introduced to the participants consisting of mainly key customers of the Italian fitting manufacturer and a delegation representing the OEM and its Finnish hose assembly supplier. The plan was to increase overall labor productivity by four, and this expectation was also shared with the visitors. One of the surprises during the demonstration was how efficiently the cell could actually produce hose assemblies in kits, without much hassle. As Managing Director of the fitting manufacturer later replied:

> "It was first difficult to accept that we would use the machine only to feed hoses to the worker in the cell and that the worker would define the speed of the production. However, now when I see the numbers, it all makes sense. "

The cutting machine needed all the orders in electronic form. Thus, in addition to the increased productivity, this information was also usable for other things within the cell. First, fitting selection could be facilitated to reduce possible human errors. Second, machine setup data for other machines could be pulled out of the IT system electronically, making the setup time shorter. Third, a dot marking machine was integrated in the cell to engrave information on the ferrules flexibly without any setup, simply using the information in the electronic orders for each hose assembly. Finally, since the IT system was controlling the cutting machine and also the work in the cell, a new system enabling full material traceability in the assembly cell was developed. Thus, the production cell eventually became the most automated hose assembly kit manufacturing cell in the world, enabling various value-added activities to be built in without slowing down the production.

After the demonstration, most of the technological uncertainties had been solved and, therefore, National Funding Agency for Technology and Innovation (TEKES) decided that their role was no longer necessary in the development. At the same time, despite the positive feedback about the new production system, the existing hose assembly supplier (i.e., the distributor) announced to the OEM the need for a double-digit price increase. The OEM sourcing encouraged the supplier to invest in the new production technology in order to prevent that, though unsuccessfully.

It was evident that the distributor did not believe in the potential this new manufacturing technology would have nor had serious commitment to the development work either. The lack of the commitment made the sourcing people of the OEM very displeased with the situation; all the parties had worked hard in order to find a solution to prevent this price increase. To maintain the fitting business with this OEM, the fitting provider agreed to establish a hose assembly factory in Finland, though as a last resort. Thus, the final intervention was to prepare budgets for the new hose assembly factory together with the fitting manufacturer and the OEM. The need for production cells was based on the OEM customer's annual volumes and the productivity estimates based on the tests in Italy. Consequently, the Italian fitting manufacturer and the OEM agreed to finance the researcher's participation in the further development of the new manufacturing concept.

First Application of Product-Centric Control Within a Production Facility

When the OEM made the decision to switch the supplier, the production concept had been defined and, therefore, the development responsibility was shifted to the Italian team. Whereas the original idea was to use the new cell for the production of the high-volume hoses, during the development process it became evident that the customer saw also potential in the other value-added features provided in the new cell. Thus, Managing Director of the fitting manufacturer decided that all those sizes that the automated cutting machine is able to cut would have to be manufactured with the new production concept. This, then, resulted in a new type of distribution of manufacturing in the shop floor: 85% with the small automated machines (containing the high-volume hoses and some other small hoses), 10% with a large automated cutting machine, and only the remaining 5% with the manual process. However, the operations management system was easily expanded to enable this and the most interesting theory contribution of the case relies on this.

For the internal logistics in the factory, product-centric control (see Kärkkäinen and Holmström 2002 for more detailed discussions) was applied. In product-centric control, the product itself knows what it wants and asks various service providers to perform these tasks (Kärkkäinen et al. 2003). For example, instead of reading a barcode in a logistics terminal and the IT system then knowing where the package should go, the parcel may have an RFID tag in it that tells the system digitally where it wants to go, resulting in a major shift in the logic of materials management. Product-centric control has been used in transportation and logistics, though the basic ideas had not been implemented in a production environment before (see Lyly-Yrjänäinen et al. 2016). In this case, the product-centric control was done in three levels: inside an automated cell, at the shop floor, and at the OEM's assembly line.

First, the product-centric control aspect within the cells arises from the ability of the cutting machine to print instructions for the operator directly onto the hose. Since the cutting machine "inserts" all of the work-order information on the product's physical platform (i.e., the hose), there is never a need to match the product to the production order information at any stage of the process; the right information is always linked to the right product. As Production Manager observed (see Lyly-Yrjänäinen et al. 2016):

> "The information system takes care of feeding the work to the cell one hose at a time, which increases the process quality. Furthermore, when the information for making a hose assembly is on the hose, the wrong assembly configurations (fitting combinations in one hose assembly) have been reduced dramatically."

In addition to the components and the location in the wheel cage (i.e., kit), the printing can also provide more detailed instructions, such as special cleaning procedures for one hose assembly. Such markings make it possible to differentiate the manufacturing process even between the hose assemblies within one kit flexibly without need for any back-office work. Interestingly, the use of product-centric control relocates the decision-making from the back office to the shop floor yet has made the production more transparent to the management, as Production Manager explained (see Lyly-Yrjänäinen et al. 2016):

> "Previously, when all the management processes were based on paper and when the hose assemblies for one order were being made in different cells to be kitted later, it was impossible to have a view of the readiness of different orders. Now, not only can the system control that in real time but when the finished hose assembly is directly placed on the wheel cage in which it is eventually taken to the OEM customer, even that can be managed visually."

Since the case company has three assembly cells, the WIP inventory contains only a maximum of three hose assemblies at any time, and the information system knows in real time how many hose assemblies are already in each wheel cage. This information can even be provided to OEM customers online so that they can track their orders, reducing the white-collar work related to answering customer requests on estimated delivery times, hence another value-added feature.

Second, when looking at the product-centric control at the shop floor, Production Manager first prepares the wheel cage and kit identifiers for each customer order, and pushes the wheel cage into the first buffer stock. The operator of the first assembly cell can take any one of the wheel cages in his buffer and bring it into the cell. For the manual cell, the identification on the wheel cage provides the right work-order information. Since all the needed materials are always available in the cell, the operator simply produces the largest hose assemblies and places them on the wheel cage. When all the hose assemblies to be made in that first cell have been completed, the operator simply pushes the wheel cage into the buffer of the next cell in line.

The operator in the next cell eventually brings the wheel cage into his cell. However, now the operator inserts the order number on the automated cutting machine and the machine asks for the right hose to be inserted in it. The cutting machine then instructs the operator when the time comes to change the hose type in the cutting machine and the process continues as before. As soon as all the hose assemblies to be manufactured in that particular cell have been completed, the operator pushes the wheel cage to the third buffer, where it waits to enter the third cell with the smallest hoses and machines. As soon as the operator in the third cell acknowledges the last hose assembly, the information system knows that the order is complete and the invoice and transportation documentation are printed automatically. Thus, the operator in the last cell seals the wheel cage, attaches the necessary documents to it, and moves the wheel cage to the shipping area to request transportation to the customer.

The product assortment in each cell is built in a way that the workload in each cell should be balanced, but because most customers customize their products, balancing the load in each cell is difficult. However, because the company is manufacturing kits, the wheel cage can visit the cells in any order. Thus, when one cell is overloaded, the operators of the other cells simply go and get a wheel cage from the buffer of the bottleneck cell and start making the hose assemblies for it. Again, as soon as the operator pushes the wheel cage into his cell, the identification on the wheel cage will pull out the production order information for the hose assemblies that can be made in that cell. After finishing his share of the order, the operator returns the wheel cage back to the buffer of the bottleneck cell.

The process discussed above eliminates waiting time for the non-bottleneck resources, but does not reduce the workload of the bottleneck. However, the workload of the cells can be adjusted without planning by making the cells capable of producing overlapping ranges of hoses. Thus, when one cell becomes a bottleneck, wheel cages visit other cells ahead of the bottleneck. The wheel cage requests that the overlapping range of hoses is now produced on the non-bottleneck cells. In this way, the workload of the bottleneck cell is reduced without any re-planning.

Moreover, this system allows the flexibility to be taken even further. When a customer sends an order to be delivered as soon as possible, it is possible to 'fast track' the order through production. As soon as the wheel cage for such an order has been prepared, it can be taken to the first cell. The operator in the first cell puts the current job on hold, takes the current wheel cage out of the cell, and brings in the fast-track wheel cage. As soon as the operator has finished all of the hose assemblies to be made in his cell for this fast-track job, the operator takes this wheel cage to the next cell, pulls the other semi-finished wheel cage back in the cell, and continues the process from where he had left it. The operators in the other cells then do the same thing, resulting in almost zero queuing time, which makes it possible to provide very short response times even in cases of large fast orders. The OEM customer interviewed pointed out the importance of increasing operational quality and reducing response times (Lyly-Yrjänäinen et al. 2016):

> "We customize our machines and, hence, our product assortment is large but the predictability is very bad. Furthermore, changes in the product configuration always impact hose assemblies, so we need the supplier to be able to react very quickly to such changes."

The identification in the wheel cage is not just used internally in the case company; the wheel cage finds its way to the right OEM assembly line with the same identification. Thus, in contrast to someone picking the right hose assemblies for each assembly job in the OEM's inventory, the wheel cage makes a request to be taken to the right place on the OEM assembly line at the right time, reducing indirect costs. Furthermore, the printing on the hose also provides features of product-centric production control for the OEM. For example, the hose assembly can also contain explicit information that tells the operator how to attach the hose to the machine; markings on the product link key data to the production, impacting final product quality. One senior executive at the OEM summarized the benefits of this approach (see Lyly-Yrjänäinen et al. 2016):

> "The more markings there are on the hose, the less skilled the assembly people have to be, both in making the hose assemblies as well as at the OEM, without quality impact."

One of the main reasons why the OEMs switched their suppliers was the pressure to reduce costs. The case company has transformed traditional manual hose assembly kit manufacturing into a capital-intensive process with expensive machines and IT infrastructure. Despite the investments that it needed for this transformation and small discount to the OEM, the case company has been profitable from year one.

Intervening Researcher as an Integrator

The discussion above has described the research process and the theory contribution of the case. As illustrated through the interventions, the role of the MA researcher has been somewhat different from most interventionist MA research projects published so far or presented in the other chapters of this book. The role of the MA researcher, therefore, deserves some more analysis. In this case, the researcher's role was to collect needs and ideas from the different stakeholders and communicate them to the others participating in the development work. These needs and ideas then would serve as inputs in different organizations, subsequently sparking new needs and ideas that needed to be communicated again. However, the key thing to point out is that, in this case, the researcher was not only a messenger; on the contrary, the researcher was playing a key role ensuring that the technical solutions developed would perform the job while, at the same time, reaching the set cost reduction targets. The role of the researcher can be well illustrated with the fact that he owns part of the IPRs for the new production concept, together with two managers of the Italian fitting manufacturer.

Thus, the role played in the game positioned the researcher truly as a facilitator in the development process and the interventions were set a demanding target: the outcome was supposed to be a production concept that not only works in practice but also reaches the financial targets set. In such a case, the researcher is 'above' the role required to passing on and communicating the theoretical interests; the researcher has the responsibility for pushing the innovation process in terms of the technical system as well as the financial targets linked to it. Such a demanding, integrative role, however, helps make the researcher 'one of us' in the eyes of the key players.

The strong role in the technical development is based on an interesting coincidence; the researcher had a personal, hands-on experience in working with hose assemblies through summer internships in the late 1990s. The internship at the shop floor provided some experience in hose assembly manufacturing processes of the time, both in Sweden and Germany. Thanks to these internships, the researcher even had personal experiences in using the contemporary automated cutting machines, including the need for calibrating the automated saws by cutting a few hoses before a batch could be cut—and after 50 or so hoses, the machine would have to be calibrated again. Thus, when the new cutting technology was introduced, the 'first cut right' concept (as later conceptualized by Sales Director and the researcher) was immediately recognized as a value-adding feature for European hose assembly manufacturers mainly producing hose assemblies in machine-specific kits. Interestingly, when the new technology was first introduced to the researcher, he was even able to recall the conversations with the managers dating back to the 1990s regarding the OEM customers being interested in sourcing their hose assemblies in machine-specific kits and the hose assembly manufacturers trying to find acceptable arguments why not to. Such an exposure to the industry, though a lucky coincidence and certainly not a prerequisite for successful interventions, helped to build a role within the team as an integrator who understands the basic fundaments and limitations of the context through first-hand experience.

The hands-on experience in making hose assemblies was a nice asset when exposed to the new hose cutting technology; the value-added of the new technology was clear. However, one of the first challenges was to convince the American owners that the market in Europe, indeed, was different. Providing the arguments for that started the integrative process of the researcher and was part of the first intervention (i.e., analysis of the new hose cutting technology and its cost reduction potential in kit manufacturing). For that, the automotive industry provided a nice analogy. Whereas US automakers make cars to stock and the right spec for each customer is usually located in the inventory of some dealer, in Europe a customer specs the car either online or with the salesperson and then waits for the car to be manufactured with those specs. That together with other similar examples helped to communicate to the US-based technology provider that there are differences in production philosophies between the US and Europe worth noting when attempting to penetrate the old continent. As a matter of fact, the top management of the technology provider later pointed out that the collaboration at the early stages helped them understand their hose assembly customers better. Thus, the facilitator role began already with helping the US-based company understand the prerequisites for entering the European market and finding the right positioning for their technology.

Finding the best way to apply the new technology in manufacturing of machine-specific kits, however, was easier said than done. At the early stages of the process the brainstorming was rather wild; the idea was to find ways to take full advantage of the new cutting speed. This first resulted in the need for an efficient material handling system for feeding multiple cells while, at the same time, keeping track of the kit structure. Interestingly, it was a video shot at one American customer that really changed the way of thinking. The company was making hose assemblies in small batches, though in a way that each hose assembly was touched only once, with the print helping to identify the components needed for each hose assembly. The cell structure was very old fashioned and there were no innovations around the cell either. Nevertheless, the video provided a powerful demonstration of the fact that, perhaps, the saw should feed the hoses into the cell one at a time. This benchmark set the grounds for the development of the new cell for kit manufacturing.

Sales Director of the US-based machine provider identified this way of applying the automated saw in the hose assembly production, making sense to people familiar with Lean principles. However, the researcher had to work hard to eventually convince the rationale of this approach; this aspect was debated almost to the end of the ramp-up of the new factory. Thus, the researcher had to find the arguments helping the stakeholders see the big picture and demonstrate that also with financial analyses. Here, for example, the comparison between the annual depreciation of one machine and the annual cost of labor when the machine is run in two shifts discussed above was a powerful tool helping the stakeholders see the point. Thus, such financial analyses were used as an integrating tool helping to weld the concept together.

It has been interesting to observe how most stakeholders automatically rejected the idea; the idea was to maximize the use of the new, expensive machine though the operator still was the most expensive one, showing the biased mind of managers in such labor-intensive business. As Managing Director of one large hose manufacturer later ironically replied:

> "Tell me professor (the researcher at that time was barely over 30 years of age and certainly not a professor), why should we invest such a large sum of money on the fast automated saw and then only cut 60 hoses per hour."

Comments such as this are painful when presented in front of a team. However, at the same time they force the intervening researcher to find the reasons and justifications to ideas that 'only seem' to make sense. Thus, finding the right questions to ask and then providing good analytics is a powerful way to integrate even such diverse teams together. Again, here the role as a neutral third-party actor also provided a powerful asset.

The video showed elegantly the power of the print as a tool for managing the workflow inside the cell and Sales Director in charge of the export in European markets was visiting the hose assembly manufacturers in Europe. However, the reception was almost the same overall; the new hose cutting technology was too good to be true. Thus, most companies showed hardly any interest in this new technology. Sales Director had contacted the hose assembly supplier of the OEM (i.e., the distributor) and even arranged a meeting with their Production Supervisor, who, similar to most customers, did not show much interest. Sales Director mentioned this to the researcher who knew that this particular OEM had always been keen to find new ways to develop their supply network. The researcher had been working with the Sourcing Manager in numerous research projects and, hence, arranged a meeting to introduce the new technology to him. Thus, the longer the interventionist researchers 'act' in the field, the larger the industry network becomes and, as a result, the more likely such networks will provide opportunities for integrating players together and gaining access to observe what happens next. Having said this, it is perhaps worth noting that researchers are not expected to become 'just' hubs for network building; managers expect researchers to use their analytical understanding and judgment before making such introductions.

When the new technology was introduced to Sourcing Manager, the one man cell concept was intended to be used in a very narrow range of high-volume hoses. However, Sourcing Director pointed out that most of the hoses they use fall within that category, hence motivating the idea that only high-volume hoses should be manufactured with such automation and the large, low-volume hoses should be done manually as before. This, again, was a major breakthrough because now the new concept would take care of the high-volume hoses yet bring down the development costs. As Sales Director later pointed out:

> "The company I used to work for invested heavily in the 1980s in the development of an automated hose assembly cell. However, they tried to have the cell cover the hose ranges form quarter inch to two inches. They eventually realized that it became too unpractical and, therefore, expensive to manage such diverse products with the same machines, especially with the components available at that time."

In that meeting, Sourcing Manager promised to give the researcher the hose and fitting use of one year, enabling the '20/80 rule' to be confirmed. Such hard fact was an important tool for the integration process since now it was easier to convince stakeholders that there were customers that would clearly benefit of the approach in dividing the production in two and managing them with totally different assets: one with new automation and the other with the old, manual way. Again, the researcher's role as a third, neutral party made it easier for the manager to provide access to such data. A machine provider alone perhaps could not have gained access to such information often considered as confidential.

Sourcing Director got interested in the new approach and orchestrated another meeting with their hose assembly supplier, this time including also Key Account Manager responsible for the OEM's business. Key Account Manager, naturally, was keen on maintaining a good relationship with the OEM and, hence, things started to move forward. Thus, the researcher facilitated the first meeting with the OEM and Sourcing Manager then became the champion (see Chakrabarti 1974) for the development work. Interestingly, soon after this meeting the planning of a new research project was started, involving also more senior managers from both companies. However, the key work done, nevertheless, remained with these three key stakeholders: Sourcing Director, Key Account Manager, and Sales Director, with the researcher working as the glue. The integrating role of the researcher was well acknowledged several years later, as was pointed out by Sourcing Manager when reading the manuscript of this book:

> "I still remember when you introduced me to the new cutting technology and visited us with Sales Director. That was a starting point of a very interesting adventure, one that still continues."

Sourcing Manager liked the idea, and introduced the researcher to Managing Director of the fitting provider. After that, the Italians took over most of the investments in the development of the production concept, fulfilling the idea of sponsor (see Chakrabarti 1974) in the development process. Thus, the two key interventions (design of the one man cell concept for kit manufacturing and demonstration in Italy) were then done in very close collaboration with the Italian team. However, whereas the Italians took care of the technical specs of the machine, the researcher worked as a 'mediator' between the OEM, Italian team, and the US-based technology provider to find out the best assembly cell layout and ways to manage the dataflow needed for efficiently running the machine in kit manufacturing. At that time, the roles of the managers working for the distributor were not that active; the main goal of the development work was to build the solution to convince them (and their superiors) to invest in the new technology. During the demonstration in Italy, the researcher gave a presentation introducing the logic of the one man cell concept and the proposed production system in general, though the technical details regarding the factory-level production control had yet to be designed. Even though many other customers were invited to join the demonstration, the key purpose was to show the OEM and its current hose assembly supplier the potential of the new technology— and in that way facilitate the integration, too.

Thus, as briefly described above, the researcher took rather holistic role in the process. However, there was one area where the researcher was not able to do much, that is the exit of the current hose assembly supplier. The fact that the demand for the price increase was lifted back on the table was shared by Sourcing Manager with practically nothing for the researcher to do about it. When such decisions are made at the top level, there is not much a facilitator nor integrator can, and perhaps even should, do. In the end, the researcher's important asset is the impartiality in the political games with the main interest in solving the problem at hand (in order to provide interesting inputs for the theorizing process). Whereas it would have been interesting to, for example, try to interview the top management of the distributor in order to find out the reasons for not investing in the new technology, this would not have added much value to the integration process. Especially when the decision was made to change the supplier and the researcher being deeply involved in the development work, the impartial role in the eyes of the distributor was, most likely, lost anyway. Thus, active work with the Italian team, perhaps, eroded the impartial role at least in the eyes of the distributor's top management.

With the Italians on board, the team for the development work was complete and the decision for them to take over the development work made the integration process less political—and things started to proceed fast, too. Thus, after that, the work of the researcher truly was the role of an integrator, with the focus on ensuring that all the different perspectives coming from the various stakeholders were taken into account appropriately and, if not, at least argued properly. For example, one important aspect was to find the right way for feeding the order information to the new saw—for the cell to be efficient, that process had to be managed well. Unfortunately the interface of the automated saw had not been designed for ERP connection. Instead, the data flow relied more on USB drives and Excel tables. This was something that also had to be negotiated with the US-based technology provider in order to find a solution that satisfied everyone. The researcher played an important role mediating the communication between the fitting manufacturer, OEM, and the machine provider, trying to balance the viewpoints of different stakeholders. The main challenge here was that the hose assembly industry had remained rather fragmented and even the large ones seemed often to be just a collection of a large amount of production cells. Therefore, there were not too many hose assembly factories with the state-of-the-art production control systems in the shop floor, explaining also why the technology provider had not focused on how their saw would be integrated in the ERP systems. This, then, required that each party was able to express what they wanted and what they thought would be possible with acceptable resources first for the demonstration and later for the real implementation. Eventually, the Italian team built the entire IT infrastructure independently.

By the time the process had developed to the level of preparing break-even analyses on the new production unit in Finland, the group had a good agreement on how the production system should work. Thus, the role as an integrating mediator was not that relevant anymore; the researcher was more like an outside consultant helping in troubleshooting whenever needed. Whereas the Italian team focused more on the development of the production cells and the factory-level production control software, the Finnish team was focusing on finding a location and designing the factory layouts and other practical matters. One aspect that, in retrospective, the researcher should have taken a more active role in was the development of the production control software, which was taken care of by the Italian team with one of the most appreciated software companies in Milan. There were some key differences between the small hose assembly factory in Italy and the factory being built in Finland that, perhaps, impacted the functionality of the production control system, eroding also productivity and, hence, profitability. First, the production volume in Italy was about 10–20% of the intended production volume in Finland. Thus, whereas the factory in Italy located in the same facility with the company headquarters was a nice ramp-up plant for the new system, the scale of operations in Finland was completely different. Second, Italian management culture is more bureaucratic (bringing stability to the operations) but perhaps not the most ideal approach when looking at the kit manufacturing for a company with a strong Lean mindset. For example, the mindset in the design process was that everything should be taken care of by the computer and the human operator should not be empowered to make decisions, a very non-Scandinavian and non-Japanese mindset for managing human resources at the shop floor. Third, it was the researcher's mindset after observing the factory in use that the production control system tended to have built-in elements of batch production slowing the operations in the kit manufacturing, explained by the fact that the factory in Italy was producing more batches than kits, at least initially. Finally, the factory in Italy was manufacturing more special hose assemblies with better margins unlike the factory in Finland; the factory in Finland was producing more simple hose assemblies, though in large volumes and practically everything in kits with a short delivery time window, meaning lower margins and, therefore, need for tighter cost control. Thus, when the factory was up and running, the local partners had a feeling that most technical decisions regarding the production system were pushed from Italy without them having much say about the process. As was mentioned by Managing Director of the Finnish hose assembly factory:

> "Our needs were never downgraded but we sort of felt that the production system was always pushed forward from the Italian perspective. They did ask our opinions and even spent time on the floor studying whatever issues we had, yet there was not much interaction when the development work started. This resulted in outcomes that certainly helped but often included elements not completely optimal for us. I think many of these could have been easily avoided with better communication throughout the process."
>
> "Having said this, I also must point out that our Italian owner has pumped large sums of money in the development of the production system and the backbone software, already very different from the one we started with."

Thus, after the factory was up and running, the integrator role sort of returned. This time the role focused on the cost management aspects and trying to find a balance in the process stability and the flexibility needed for manufacturing the kits cost efficiently. Thus, an important role of the researcher as an integrator was to ensure that these 'ideological' differences were balanced in order to reach the needed process stability to ensure profitability and production control yet at the same time the flexibility for the kit manufacturing and problem solving at the shop floor. As Managing Director of the fitting manufacturer pointed out:

> "Initially I thought that every country unit has to have the same way of operations. If we give some freedom to the country units, a few years later we wake up in a situation that they all have totally different ways of doing things. However, later I have realized that we will need to be able to better respond to different types of customer needs. Thus, we need to have several interfaces how customers with different types of logistics needs can efficiently work with us. At the same time, there are certain 'philosophical' elements on the background of our system that must not be lost in the process. This is something we are working on now."

The different country teams have now started to meet a few times per year to exchange ideas and needs for further development. The researcher still plays a role in mapping what the contemporary needs of the country units to be lifted on the table are. In addition, the researcher is also taking a stronger role in developing tools for communicating the benefits of the new production concept to the potential new customers. Interestingly, the new hose assembly factories are—instead of hose assemblies—increasingly selling logistics solutions (such as kit or kanban deliveries), traceability for quality control, marking options for traceability, or even to support after sales services, not in the traditional comfort zone of hose assembly salespeople. This, then, means that the country units need more support in succeeding in the sales because very few OEM customers change hose assembly suppliers for 10% price reduction; the risks involved are simply too high compared to the financial gains. Thus, the researcher in the future is likely to work as an integrator with potential new customers, a position very interesting for an MA researcher. It is noteworthy that this is in line with the current interest of universities in pushing research-based inventions in the market to make larger societal impact, and at the same time attaining access to settings with different types of theory contribution potential through engagement with the industrial development.

Discussion of the Case

With regards to this case study, the starting point was an interesting opportunity to observe a new technology being diffused in the European markets. The starting point of the research collaboration, therefore, can be seen to lean strongly towards practice (techne), as shown in the figure below.

According to Jönsson and Lukka (2007), IVR projects should be established with the theory contribution in mind already at the outset of the project. In this case the expected theory contribution was to be related to the role MA information can play in such a technology diffusion process. However, as shown with the dashed line in the figure above, such contribution was never explicitly argued for. Instead, the theory contribution was positioned more in the field of operations management, thanks to the first implementation of product-centric control in factory operations, complemented with visual control for the materials management and special emphasis on kit manufacturing.

When looking at the solution, the operators on the shop floor can handle production management independently when the assembly cells together contain all of the active materials needed for the OEM customers (managed visually), when the cells have overlapping material stock, and when product-centric control is implemented. This method of production control not only reduces the costs of indirect production work but also increases the utilization of the bottleneck resources, improves flexibility, and effectively supports OEMs of customized machines. As was mentioned by Sourcing Manager of the OEM customer (see Lyly-Yrjänäinen et al. 2016):

> "Every second order has to be delivered within the same day. Nevertheless, delivery performance is constantly over 90%. This delivery performance level is superior compared to our previous supplier and competitors."

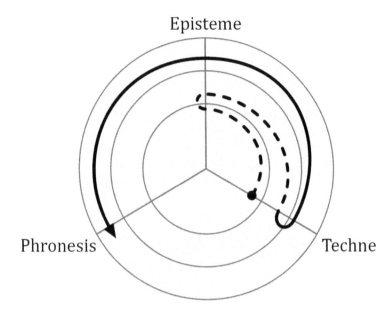

Figure 5.3 Interplay Between the Three Perspectives in the Case Study.

As pointed out by Sourcing Manager, the OEM has been very pleased with the production system developed in collaboration with the researchers. Later, the system has been applied in three countries, with a fourth one under implementation. In addition, the production concept has been further developed in a way that the entire factory can be shipped to a new location and set up in a matter of days, even inside some OEM customers' facilities and even run by them. When the current status of the production system was recently discussed with the team consisting of the country managers using the new production system, the tone was very positive. As mentioned by Managing Director of the production unit in Finland:

> "The fact that we have been breaking even every year since we started proves that the production system works as planned."

Thus, considering the practical relevance, not only within the case company but more broadly within the network, the outcomes have been considered good and the researchers first as integrators and then as external observers playing an important role. As was pointed out by the Managing Director of the Italian fitting manufacturer:

> "I have been happy with the development. The researcher involved is deeply knowledgeable about the things. Naturally the researcher misses

some details related to the hose assemblies but then he brings views from the outside, which makes it very interesting for me."

The production system was even patented (patent app. PCT/IT 2015/000102) by the Italian fitting manufacturer, with the researcher mentioned as one of the inventors.

However, the identification of the theory contribution (episteme), as pointed out by Suomala et al. (2014), again needed some outside perspectives. When the production concept was introduced to an academic who had published articles on product-centric control (Professor Holmström from Aalto University), he immediately pointed out the special application in internal, shop-floor logistics and the three levels (inside the cell, between the cells, and at the OEM customer). Thus, the final theory contribution was then built in collaboration with an extended research team with specialists in complementary fields (Lyly-Yrjänäinen et al. 2016).

In some sense, the researcher played a very active role, following the spirit of IVR, in the development of the production system while, at the same time, keeping eyes open for interesting theoretical discoveries. After the OEM customer made the decision to change the supplier, the researcher's role shifted from the practical development of the production concept more to the ramp-up. This, however, enabled the researcher to invest more time in the theoretical development regarding the new production system. The technological uncertainties in such development process, combined with the evident business-related uncertainties, consumed the 'brain capacity' of the researcher, making it hard to focus on the theory development. In addition, as was the case here too, someone coming from outside the box can also see the theory linkages better and is able to help the researcher conceptualize the key findings by asking the right questions.

It would be nice to argue the societal impact (phronesis) simply by emphasizing the changes within the hose industry. For example, the researcher involved in the development of the concept has been asked for consulting services by most major hose assembly manufacturers in Scandinavia, indicating the first-mover role of the case company in this industry. In addition to that, making hose assemblies is physical work and a typical hose assembly factory may have almost 10% of their operators constantly in a sick leave on work-related problems. Interestingly, the case company during the first five years in operation has zero work-related sick leaves, another interesting societal impact one could argue.

In this case, however, the societal impact is related more to the role IVR can play in government research policy making. Thus, from the phronetic point of view, we would like to argue that this case shows how management research can be conducted while, at the same time, leaving a strong mark on the industry under examination. Thus, the societal implication is positioned more in the area of research policy; research work can have very interesting pragmatic outcomes while at the same time providing interesting empirics for theorizing. Interestingly, the way the independent cells were managed has similarities to 3D printing, providing ideas for how production control systems work in an additive manufacturing context. Thus, the key lesson learnt regarding research policy making is that episteme and techne are not mutually exclusive but can actually support each other. Encouraging research with such approaches could be one way to increase societal relevance of MA research in the future.

References

Chakrabarti, A. 1974. The role of champion in product innovation. *California Management Review*, 17(2), pp. 58–62.

Jönsson, S. and Lukka, K., 2007. There and back again: Doing IVR in management accounting, in: Chapman, C., Hopwood, A. and Shields, M. (Eds.), *Handbook of management accounting research*, Vol. 1. Elsevier, Amsterdam, pp. 373–397.

Kärkkäinen, M., Ala-Risku, T. and Främling, K. (2003). The product centric approach: A solution to supply network information management problems? *Computers in Industry*, 52(2), 147–159.

Kärkkäinen, M. and Holmström, J. (2002). Wireless product identification: Enabler for handling efficiency, customisation and information sharing. *Supply Chain Management: An International Journal*, 7(4), pp. 242–252.

Lyly-Yrjänäinen, J., Holmström, J., Johansson, M. and Suomala, P., 2016. Effects of combining product-centric control and direct digital manufacturing: The case of preparing customized hose assembly kits. *Computers in Industry*, 82(October), pp. 82–94.

Suomala, P., Lyly-Yrjänäinen, J. and Lukka, K., 2014. Battlefield around interventions: A reflective analysis of conducting interventionist research in management accounting. *Management Accounting Research*, 25(4), pp. 304–314.

6 Management Accounting Research and National Innovation Policy

The researchers, who engaged in the development of hose assembly manufacturing (discussed in the previous chapter), identified a bottleneck in the production process. When looking at the manufacturing process of a hose assembly, the capping of a finished hose assembly tended to take an unacceptably long time, especially when compared to the other, more value-added stages in the manufacturing cycle. The management team also came up with an interesting solution to the problem. However, although the company and its parent had invested a considerable amount of money into developing the state-of-the-art hose assembly kit manufacturing system, the development of hose capping was considered to be outside the core competence.

The hose assembly manufacturer was distributing safety spirals and safety sleeves of a Finnish manufacturer. That particular manufacturer was repositioning itself more as a manufacturer of hose-assembly-related accessories, motivating the team to inquire whether the company would be interested in taking over the development of the hose capping process. In the end, the company had special knowledge on extrusion of plastic products (plastic safety spiral), hence providing some manufacturing-related synergies for the hose capping. The hose capping could also be seen as a hose-assembly-related accessory and, therefore, the researcher approached this particular company. The company management, unfortunately, was not interested.

The management, however, liked the process of how the proposed capping solution had been developed. Business Unit Manager pointed out that their customers using safety sleeves and spirals were not satisfied with the existing processes for installing them on hose assemblies. Thus, Business Unit Manager proposed collaboration in finding ways to streamline the use of these safety products in hose assembly manufacturing. In the development process, he insisted on following the same method used with the hose capping, i.e., using mockups and simple prototypes not only for 'proof of concept' but also for analyzing potential process cost implications at the early stages of the development process. At the beginning, the collaboration focused mainly on the technical development (i.e., techne) though, at the outset of the research collaboration, there already was some element of phronesis in sight, too.

Making mockups and low-fidelity prototypes is a common practice in the software industry, and widely adopted by startup companies. Especially with the latter, the lack of cash and other internal resources force companies to test ideas with innovative prototyping methods. The purpose of such tests typically is to have a 'proof of concept' and get some customer feedback. The case company working in the textile commodities can be seen to operate in a rather mature industry. In addition, as a middle-sized company, it had limited resources for product development, hence welcoming such a new approach for concept development. In this case, however, the focus was not only on the use of mockups in mature industries for 'proof of concept' but using them for gaining ex-post financial information at the early stages of the product development process.

Interestingly, Finnish Funding Agency for Technology and Innovation (TEKES) encourages companies in more mature industries to adopt similar approaches in their R&D. This case provides insights on how companies in more mature industries may apply mockups and other agile experiments in their development processes. Thus, already at the outset of the research collaboration, there was some element of phronesis in sight, too.

Introduction to the Case

The case company is a business unit of a larger textile company. This business unit focuses on manufacturing of hose assembly accessories for the hydraulics industry. This case focuses on two main product categories within their portfolio: safety spirals and safety sleeves. First, safety spirals are placed on top of a hydraulic hose in order to reduce external wear. For example, in mining or tunneling machines, the hoses may be under constant rock rain, and the safety spiral works as an extra skin taking the external wear. In addition, spirals are used for bundling several hoses into a larger bundle, seen for example in excavators of forest machines. Whereas spirals protect the hose from wear and tear, safety sleeves on the other hand are designed to protect the operators and other personnel located close to the machines. In case the hose has a small leak (called pinhole), the sharp hot oil spout can be lethal up to several meters. However, the safety sleeve is designed to absorb this force and, hence, protect the operators in case of such a hose failure.

This case is connected to the one discussed in the previous chapter. When the hose assembly factory was up and running with the new manufacturing concept in full speed, the capping of the hose assemblies was identified as a bottleneck; the time needed for capping one hose assembly (to ensure that the hose assembly is not contaminated during the transport) was rather long compared to other activities within the cell. The management team did some brainstorming and came up with a new idea. If the caps were attached in a belt and there was a feeding machine for the belt, it would be much faster to push the cap on the hose compared to picking up a cap manually and positioning it on the hose properly.

The idea was tested with a very simple mockup. First, a piece of duct tape was placed on a table, with the sticky side on top. Then hose caps were placed on it in a way that the side coming to the hose was up. Finally, a cardboard box was utilized as a machine feeding the caps to the front edge. With this 'machine' the operator only had to push the hose against a cap to seal the hose, turn the hose around and plug the other end—the caps would always be positioned in the right way, hence enabling faster capping. This simple setup also allowed the cycle time to be defined, as shown in Figure 6.1.

The price of one cap is one to two cents (depending on the size), and the average cost of blue-collar work in Finland is 30 Euros per hour, i.e., approximately one cent per second. Thus, the price of one cap in such a belt can be about two times higher for the solution to save money in the production, though still ignoring the cost of the feeding machine itself. Thus, the simple mockup not only showed the cost reduction potential in the assembly process but also provided a target cost for the new way of packaging the caps as well as for the feeding machine, without hardly any investment in the product development.

The Italian fitting manufacturer and the OEM were investing money in the development of a new concept for making hose assemblies and, hence not willing to develop everything in-house. Thus, the hose capping idea was demonstrated to the case company; the company had been adding new products in its product portfolio over the past years and was interested in hose-assembly-related accessories. However, the case company did not see the potential in the capping solution. As phrased by the manager in charge of the business unit (referred to as Business Unit Manager):

"We were interested in some new products to add in our portfolio. However, at that time we had some other needs, based on the inquiries of our customers. However, we liked the approach used in the development process."

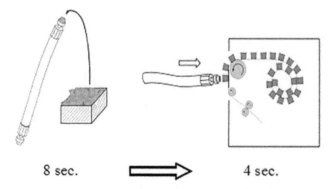

8 sec.　⟹　4 sec.

Figure 6.1 The Concept of a Hose Cap Feeding Machine Reducing Capping Time 50%.

Thus, the manager was interested in the approach on the development of the concept with simple mockups. Consequently, he proposed two other issues to work with—also with more immediate market need—using the very same approach.

First, the latest machine directives require that hoses located close to the operators must be covered with safety sleeves. These sleeves are woven from nylon (or similar materials depending on whether they need to be, for example, fireproof) and, therefore, once they are cut they tend to unravel themselves. To prevent this, the sleeve edges are often melted with hot iron after the cutting. According to Business Unit Manager, many companies offering cutting devices have been eager to offer different types of hot knives for this purpose. These devices are often used for cutting nylon ropes or nylon belts in order to prevent them from unraveling. However, once some samples have been sent to these suppliers, they no longer have been so convinced about their solutions. If such devices are used for cutting the nylon sleeve, the two sides melt together; instead of a sleeve, the output is a bag sealed from both ends.

Second, one of the challenges in placing the safety spiral on top of the hose assembly is that, for the spiral to sit tightly on the hose, the inner diameter of the spiral must be smaller than the outer diameter of the hose. This results in a situation that the length of the spiral is reduced once the spiral has been placed on top of the hose. If the spiral is too short, the hose assembly has to be spiraled again and, if the spiral is too long to play it safe, some of it is wasted. In addition to that, placing the spiral on top of the hose is tough on the wrists and elbows plus doing that for a long time is mentally consuming, too. Again, OEMs would like to spiral the hose assemblies used in their machines, yet the hose assembly providers are not very keen on doing that, thanks to the laborious process.

Thus, the case company had two products with increasing demand. At the same time, the hose assembly manufacturers were not very happy with the processes when using these products in their production. As phrased by Business Unit Manager:

> "Our customers keep asking us solutions how to use these better in their production, but we do not have much to offer."

Thus, a project was set up for developing new ways of using these two products in the hose assembly manufacturing. It was agreed that the researchers would be brainstorming new ideas together with the management team and the key customer and, as soon as there were some ideas, these ideas would be tested with very simple mockups. The mockups, however, would not only be used for enabling the 'proof of concept' from the feasibility point of view but also include the analysis of the potential process implications, including also the cost impact. In other words, the idea was to develop the two new products with the same development process used for the hose capping idea, following the policy recommendations of TEKES. Therefore, the idea of using such mockups not only for the 'proof of concept' but also including the cost implications of the new idea at the early stages of the development process provides a new perspective to the policy recommendations of TEKES, arguing for the flavor of phronesis already at the outset of the project.

Interventions

The collaboration was started with the development of the machine for sleeve cutting. Interestingly, since the researchers had good access to the facilities of the hose assembly factory, most of the development work took place there, though with active collaboration with the management of the case company (mainly with Business Unit Manager and their Production Engineer). Whenever there were some interesting ideas, since the companies were located about 500 meters from each other, a short audit was arranged. In this case, the interventions provided the researchers a way to familiarize themselves with the product development procedures more common in the software and startup worlds. Thus, the main interventions were:

- Brainstorming for new ideas and testing them with mockups
- Discovery that most sleeves are short
- Development of fully-functional mockups
- Time studies for different fully-functional mockups
- Testing the machine in customer's production
- Further development.

First, when attempting to solve the issues, many out-of-the-box ideas were brought up, some more and some less successful. For example, one attempt was made to blow air in the sleeve in order for the two sides to be separated while using the hot knife for cutting. The air blow, unfortunately, tended to cool down the blade, not resulting in a smooth cutting process. A rotating hot blade was tested too, without much improvement. The most interesting test was made using four vacuum cleaners to open up the sleeve before cutting. Two vacuum cleaner tubes were placed against each other. When the sleeve was between these two tubes, the vacuum cleaners were turned on and pulled away from each other, thus separating the sleeve sides from one another. Though impressive as a test setup, the suction created some wrinkles on the sleeve and, hence, the quality of the cut was not acceptable either. These tests, however, helped to understand the challenges related to cutting the sleeves. In other words, even though the experiments were not providing any concrete results, the researchers were accumulating knowledge that facilitated discussions with the management team on what to pay attention to in the development.

Second, one of the managers in the hose assembly manufacturing company, during some very informal discussion, pointed out that most sleeves they cut are less than two meters. This simple observation resulted in a completely new approach for sleeve cutting. Thus, if there were a tube on top of which the sleeve would be stretched, the hot knife could be used to cut the sleeve right at the edge of the tube without melting the two sides on each other and resulting in a clean cut. The idea was tested immediately (Figure 6.2 left) and the managers were very pleased with the cut. This proof of concept then initiated a new development cycle. It is important to note that, thanks to the unsuccessful attempts, there was a hot knife in the company, enabling the proof of concept to be done within minutes of the new idea.

Because the idea seemed feasible, the development work was pushed forward. The next step was to develop a machine that, instead of one tube, had two of them that could be separated from each other with a pneumatic cylinder. The idea was that, once the tubes were connected, it was easy to place the sleeve on top of them both but, when the cylinder was activated, the sleeve would be stretched (i.e., 'opened') from side to side, hence ensuring a very nice cut at the end. In addition, that solution would have made it possible to use the same machine for different sleeve widths without any setup time. This idea, unfortunately, did not work out; it was simply impossible to find tubes that were rigid enough to ensure that the sleeve would be completely opened at the end where the cut was to take place.

However, by accident, an idea was born that it may not be necessary to stretch the sleeve completely open; as long as there was a tube inside the sleeve, it was enough to separate the two sides from one another for a clean cut. As soon as this was discovered, a more powerful hot knife was purchased, meaning faster cutting speed. The cutting process was also eased up by attaching the hot knife on a pneumatic cylinder controlled with a foot pedal. This freed the operator's hands for holding onto the sleeve that was

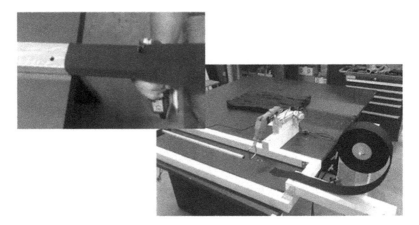

Figure 6.2 The First Proof of Concept and Fully-Functional Mockup for Sleeve Cutting.

now only loosely around the tube (in the previous version, when the sleeve was stretched, the operator did not have to hold the sleeve while cutting). In addition, when the sleeve roll was placed properly, pulling the sleeve on top of the tube became easier, too.

Figure 6.2 (right) shows the fully-functional mockup of the sleeve cutting machine. The mockup is called a fully-functional mockup because it was operated just like a real production machine even though the frame was made from cheap materials (wood and plywood), as mockups typically are. Even though the machine did not look very professional, it was used for cutting some real customer orders. The only limitation was that, since the hot knife was not designed for continuous production, the hot knife had to be cooled down after a dozen or so cuts. Nevertheless, this simple mockup enabled the team to cut sleeves in small batches, simulating the real production process. Interestingly, not only did the mockup enable the process to be tested, it also enabled the team to study the cycle times when using the new solution. In addition, the team got some cost information on the process implications, before major investments in the development work had been committed. Thus, the fourth intervention was to do a time study using this fully-functional mockup. The case company had been offering its customers a sleeve cutting service using an automated cutting machine. However, after cutting the sleeve ends have been melted with a hot iron plate. In this process the time needed for one sleeve is about 40 seconds. The new method cut the time to about one fourth, i.e., ten seconds, despite the fact that the machine had been built using wood, plywood, and aluminum tubes.

The above process and the time study confirmed that, from the process development point of view, the new sleeve cutting solution seemed to work nice in streamlining the cutting process. However, the cut was not perfect yet; the sleeve sides tended to slightly stick to each other at the edges of the sleeve. In other words, simply putting something inside the sleeve did not open the sleeve wide enough for a complete cut. Managers in the hose assembly manufacturing would have been completely satisfied with the quality. However, especially if the idea was to use the machine for offering sleeve cutting services, the quality would have to be better. As one of the managers pointed out:

> "For us the quality is good enough when we cut the sleeves ourselves. However, if an OEM purchases these from an external supplier as pre-cut sleeves, I am sure someone will be complaining about the outcome."

The development process, however, had increased the knowledge about the challenges related to the sleeve cutting process. Interestingly, one customer provided a video in which a sleeve was cut by feeding it through a device that 'tilted' it in a way to have the edge make a crease in the middle (like with trousers when they are hanging vs. put on), hence opening up the edges of the sleeve completely. Thus, this idea seemed to solve the problem identified in the previous version, immediately tested with a mockup. This very simple and low-cost solution enabled a complete cut without any increase in the cycle time. However, the changeover time turned out to be inconveniently long and, therefore, a mockup was made with the most widely used sleeves already set up in a large vertical magazine. The operator only had to adjust the column full of sleeves using the stacker attached to the cutting machine and start pulling the right one to cut. This solution worked elegantly when tested; however, when the machine was placed in one customer's production (fifth intervention), the sleeves tended to return to the original position, resulting in a poor cut again. The machine seemed to work nicely only when it was carefully used, though not feasible in normal hose assembly production. After a few months in production, the machine had to be taken away.

Interestingly, the company management came up with an idea of making the end of the 'rod' spreadable in order to maximize the opening of the sleeve before cutting. The idea was first demoed with Legos and then with a mockup, until a first fully-functional mockup was made. The solution was tested but somehow it did not feel right. First, the cut tended to be not straight because the sleeve was stretched nonlinearly. Second, the rod had to be thicker, making it a bit challenging to feed the sleeve on the rod resulting in longer cycle time. As Business Unit Manager pointed out:

> "The cut is not completely straight, though quality of the cut is now good enough. However, when I look at the process, it is no longer as fast as it used to be (with the other mockups). Thus, I do not see such clear benefit compared to the process we currently use."

Thus, the management team was about to turn the new idea down. Nevertheless, Business Unit Manager pointed out that there is an increase in the demand of precut sleeves from them, and he insisted on continuing the development work. New ideas are being tested and, as soon as there is some proof of concept, a fully-functional mockup will be made to test the process implications to see immediately what is, not only the output quality, but the process speed, too.

The development of the spiraling machine was started a few months later, though with the same philosophy. The key interventions were as follows:

- Brainstorming for new ideas and testing them with mockups
- Development of the fully-functional mockups
- Time studies
- Testing the machine in customer's production
- Patented table-top machine.

The initial idea was to be able to place the spiral on top of the hose straight from the box without cutting the spiral first, hence eliminating work phases and possibilities of errors and rework as well as waste. The first intervention was to experiment with the spiraling process. Some attempts were made without much success. Thus, the key design principle was provided by Business Unit Manager:

> "In all the spiraling applications I have seen, the spiral is coming to the hose with a 90-degree angle using some sort of a pin. The spiral then goes on the hose by rotating the hose itself."

This idea then was tested with a small spiral, pen, and a stick as shown left in Figure 6.3. When the pen was rotated, this rotational movement simply pulled the spiral on top of the pen. Furthermore, when the spiral came directly from the box, also the spiral box had to be rotated, well-illustrated by this simple experiment. Thus, this simple setup made it easy to communicate to the management what the requirements are if the hose is to be spiraled without cutting the spiral first.

The other interesting discovery was that the spiral, when climbing on the hose, pushes the hose forward. This results in a situation that there is no need for a control system that pushes/pulls the hose; thus, changing the rotating speed hence requires no control mechanism to manage the horizontal movement of the hose. The only prerequisite was that the hose and the drive simply have to be able to move when the spiral pushes them forward. This was then tested with a Lego mockup with two drives, shown in the middle in Figure 6.3.

Since the Lego mockup seemed to work, the idea was pushed forward. The next step was to make a fully-functional mockup using plywood and plastic tubes. In that fully-functional mockup, two battery-driven screwdrivers were used as drives, connected in series. This simple mockup enabled two-meter hose assemblies to be spiraled, hence providing again data for cost analysis. The process required three activities: (1) attaching the hose assembly in the machine and connecting a few rounds of spiral on the hose, (2) spiraling the hose assembly, and (3) cutting the spiral at the right place and detaching the hose assembly from the machine. Table 6.1 shows the results of the manual spiraling process and the time needed when using the mockup.

Two industrial scale machines were built and sold to the customers. However, one of the challenges was that the synchronization of the two

Figure 6.3 Different Mockups for Spiraling a Hose Assembly.

Table 6.1 Results of the Time Study with Manual Process, Mockup, and the Final Construction.

	Measuring and cutting the spiral	Attaching the hose	Spiraling	Detaching + packing	Total
Manual	15 s		250 s	0 + 5 s	275 s
Mockup	–	40 s	15 s	5 s + 5 s	65 s
Spiraling machine	15 s	20 s	20 s	0 + 5 s	60 s

drives required an expensive control system, bringing the machine cost over 10,000 Euros and making most customers unhappy; only some very sophisticated customers were interested in the machine with such a price level. In addition, the fact that the hose was traveling freely (pushed forward by the spiral climbing on the hose and, hence, making the hose itself a linear guide) in a tunnel made it possible to spiral only rather small hoses. A hydraulic hose has steel wires inside and, therefore, they tend to have 'memory' and want to go back to the original curvy shape as they were in the coil, hence making it difficult to rotate the hoses in the tunnel.

Thus, the researchers invented a solution that uses pneumatic grippers at both ends of the hose and a third pneumatic cylinder to pull the hose straight. In other words, while the two grippers hold tightly both ends of the hose, the third pneumatic cylinder pulls the hose straight and makes the flexible hose behave like a rigid tube, much easier to manage in the spiraling process. Furthermore, the company decided to abandon the requirement for spiraling the hoses directly from a spiral box and, hence, a tabletop machine was designed. In this machine, the hose no longer had to move but, instead, the rotating hose pulls the spiral on top of itself and pushes the pin guiding the spiral forwards. A patent has been applied for the solutions (patent app. FI-20160139). The bottom row in Table 6.1 shows the time study of the setup times using the fully-functional mockup with the patented solution. Thus, the time for spiral cutting and detaching the hose are more or less the same, though attaching the hose in the machine is made faster with the pneumatic grippers compared to a manual screw-based gripper. However, since the pneumatic grippers are heavier and the precut spiral is fed to the machine by the operator, the spiraling speed had to be reduced. The cycle time, nevertheless, remained about the same. The company management seemed very pleased with the solution.

"We have invested in an automated machine for providing precut spirals for our customers. Our cutting machine enables nice finishing of the spiral ends and, naturally, speeds up the spiraling process of our customers. Thus, we see this spiral cutting service and our spiraling machine together offer interesting solution to our customers that our competitors, at least not at the moment, can offer."

When the ambitious original idea of feeding the spiral from the box was abandoned and the machine was designed to use precut spirals with hose locked at both ends and stretched straight, the case company was able to offer its customers a low-cost solution making the spiraling process significantly faster. For high-volume customers, the use of precut spirals would also provide a way to enhance the relationship with the case company, adding a service feature to their business, too.

Customer-Experienced Value at the Early Stages of the Development

Overall, companies should offer products and services that customers find attractive. However, customers consider a product attractive only if the benefits perceived from product usage surpass the sacrifices necessary for acquiring the product (Khalifa 2004). Thus, the offering should result in customer perceived value, and that value should be quantifiable. Quantifying the perceived value is challenging, as it requires in-depth knowledge about customers' processes and their key value drivers. However, one of the main challenges in gathering reliable customer feedback on customer perceived value is that customers perceive the real value of the product, by definition, only after experiencing the product in use (Lanning 1998; Woodruff 1997).

The use of mockups and prototypes has grown significantly as a means to help companies communicate their ideas more easily in the development process and to give customers a chance to experience the product in use. On the one hand, in early stages in the development process, mockups and prototypes are built to test the core functionalities of the final products, commonly known as low fidelity prototypes (Preece et al. 2002). On the other hand, during later stages of the product development process, prototypes are built out of the same materials and components as the final product and offer an equal level of functionality (Yang and el-Haik 2003). These prototypes are referred to as high fidelity prototypes (Preece et al. 2002). However, there has been a large gap between prototyping methods (see Karimian Pour 2015) and, as a result, customers have only been able to experience the real product usage very late in the development process yet, at this stage, over 80% of product life-cycle costs have already been committed (Turney 1991). Hence, even if the company received valuable customer feedback, it would be very costly to apply any modifications to the product (Dowlatshahi 1992, cited in Asiedu and Gu 1998).

Mockups have typically been used in three different ways. First, different types of low-fidelity prototypes (i.e., mockups) are often used for proof of concept to illustrate the new idea to the development team. Second, sometimes such mockups are also used for gathering some initial feedback from the end users. This is very common, for example in the development of software products or apps; the developers may only design a user interface of the new product in order to show it to the customers to get an idea whether customers would find something as proposed useful or not. There are even software products for only illustrating such user interfaces and rough functionality of a software. However, more traditional industries may not even welcome such an approach; it may jeopardize the credibility of engineering work in the eyes of colleagues, not to speak of customers. However, at the same time, such an approach may offer faster product development cycles also for more conservative industries.

Third, mockups can be shown to the customers to estimate how much customers would be willing to pay for such products or solutions. Thus, instead of just interviewing customers on product features they seek, mockups can be used to get more accurate data to confirm the customer's needs. Interestingly, some companies use mockups to test the customers' willingness to buy with a real transaction—until the sales process is terminated at the very last moment. A fast food restaurant, for example, can run a test in one restaurant by adding a new course on the menu with a price. Then, in case a customer wishes to order one, the order is inserted in the IT system until it notifies that the restaurant happens to be out of the key ingredients and the customer must choose something else instead. Nevertheless, the customer preference was as close to a real order as possible; the customer was willing to pay for the purchase with the price set. Such an estimate provides some guidelines for the price level, but that should not be confused with the customer perceived value; in order to define the customer perceived value, customers, by definition, would have to experience it first (Lanning 1998; Woodruff 1997). However, developing a product to the level that a customer can be judged based on a real purchase decision is oftentimes rather costly, especially in the more mature industries.

Low-fidelity prototypes (i.e., mockups) are typically built in a way that real customer experiments are not yet possible; these prototypes made of cheap materials do not enable testing in real usage situations. This case, however, argues that by combining the characteristics of low- and high-fidelity prototypes in a 'fully-functional mockup,' it is possible to test a new product idea in the context similar to the real production environment at the early stages of the product development process. Thus, the usage situations based on such a fully-functional mockup can, then, be used for making time studies, hence providing ex-post cost information on the process implications the new idea would have on the customer's process. In other words, instead of merely customers' opinions, the development team will have ex-post cost information on the implications the new product will provide to the customer. Furthermore, when the customer has been able to 'experience' these cost benefits, there not only exists ex-post cost information, but one can even consider having access to the process implication component on the customer perceived value, especially if the new idea is mainly designed for cost management purposes. Thus, it is possible to build a value proposition for the new offering at the initial stages of the development process based on 'experienced' value in use. Such information is a powerful input on go/no-go decision at the initial stages of the development cycle when only a limited amount of resources have been committed to the development work.

In this case, already at the beginning of the collaboration, the company was very interested in the idea of using mockups for proof of concept; the way the new capping solution was demonstrated to the management team was rather convincing. Already in that simple experiment, the output was the process implication of the new idea. The first mockup shown to the management was indeed a very simple one and did not provide really any real means to be used in practice—there was no real solution for having the caps in a belt. The others developed, however, already were machines that were usable in a real production setup with real components and materials, enabling customer-experienced process implications, hence providing not only ex-post cost information but the inputs needed for a valid value proposition. As mentioned, the development work was mostly carried out in the facilities of the hose assembly manufacturer and, therefore, the process implications were tested immediately when there was something to be tested, resulting in fast user feedback on 'experienced value.' Interestingly, the cycle times measured with the mockups were almost the same as eventually with the final products. Nevertheless, the question regarding how close the cycle time measured with the fully-functional mockup was to the real one is not that relevant. When the cycle time of sleeve cutting came down from 40 seconds close to ten seconds, that indicates a major productivity jump anyway; as long as the cycle time with the real one is between five and 15 seconds, the development team can be satisfied. Similarly, when the cycle time for spiraling came down from over four minutes to about one, the 'magnitude' of the process impact became evident, and some fluctuation would no longer erode the value potential. In other words, the most important role played by the mockup was to show the range regarding the productivity potential of the new ideas. In real life, the setup times were practically similar with the mockups and the real machines. The key drivers on the cycle times with the real machines were based on rotating speed and cutting speed, not impacted by the shift from the mockup design to the final product, but rather based on the limitations of the final components selected.

Finally, with both machines, thanks to the use of fully-functional mockups and the experiments based on them, the sales material was prepared at the early stages of the development process. This, again, was possible when the cost implications on the customer's operations were taken into consideration at the early stages. For both machines, the initial sales material drafts included payback tables with different annual production volumes, enabling the customers (as well as the development team) to do the payback analysis easily. As Business Unit Manager pointed out:

> "These payback period tables must be very useful for our customers. Whenever we are investing in new equipment, our controller always

asks for the payback period. Usually we cannot really answer anything; we just know that the new equipment will help in the production."

Thus, it is not enough that the customer perceived value is quantifiable, it is also important to consider the performance indicators customers use for evaluating the value creation. The very same perceived customer value can be explicated using different performance indicators.

Different Dimensions for Participation in the *Emic* Level

In the two previous chapters, the focus on the IVR has been on the role of the researcher, first regarding the evolution from a comrade to an expert and then as an integrator welding the team together. In both chapters, the focus has been on how the researcher has been able to penetrate deep in the *emic* world, later then going back to the *etic* mode and possibly doing this transition iteratively. In this chapter, we will analyze more how the researcher also gained deep access to the *emic* world, yet the researcher's role in the *emic* world kept changing, too.

The researcher has played a key role in developing the solutions enabling the new machines/services, meaning a very deep penetration in the *emic* level in terms of the technical development and the dialogue with the managers on the technical aspects. However, at the same time, the researcher has had a role of an outside facilitator, bringing the ideas needed for validating the value propositions and in that way a broader perspective to the development work, though still at the *emic* level. In other words, although the interplay between the *emic* and *etic* roles of the interventionist researcher is something already well-recognized in IVR; yet in this case, quite uniquely, the interest is on interplay within the *emic* level (i.e., techne) alone.

When the researcher first got involved with the case company management, the focus was on the development of the new hose capping solution. However, even though the case company was not interested in the solution itself, they nevertheless appreciated the process. Since the case company is rather small (especially the business unit) and works with commodity products, they end up with low margins and, therefore, have no large product development budgets either. Therefore, the case company was interested in new ideas, yet, looking at the innovation process with a new lens as well. Thus, the company was interested in sort of Lean product development with financial analyses deeply integrated in the development process based on mockups, i.e., use of fully-functional mockups as tools for, not only the proof of concept, but also for the validation of the value propositions at the early stages of the development process. As a result, collaboration was started with two areas in which they had more imminent needs amongst their customers: spiraling machine and sleeve cutting machine.

With the sleeve cutting machine, the first step was to brainstorm new potential ways to cut sleeve and test these ideas with mockups. First, the focus regarding the use of mockups was to test possible ways to cut the sleeve with an acceptable quality, meaning very practical development work on the technical solutions. Interestingly, the development process for hose capping had been very straightforward—as soon as the idea of having the caps on a belt emerged, the idea was tested with the mockup, the mockup also enabling the time study. However, with the sleeve cutting, finding a way to do that in the first place turned out to be challenging, since most ideas with hot knives and even the use of the vacuum cleaners to open up the sleeves did not seem to lead anywhere. Nevertheless, the researcher was deeply involved in the case, though with the main focus on the practical development for the sleeve cutting solution, i.e., on 'low *emic* level' so to speak.

One key error in the development of the sleeve cutting was that the idea was to enable a continuous flow of the process. Thus, the idea that most sleeves are short provided a major breakthrough for the development. The managers originally would have preferred a continuous process (similar to the automated cutting machines), whereas the researchers were able to demonstrate that i) pulling the sleeve on top of two support 'rods,' ii) using the 'rods' to open up the sleeve completely, iii) cutting, iv) bringing the 'rods' back together, and finally v) pulling the sleeve out, enabled the process to be performed four times faster compared to the old method, even if not following a continuous process. In other words, even though the process required the sleeve to be pulled back and forth, the process still provided significant time savings compared to the old way of cutting sleeves. Interestingly, even if at this point there were no mockup to study the process implication (a simple square tube was used as shown left in Figure 6.2), the time difference was nevertheless notable. With the time analysis on the table, the researcher shifted from 'low *emic* level' to the more 'abstract *emic* level,' though still remaining in the *emic* level.

When the first fully-functional mockup was being tested, yet another idea emerged; it was enough to have something inside the sleeve to open it up. Thanks to the fully-functional mockup in progress (though not yet successful), it was possible to test the new idea in a matter of hours, including also its cost implications. Thus, the fully-functional mockup was modified in order to test the solution in a production-like setting. The only limitation in the test was that the hot knife had to be cooled down after ten products; otherwise, the mockup could be used just like in real production. Now the mockup was providing something more than just the proof of concept; now it enabled the customer value potential to be estimated, too. Again, while fine-tuning the process itself (meaning working on the 'low *emic* level'), the process and cost implications were evaluated (meaning simultaneous work on the more 'abstract *emic* level') to ensure that the process targets were reached.

The sleeve cutting machine, in addition to the theoretically interesting discovery regarding the use of fully-functional mockups in verifying value propositions at the early stages of the product development process, was an interesting case because the further development took rather colorful steps. First, the idea discussed above did not result in a perfect quality and hence was terminated. Another solution was also developed that, in the tests, seemed to work very nicely; though it required very careful use from the machine operators, eventually becoming too challenging in the real production environment. Interestingly, the way the sleeve was opened by 'tilting' it enabled a continuous process without pulling the sleeve back and forth. This solution would have enabled also long sleeves to be cut too, though the production tests proved it unpractical. Despite the fact that the solution did not require extra movement, the cycle time was still more or less the same as with the other, showing that a continuous process appeared more professional but did not really impact cost efficiency. Thus, after a few mockups, the researchers were able to reason that the cycle times tended to be more or less the same; one needed to pull the sleeve and then the cutting speed was a function of the melting speed of the different sleeve materials—the most important cost driver for the cycle time. This illustrates the analytical cost management approach to the development work resulting in some 'costing laws' to be used in the further development. In other words, working on the more 'abstract *emic* level,' the researchers were building better understanding of the key cost drivers of the different elements needed for sleeve cutting.

Interestingly, when the latest product idea was demonstrated to the case company management, the sleeve cutting process started to approach parametric costing: one first pulls the sleeve, then there is the mathematics for cutting speed, and finally there is some work needed to pull the sleeve out from the 'rod' in order for the cycle to start again. However, the problems in that version were that the size of the 'rod' made the pulling process inconvenient and slow, providing the arguments for not proceeding with the idea. Even though no superior 'killer solution' was discovered during the development work, the team learnt a lot. When the latest ideas had been explored, there were not only more knowledge about the cutting process (findings at the 'low *emic* level') and the 'time functions' related to it (findings at the more 'abstract *emic* level'), but there were also plenty of components and semi-stripped fully-functional mockups providing a good starting point for fast experimentation with new ideas, including also the testing of the potential cost implications.

Concerning the spiraling machine, the process started more or less in a similar way; the team had to brainstorm ideas for the spiraling process. In this case, the key idea was provided by Business Unit Manager and, once the idea was on the table, building of the mockups was rather straightforward. In fact, the first fully-functional mockup using two screwdrivers was built within a month of the idea, and that enabled both the proof of concept as well as the first time studies. The connection of the hose to the machine, however, remained a problem quite long, yet data from the first mockup and parametric estimations of the spiraling process nevertheless enabled rather accurate estimates of the process implications. Again, the case shows how the researcher was first needed to work on the 'low *emic* level' in order to find feasible solutions to the practical problem and, as soon as there was an idea regarding the potential solution, the researcher had to reposition the work more towards the more 'abstract *emic* level' to bring the cost analyses and financial understanding to the process, though still remaining at the *emic* level. In other words, the 'abstract *emic* level' is not *etic* in the sense that is resembles the contribution potential of the case, but it helps by taking distance and providing new viewpoints to the development work within the *emic* level.

When the first machine was sold to the customer, the extensive testing provided interesting opportunities to learn about the 'industrial scale' spiraling process. Again, all that understanding is connected 'only' to the more 'abstract *emic* level' and not yet providing theory contributions to the MA field. Again, as this case shows, both *emic* levels were very important for (1) keeping the development process going and (2) adding value to the development process with the analysis of cost implications. The first one was important for maintaining access, yet the second one was important for providing management understanding on pros and cons of different ideas in terms of their process implications. As Business Unit Manager pointed out during the process:

> "Even though we have not been able to develop a well-functioning sleeve cutting machine and the spiraling machine turned out to be much more expensive than planned, I am very pleased with our collaboration. Now when I talk to the customers, I know exactly what they mean when they are talking about the problems they have in their sleeving and spiraling processes. Thus, we have learnt a lot and it seems that customers also appreciate our knowledge. In the end, most of our competitors mainly sell sleeves and spirals, not being able to have such deep dialogue on the customer's processes."

Eventually, there was an idea for using pneumatic grippers to attach both ends of the hose and then use a third pneumatic cylinder to pull the hose straight (i.e., the patented table-top machine), resulting in a very convenient spiraling process even for thick hoses. Thanks to the development work, the case company was able to offer their customers both a more expensive (and more professional) as well as a relatively low-cost solution for spiraling. Eventually, there may be a solution in sight also for the sleeve cutting. However, the key thing from the research point of view is, nevertheless, the possibility to extensively play with the fully-functional mockups in order to study their role in evaluating perceived customer value at the early stages of the development process. Thus, both *emic* levels ('low *emic* level' and more 'abstract *emic* level') eventually served as access providers to do scholarly work on the role of the fully-functional mockups in estimating process cost implications.

However, it is important to emphasize the uncertainties an MA researcher faces when engaging in such development processes. Combining the *emic*-level roles with the *etic*-level needs is a challenging task, requiring expertise in many areas. In the end, very detailed technical aspects had to be tackled in order to have customers test the new machine to verify the value potential estimated with the mockups. In a similar way, building a costing model or PM framework may require working at the 'low *emic* level,' for example in gathering or analyzing data, as well as at the 'more abstract *emic* level' when designing such frameworks—both seen as work in the *emic* level. The former may also have connotations with the role as a 'comrade,' whereas the latter more to the expert. However, understanding better the roles played in the field helps to improve the knowledge on what IVR is and can be.

Supporting Government Innovation Policy

Both machines developed in this project enabled the customers to reduce their operating costs when using the spirals and sleeves of the case company. Thus, the case was initially positioned to focus on the practical development work (techne) in the area of cost management by helping the company develop low-cost solutions for its customers to use sleeves and spirals in their operations (see Figure 6.4).

As shown in the figure, the use of low-fidelity mockups in the machine construction industry was seen as one interesting feature, following the

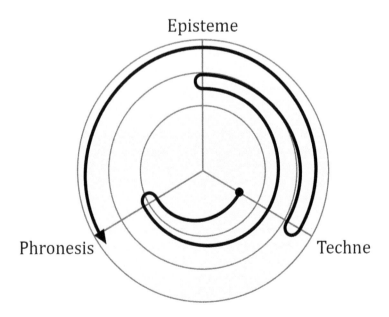

Figure 6.4 The Interplay Between Techne, Phronesis, and Episteme.

suggested R&D policies of Finnish Funding Agency for Technology and Innovation (TEKES). Thus, already at the outset of the research collaboration, the societal impact (phronesis) was present. However, plenty of effort was needed in order to work on the feasible solutions for solving the process needs of the customers using the spirals and sleeves of the case company. Thus, the main empirical work was related to the development of the solutions needed for the machines (techne). However, after some development work, the researchers came up with the idea of using the mockups for making time studies needed for cost analysis, providing some interesting theoretical insights (episteme). Thus, instead of simulated time studies providing ex-ante cost information, the idea of using fully-functional mockups to provide ex-post cost information at the early stages of the product development process was proposed. When this idea was introduced to one of the Senior Technology Advisers in TEKES, she pointed out:

> "I am impressed. It seems that you are one of the first movers in using mockups for verifying value propositions at the early stages of the development process, especially in the machine construction sector."

This comment, then, gave motivation to continue working on the improved versions of the mockups with time studies as an integral part of the development work, again positioning the work in practical development (techne). At the same time, if interventionist MA researchers are allowed the position of first movers with respect to significant mechanisms in the innovation processes, it opens several new avenues for interpreting and intentionally extending the societal impact potential of interventionist MA research.

Interestingly, when the mockups were being built and cost implications studied, the team came up with an idea to prepare some payback analyses on the behalf of the customers. In these studies, the process implication was a known (even at the level of ex-post cost information) though the machine price remained a variable. When this information was then connected to the literature on customer value (episteme), the fact that the customer was able to use the mockup in real production to 'experience' the cost reduction positioned the theory contribution from MA literature to the marketing literature and, more precisely, to the customer value literature.

This theoretical idea, however, made the idea even more interesting considering the government innovation policy (phronesis); it repositioned the use of mockups from proof of concept to testing of value propositions at the early stages of the product development process. Thus, already at the initial stages of the development, it would be possible to show management and potential customers cost analyses on the process implication based on ex-post cost data generated using these mockups. Thus, not only can mockups be used as tools for shortening the development cycles, the use of them in analyzing customer perceived value at the initial stages of the development process also provides an interesting tool likely to improve the success rate of the development projects. This could provide yet another interesting 'sales argument' for TEKES when promoting the use of rapid prototyping for renewal in more mature industries.

References

Asiedu, Y. and Gu, P., 1998. Product life cycle cost analysis: State of the art review. *International Journal of Production Research*, 36(4), pp. 883–908.

Dowlatshahi, S., 1992. Product design in a concurrent engineering environment: An optimization approach. *The International Journal of Production Research*, 30(8), pp. 1803–1818.

Karimian Pour, N., 2015. *Fully-functional mockups in constructing value propositions* (MSc Thesis). Tampere University of Technology, 114 p.

Khalifa, A., 2004. Customer value: A review of recent literature and an integrative configuration. *Management Decision*, 42(5), pp. 645–666.

Lanning, M. J., 1998. *Delivering profitable value: A revolutionary framework to accelerate growth, generate wealth, and rediscover the heart of business.* Perseus Book Group, New York, 324 p.

Preece, J., Rogers, Y. and Sharp, H. (2002). *Interaction design—beyond human-computer interaction.* John Wiley & Sons Inc, New York, 519 p.

Turney, P., 1991. *Common cents—the ABC performance breakthrough.* Cost Technology, Hillsboro.

Woodruff, R., 1997. Customer value: The next source for competitive advantage. *Journal of the Academy of Marketing Science*, 25(2), pp. 139–153.

Yang, K. and El-Haik, B., 2003. *Design for six sigma.* McGraw-Hill, New York.

7 Accounting and Control for Supporting New Service Development in Machinery Manufacturing

This chapter presents an exploratory process towards designing and enacting accounting and control techniques for New Service Development (NSD). The chapter is connected to the timely servitization phenomenon, where machinery manufacturers are increasingly interested in and focused on developing new services for their machinery in use at the customer's site. Essentially, refocusing the business on the services throughout the machinery life cycles represents also a change in the focus of the accounting and control tools and practices. The chapter takes advantage of an interventionist case in one machinery manufacturing company (Fastems), providing its customers with comprehensive production systems and related after sales services. Unlike in the previously presented cases, the starting point of this case was the contribution potential ('episteme' as a starting point in contrast to many other cases presented in this book) that was identified in better understanding the possibly supportive role of accounting and control in NSD within the servitization (see, e.g., Tenucci and Laine 2015). At the same time, it is noteworthy that antecedents of this particular case also feature development of tools and techniques needed for planning and controlling innovation activities ('techne').

In fact, servitization has been recognized as an influential business phenomenon for three decades (Vandermerwe and Rada 1988), and its scope and content have been defined in numerous more recent articles (see, e.g., Oliva and Kallenberg 2003; Gebauer et al. 2005). Despite the increasing interest in the phenomenon among scholars and the timely research stream related to it, the tools and techniques that are required by (or would be potentially beneficial to) the machinery manufacturers have not been sufficiently examined. In fact, many machinery manufacturers have been disappointed about the financial results of their servitization initiatives, although many benefits have been at least implicitly promised to all the machinery manufacturers in studies reporting servitization success stories (see, e.g., Gebauer et al. 2005). More particularly, the role of accounting and control in supporting servitization, e.g., their potential of providing relevant tools and techniques for overcoming the experienced challenges in realizing the business benefits of servitization, has not been addressed in the existing literature (see

Laine et al. 2012a, b; Lindholm et al. 2017; Tenucci and Laine 2015 as few exceptions).

To specify further the contribution potential underlying this case, the so far published articles on the matter have been largely conceptual (Laine et al. 2012a) or provided an overview on the topic. Practical, yet scientifically examined cases on support from accounting and control for particular (actual) NSD projects have not been available. At the same time, this specific topic fits well in the research agenda of CMC, as the idea is to examine how MA researchers could contribute in finding better support from accounting and control to timely business phenomena, such as servitization.

A unique feature in this contribution potential is the fact that accounting and control for New Product Development (NPD) still remains a timely research topic, with an articulated lack of studies with in-depth empirical access to NPD accounting practice (see, e.g., Nixon 1998; Jorgensen and Messner 2010; Laine et al. 2016a; Tervala et al. 2017). It is noteworthy that still in the recent studies on this topic, the role of emerging strategic initiatives in the NPD accounting practices have not been addressed. Besides, the possible differences between tangible products and intangible services as accounting and control objects have not been thoroughly examined in the accounting literature, despite a few examples (Modell 1996; Brignall 1997; Laine 2009). Potentially, examining the NSD efforts of the machinery manufacturers could not only reveal some peculiarities embedded in NSD as an accounting context, but also reveal several new insights into accounting and control practice that would support the business renewal processes.

Episteme viewpoint as a starting point of this case does not mean the absence of the other two perspectives. In fact, as mentioned in the very beginning, the focus of the case on developing the potentially supportive tools and techniques for NSD represents an explicit link to techne. Besides, the case presented in this chapter was taken from a nation-wide research program on enhancing the service businesses of the Finnish machinery manufacturing companies that aim at better supporting their machinery fleets at use in the customers' sites. Therefore, the case is connected to the timely and remarkable industrial renewal that is essentially related to the newly identified sources of competitive advantage of the Finnish machinery manufacturing industries (phronesis). As a result, positioning the starting point in episteme implies also an active interplay with the other two perspectives, when examining the implications of this case.

Introduction to the Case

The chapter takes advantage of the access of the researcher(s) to a company called Fastems, providing its customers with comprehensive production systems and related after sales services. The MA researcher(s) have been earlier involved in research projects focusing on planning and controlling the company's R&D activities by introducing a new tool for selecting and steering different kinds of R&D projects (the first research project was in 2011–2014, as referred to in this chapter). Now, since the beginning of 2015 the research was focused on identifying, selecting, and steering NSD activities (the second research project). The second research project was a part of the wider, national research program, and the case featured the presence of a multidisciplinary team in this case. However, the second research project is reported here solely from the perspective of the MA researchers in the CMC research team, and limited to the primary findings of the MA researchers with respect to the case, although the MA researchers acted within the multidisciplinary team as the second research project proceeded.

The second project intentionally builds on the previous cooperation between Fastems and the MA researchers, but at the same time, also new features stemming from the peculiarities of the company's service activities were integrated in the research plan. Especially, the focus of the second research project in 2015–2016 was on the analyses of the service business profitability now and in supporting selected NSD activities with suitable accounting and control tools and techniques (techne).

Altogether, in 2011–2016, the MA researcher(s) were involved in the two research projects that included around 25 relevant meetings and workshops as the primary research data of this chapter. In between those events, numerous phone calls and emails were exchanged. This longitudinal setting features a unique characteristic of engaged research in long-term industry collaboration. As outlined above, besides the longitudinal nature, the multidisciplinary research team employed by the company is a unique characteristic of this case. Although the focus in this chapter is on the research agenda conducted by the MA researchers, the implications of the multidisciplinary work are brought up whenever needed. Especially, when reflecting upon the role of the MA researchers at the end of the chapter, the evolving roles of the MA researchers in the multidisciplinary team are brought up and thoroughly discussed.

The first research project focused on designing a BIA tool for R&D control. The project included discussions, where the MA researcher(s) and the company representatives discussed the decision-making criteria and related quantitative and qualitative analyses in a detailed manner. Therefore, already during the first research project, the parties involved already discussed the characteristics of different kinds of projects ranging from the development of new generation systems to product safety improvement projects. Besides, the development of complex entities of new products and related services were already discussed from the financial perspectives. For example, the role of the services as amendments to the tangible products or as "stand-alone" products was discussed, and it was found out that in order to understand the business impacts of new products and services, the scope and content of the products and services under development require careful examination case-by-case.

This first research project can also be seen as a series of interventions, starting from the need for identification and continuing to the iterative process of designing and testing the tool for selecting and steering the R&D projects. However, from the perspective of this chapter, this process as a whole represents an intervention that paved the way towards the series of interventions taken regarding the servitization initiative and the NSD activities in the second research project.

In the first research project, the researcher was first involved in analyzing the potential business impacts of a few radical innovations under development in the company (autumn 2011—spring 2013). After that, the focus shifted to designing and testing a tool for selecting and steering different kinds of R&D projects according to the objectives and preferences of the company (2013–2014). The challenges related to the assessment of the business impacts of the radical innovations highlighted the need for a more generally applicable tool for business impact analyses. As stated by the R&D manager of Fastems, the main aim of the tool was to help planning and controlling R&D projects:

> "[The tool] helps choosing good projects. . . . And afterwards we are able to assess how well we actually chose."

As an outcome, the (Excel) tool for selecting and steering the R&D projects consisted of separate sheets for different projects that included the following considerations: i) an assessment of the relative newness of the project (new to the company, new to the customers), ii) a qualitative assessment of the impact of the project (customer value and strategic fit), and iii) economic evaluation. The economic evaluation followed a logic of a Business Impact Analysis (BIA) (see, e.g., Laine et al. 2016a), i.e., it contained the estimates of the future process, volumes, product costs, and the project costs. Moreover, the analysis included considerations of the cannibalization effects of the new product, after sales business estimations and considerations of other indirect effects. As a result, the tool enabled calculations of the overall business impacts of the new products as well as estimates of the Net Present Value and payback time of the new product under consideration. Besides, as different R&D projects were included in the tool in a separate sheet, an overview of the R&D portfolio as a whole could be presented in a report sheet. This allowed the examination of the overall value and characteristics of the company's R&D activities.

During the design process of the tool, the researcher had several meetings with the R&D manager in order to understand the scope and content of different R&D projects and to find ways of using the tool as effectively as possible in different cases. In fact, the nature of particular R&D projects was further elaborated by considering their business impacts, either through their direct or more indirect effects. For example, designing new subsystems to the production systems could result in direct sales of such a feature within the overall system sales. Another viewpoint is to consider the probability of new system sales after the launch of the new feature. In both cases, also the cannibalization effects, i.e., the sales that will be replaced by selling this new feature, need careful considerations. Technically, it is important that the positive benefits are not counted twice, if the business impacts are considered by calculating both the extra price of the new feature and the overall margin of the potential new system sales. From the behavioral perspective, it is important to consider what the actual nature of the new product (or service) under development is, and how it would be translated into positive business impacts. From the perspective of the R&D stakeholders, realizing the potential positive benefits attained from the new product (or service) requires detailed, in-depth understanding about it.

One may conclude that using the new BIA tool enabled refining the idea and role of the new product(s) within the overall product offering of Fastems. At the end of the first research project, the new tool was test used by the product managers and, as a result, the company's decision-making on the R&D projects adopted the principles of the tool, both at the level of single R&D projects and with respect to the overall R&D portfolio management. However, the tool as such (Excel) was not widely implemented.

At relatively late phases of the first research project, the MA researchers planned a new cooperative project, with a focus on supporting the NSD of the company according to the servitization initiative in place in the company. As noted, this second research project (2015–2016) was intended to be part of the wider research program aiming at enhanced service businesses for Finnish machinery manufacturers serving the machinery fleets at their customers. When the new research project started, with the focus on NSD activities, the researchers had already been familiarized with some of the key measurement and valuation challenges in this particular business context. On the other hand, the key personnel of the company had the impression that the MA researchers could help them in the NSD activities, in particular with respect to the business impact analyses connected to the new service businesses.

More particularly, the second research project was part of a larger scale Finnish research program, with a focus on service solutions for fleet management, supporting and enhancing the use of the machinery at the customers' sites throughout their life cycle. In the program, several strategic, operational, and technological aspects were studied from multidisciplinary perspectives, in many cases in a close collaboration between the researchers and industry partners. The program involved almost ten universities and more than 40 companies as a whole. The planning of the program featured detailed examination of the status of the service business in different companies, and critical examination of the most potential avenues of further developing the servitization initiatives within those companies. Fastems as well as some other companies were actively involved in designing the research activities with the university partners that could best support them in the long-run, with respect to their service businesses.

Within the program, one subproject focused on profitability-driven service business renewal, that is, the potentially supporting role of management accounting and control in the servitization that has not been previously sufficiently examined in the literature, as discussed above. This subproject was managed by the MA researchers, and the second research project reported in this chapter is a part of this subproject. The MA researchers were involved also in other cases, where the aim was to enhance the practice of accounting and control in the servitization context and thus support the companies that aimed at developing innovative new services and a better performance in their service activities. This overall agenda is in line with the research gap outlined above. However, the topic is also societally relevant in Finland, due to the important role of the machinery construction industry in Finnish export business, and thus relates to the overall well-being of the society.

Interventions

The process of interventions in the Fastems case could be outlined in the following way. In the beginning, in the first research project, the researcher designed an Excel tool based on the requirements set by the R&D manager and other managers in Fastems. Several meetings were organized that focused on familiarizing with the R&D control within the company, on identifying timely R&D project ideas and their characteristics, and discussing the projects, project ideas, and R&D control with the help of prototypes of the BIA tool (Excel) (see, e.g., Wouters and Roijmans 2011, for accounting prototypes).

In the second research project, in order to organize the workshops for supporting timely NSD ideas, the MA researchers conducted a current status analysis of the service contracts of the company in selected market areas and reviewed the existing business models related to those contracts. The analyses were beyond the routine financial reporting of the company, and the results of these analyses were used in the workshops to introduce the current status of the service business. Similarly to the MA researchers' tasks, also other research parties had their own tasks for preparing the workshops on NSD. These included analyses of different service offerings and customer experience related to them.

When organizing the workshops, essentially, the MA researchers utilized their background in R&D control tool development to facilitate the workshop, where the business potential and impacts of three promising new services were addressed. Essentially, in addition to using the tool itself, the researchers presented their insights on estimating business impacts under uncertainty and complexity. As a result, the expected business impacts were made tangible to the parties involved.

As a unique feature, this series of interventions was not only based on the contribution potential in the MA literature (or other research domains), but the series of interventions was also largely steered by the company representatives, despite the articulated research gap (episteme) underlying the project. From the perspective of IVR, the MA researchers got access to an authentic development project, and could observe the discussions as they appear when selecting and steering promising new services (see Laine et al. 2016b as another example of using discussions in outlining the financial impacts of new offerings).

Altogether, the series of interventions made during this research process may be summarized as follows:

- Planning the three workshops on NSD management
- Co-organizing the workshop on ideas for new services (active participation)
- Co-organizing the workshop on selecting appealing new services (active participation)
- Co-organizing the workshop on Business Impact Analysis (BIA) of new services (facilitation of the workshop).

The first intervention focused on planning the workshops for NSD management. This intervention is tightly connected to the wider research program and was designed jointly by the company representatives and the multidisciplinary team of researchers. This intervention can, again, be divided into smaller scale interventions including the current status analyses of the service business of the company and the multi-phase process of designing the workshops according to the evolving needs of the company.

According to the objectives of the second research project on "profitability-driven service business renewal" (2015–2016), the research process began with i) current status analyses on the business logics of the machinery manufacturers and their customers. After that the research effort focused on ii) selected service business renewal initiatives, such as NSD projects. Finally, the idea was iii) to examine the actual business impacts of the actions taken in the previous phase. In this particular case, the aim was to focus on the NSD activities, by taking advantage of two factors enabled by the previous cooperation between the researchers and Fastems:

- The MA researchers had familiarized themselves with the financial reporting of the company
- The MA researchers had developed the R&D control tools and procedures together with the R&D organization.

As a result, the MA researchers were assigned tasks of performing a (brief) current status analysis of the service business and proactively participating in a series of workshops that were organized for developing the NSD management within the company (in 2015). The analyses were beyond the routine financial reporting of the company, and the results of these analyses were used in the workshops to introduce the current status of the service business.

The findings of the current status analysis were twofold. First, the company has already a relatively comprehensive service offering, including services based on the online access to the machinery owned and operated by the customers, but the financial performance of these services is not managed in a unified way. Different contracts and services appeared in different ways in the financial reports, which highlighted the need for current status analysis. Second, the current status analysis revealed a potential of increasing the service business in different market areas both by refining the existing service offering for current and new customers, and finding new service concepts to extend the service business and open new market opportunities. Based on the challenges in the earlier reporting, such a detailed business potential analysis was not previously available in the company. Altogether, this analysis provided one natural starting point for the workshops.

The three workshops for NSD management are interpreted as interventions two through four presented in this chapter. The second intervention was co-organizing the first workshop on new service ideas. In fact, the first step taken in the workshops was to identify different new service ideas potentially available for the company. In addition to active participation in general, the MA researchers contributed to this workshop by introducing the current status analysis results as outlined above. Moreover, all the workshop participants brought up examples of innovative services during the discussion.

As the third intervention, in the second workshop, the focus gradually shifted to the initial screening of the most promising ideas. During the second workshop, primarily organized by the company itself, the company representatives identified and tested new ways to manage the process from service ideas to new services. The MA researchers were engaged with the process of preliminarily selecting the most promising service ideas. The role of the MA researchers was to actively contribute to the discussions during the workshop.

It is noteworthy that the workshops were organized according to the company's development agenda, and they involved several viewpoints and managerial roles of the company (R&D, service operations, NSD, technical support, etc.). Besides, there was a cross-disciplinary research team employed in facilitating and supporting the execution of the series of workshops, including management accounting researchers, service and operations management researchers, and psychologists (cf. Van de Ven and Johnson 2006).

The fourth intervention, i.e., the BIA workshop, was designed and facilitated in a close cooperation between the MA researchers and the company representatives (especially R&D manager, service operations manager, and an engineering student). The MA researchers had the greatest role in the facilitation of this workshop, and thus the analysis of this chapter largely focuses on it. The BIAs conducted in the workshop focused on three NSD ideas, selected during the previous workshops (interventions two and three). The relative newness of the NSD ideas varied from refinements of the existing maintenance program to wider renewal of the particular industrial operations at hand. During the workshop, the participants worked together in small groups, in order to better understand the nature and potential of each NSD idea.

More particularly, the workshop agenda was as follows:

- Describing each NSD idea and discussing their special features and relative newness (together)
- Elaborating on the 'identity' of each idea and its qualitative impacts (customer value and strategic fit) (in groups, each group, each idea)
- Estimating the business impacts of each idea (in groups, one group focusing on one idea)
- Synthesizing the findings and reflecting upon the business impact analyses.

As can be seen in the agenda of the workshop above, the BIA workshop followed the routine designed earlier in the company with the help of the R&D manager for selecting and controlling R&D projects. Furthermore, the workshop enabled not only using the technical tool, but discussing the business impacts of the new services from multiple perspectives, and actively outlining the desired further steps with respect to each idea.

Table 7.1 conveys the structure of the analysis followed in the workshop. Table 7.1 provides more detailed content of the analyses and outputs of the different phases of the workshop.

It is noteworthy that the discussion started with topics that were relatively easy to understand by the non-accountant personnel of Fastems and

Table 7.1 The Analysis Structure Used in the BIA Workshop as a Basis for Discussion.

Discussion topic	Idea description and analysis	Qualitative analysis of the idea	Financial analysis of the idea
More detailed content	— Name — Relative newness — Time frame — Budget	— Value to the customer — Strategic importance — Technical feasibility	— Volume — Price — Direct and indirect costs — Development costs — Cannibalization — Indirect effects
Output	Outline of the scope and content of the overall idea	Assessment of the identity and the preliminary value of the idea	Assessment of the financial impacts of the idea

non-accountant researchers involved. Regarding each NSD idea, there was a person who was able to present the idea in essence, with respect to its name, relative newness, and possible role in the future offering. This discussion paved the way towards more detailed qualitative and financial assessments of the ideas in groups.

Indeed, all three workshops involved several company representatives that had not been earlier involved in the BIA work at the company, due to the earlier distance between the operations focusing on the machinery systems and related services. However, the BIA workshop enabled all the participants to follow and contribute to the assessment of the NSD ideas at hand. In fact, feedback received from one participant, whose work previously did not include financial estimations, confirmed this observation:

> "The Excel platform was surprisingly easy to use and the logic enabled the participation of us who are not used to work with financial numbers . . ."

As a result, the following observations were made during the BIA workshop. First, in addition to the tool and its structure, the MA researchers presented their insights on estimating business impacts under uncertainty and complexity. During the workshop, the expected business impacts were made tangible to the parties involved. Regarding the qualitative analysis, it was found that the concept that was closest to the existing business performed best, whereas the two other concepts suffered from the ambiguities in their definition or from the uncertainties related to the actual fit to the strategy or the customers' processes.

Second, the analyses regarding the monetary effects provided a basis for important discussions. The attained figures of Net Present Value (NPV) or payback time were relatively positive, which conveys the message that the parties involved actually see the value and customer potential in the new concepts. The positive figures are, however, at least partly due to the fact that the total costs of the relatively new concepts were not that well known by the parties involved. It seemed to be easier to estimate the number of customers and the expected price of the new concept than the development costs, direct costs, and especially the overhead costs related to the new concepts in use.

Overall, third, the participants found it especially useful that they were 'forced' to give estimates as a basis for further discussions. The detailed structure of the BIA tool required estimates on the development costs and operational costs related to the new services, and those were not previously analyzed in such a detailed manner. Although it is not extremely important to estimate all the cost elements in detail, the examination of the future processes related to the service under development unveils resources and activities that require further consideration prior to the launch of the new service. For example, if the new service requires certain technical skills and capabilities, the availability of such skills and capabilities to the desired extent needs examination. Through these kinds of cases connected to the new services under development, the company representatives got new information both about the concepts themselves, but also the uncertainties and ambiguities related to them.

Impact of the Case—Business Potentials of the New Services

The contribution potential of this case focuses on the potential support of accounting and control in NSD activities within servitization (Laine et al. 2012a, b; Tenucci and Laine 2015). As the findings revealed, the R&D control tools and approaches, previously designed and enacted in NPD settings, are suitable for the NSD context as well, if the relative newness of the NSD ideas are taken into account and a particular attention is paid to the organizational structure and governance related to the servitization initiative (Laine et al. 2012a).

However, in this particular case, the transferability of the tool primarily designed for selecting and steering NPD projects was enabled by the fact that, already in the first research project, the parties involved had discussed the peculiarities of the R&D projects in this context and related measurement and valuation challenges. It is also fair to say that, in the interventions reported in this chapter, the tool was used to analyze NSD projects at a relatively early phase. In other words, the tool serves well the purpose of defining the identities of the new service ideas, qualitatively assessing them, and preliminarily addressing their potential financial consequences. So far, the tool has not been used in supporting the decision-making in a wider sense, but more readily it has fostered and put forward valuable discussions regarding the future offerings of the company.

After the series of workshops, the selected NSD ideas have become projects (2016) and the MA researchers have been involved in more detailed BIA analyses of some of the ideas. Other research teams involved in the workshops have been involved in identifying and examining more detailed customer expectations and requirements related to the new services. Overall, the series of workshops as organized in this case represents a boost in the NSD management in Fastems—better in line with the modern R&D management ideas and the overall servitization initiative of the company.

In particular, the case involved several different managerial roles of the company, including R&D manager, service manager, and experts who now together built a shared understanding about the current and desired role of service business in the company. The multidisciplinary research approach enabled versatile discussions on the topic and different viewpoints brought up were taken into account. In spring 2017, a new workshop is under preparation that will summarize and synthesize the lessons learned from this project. The series of workshops seems to have established new discussion avenues and routines within the company (see, e.g., Laine et al. 2016b).

This is important especially in the context of the servitization initiative that essentially challenges, and possibly renews, the organizational responsible structures as the offerings and customer relationships are substantially under development.

From the MA perspective, the current status analysis made visible the existing service offering and its current financial consequences. Based on this new information, the service personnel and other experts became more interested in extending the share of the service businesses and finding ways to articulate the value of the new services both to Fastems and its customers.

During the workshops, both the R&D manager and the service manager brought up the idea of the company to either increase the revenues or cut costs in their customers' operations as a basis for their service offering. The starting point of the discussion was thus tightly connected to the MA viewpoint (see, e.g., Laine et al. 2012b). Based on this, it was relatively natural to start discussions on the customer value of the new concepts, their appropriate pricing, and other profitability impacts. The multidisciplinary approach during the workshops was important because the discussions on the financial aspects were not discussed separately from the customer preferences or strategically important aspects, but the participants 'were forced' and were willing to share their insights and find the best possible estimates regarding the business impacts.

An important outcome of the workshops was that the 'identities' of the new service concepts were now discussed earlier than previously within the company. At the same time, it was found out that some of the more futuristic service ideas were seen as ambiguous and their fit to the customer needs was not known by the parties involved. However, understanding such uncertainties and ambiguities at a relatively early phase enables overcoming them during the NSD project execution (Laine et al. 2016b). As discussed by Laine et al. (2012a), the role of accounting should evolve along the way the servitization initiative proceeds in a given context. In this case, the workshops were one source of inspiration (see, e.g., Burchell et al. 1980) for the new service development and thus represented this important role of accounting in decision-making, as opposed to accounting as answer machine (Burchell et al. 1980).

Regarding the potential support from accounting and control in servitization, examinations of the NSD projects from this perspective have been extremely rare (Tenucci and Laine 2015). Importantly, Fastems represents an example of an advanced approach in supporting NSD projects within servitization. Advanced methods for selecting and steering R&D projects were used also for NSD purposes, and the company sought to examine the most suitable ways for this practice. As a result, the consciousness of the objectives of the servitization initiative increased during the process. In MA terms, the objectives of the decisions related to the servitization included thus less uncertainty, and during the NSD projects and afterwards, the company will learn much more about the financial consequences of its service businesses ('learning machine,' in Burchell et al. 1980, used also in Laine et al. 2012a).

At the same time, it is noteworthy that the servitization initiative does not go towards decreased uncertainty at all the levels, but also the NSD portfolio should include a set of different types of projects with significantly different levels of uncertainties. Also in this case, there are new service business ideas that are new both to the company and its customers. At the same time, there are ideas that represent merely improvements for the existing services. Therefore, to be supportive, an MA tool should be flexible enough to enable decision-making regarding different kinds of projects. In other words, MA tools should reduce uncertainties and ambiguities to a sufficient extent so that strategizing, i.e., decision-making without financial information is not needed, if the parties know actually something about the financial consequences (cf. Jorgensen and Messner 2010). As this case suggests, there is a lot of potential in discussions among the key stakeholders to build a shared awareness of the identities of the new products and services and their qualitative and quantitative (financial) impacts.

Reflection on the Interventions—Evolving Roles Within the Multidisciplinary Team

The interventions that took place in this case can be labeled as MA interventions within a multidisciplinary team (cf. Van de Ven and Johnson 2006). In this particular case, the first research project was an important phase in building trust between the MA researcher(s) and Fastems. As a result, CMC was seen as a suitable partner with respect to the second research project, with capabilities on assessing and analyzing business impacts. In fact, the R&D manager of Fastems usually labeled the viewpoint of the MA researchers in CMC as 'business impact' examination. This can be seen also in the structure and division of tasks and responsibilities of the workshop series, where MA researchers held the responsibility for the workshop focusing on the BIAs. Similarly to this label of the MA researchers' capabilities, also other research groups had their unique profiles within the multidisciplinary team, such as service operations, customer value, user experience, and service acceptance.

It is noteworthy that the planning of the second research project in Fastems was largely directed according to the company's servitization agenda, influenced by the planning of the national research program on this topic. Therefore, establishing the multidisciplinary team was also largely directed by Fastems, which chose the research teams they wished to cooperate with. However, the actual configuration of the multidisciplinary team was refined by the research teams that sought the most suitable people to take part in this particular project. This is a remarkable finding in line with the idea of interventionist research in a battlefield of competing (or at least varying) forces (see Suomala et al. 2014). Additionally, in the process outlined in this chapter, the company had an overall understanding about their servitization initiative and the scope, within which the research effort would make the largest impact. As a result, the battlefield where the MA researchers operated was largely influenced by the company and its strategic initiatives, and refined by the engagement within the multidisciplinary research team.

It is noteworthy that the examination of the actual NSD projects highlights the interest of the company representatives in the research project. Therefore, since the beginning of the second research project, the company representatives were eager to hear about the new ideas and stream within the servitization phenomenon. Besides, the overall research agenda included aspects that were relatively new to all the parties involved. In essence, the different research groups and also the company representatives brought up their own viewpoints and contributed to the overall understanding since the very beginning. It was not a matter of acceptance of the MA researchers by the company representatives to the multidisciplinary group ("one of us" in Suomala and Lyly-Yrjänäinen 2012), but all the parties involved constituted the team that was responsible for putting forward the overall research agenda that was supposed to contribute to the actual NSD projects. At the same time, it is noteworthy that the company was in charge of the overall process and their servitization initiative as a whole.

As described above, the MA perspective or business impact analyses were not in the focus of the other research teams involved. However, the multidisciplinary team as a whole was present in all the workshops, and there were other engagements such as joint planning meetings and some joint interviews among the stakeholders of the research project. Besides, in the workshop, focusing on the ideas of new services, the MA researchers initiated a discussion session where each participant (the company representatives and other research teams included) brought up examples of innovative new services and related business models. The idea was to collect ideas on services, where really something new had taken place. This discussion session revealed that such examples were found interesting not only from the perspective of the MA researchers and the company but also from the perspectives of the other research teams. For example, a researcher with a background in psychology brought up an example of a cafeteria where the second cup of coffee had a negative price of five cents. This business model was initiated by the owner of the cafeteria to provide a positive image about the cafeteria, to invest in long-term relationships—and potentially gain extra revenues if the length of the average visit in cafeteria increases, thus yielding indirect sales. Unconventional thinking in the service business development, as well as a multitude of different aspects related to it, were discussed through these real-life examples. Again, all the parties involved contributed significantly to the discussion.

Another level of engagement in this particular case was the established direct links between a) the MA researchers and the parties involved in NSD, such as R&D and service management, and b) the MA researchers and the financial department. The background of the cooperation between the MA researchers and R&D was outlined in this chapter earlier. The cooperation between the MA researchers and the financial department was of course only natural due to the focus and tasks in the research project. However, during the research projects one and two, the structure of the financial department changed and so did the personnel working for it. Remarkably, as CMC has a relatively long history in MA research within the region, some of the financial department representatives had previously worked in or cooperated with CMC. Therefore, it was relatively easy to gain access to the essential materials to conduct analyses and open discussions about the avenues for further development. Besides, quite essentially, also new representatives of the financial department joined the cooperation and contributed to it remarkably.

In all, the case is an example of engaged, interventionist research within a multidisciplinary team (Van de Ven and Johnson 2006; Suomala et al. 2014), with peculiarities stemming from the active role of the company in designing and steering the research agenda, and the versatile, yet fruitful cooperation within the multidisciplinary research team. The role of the MA researchers was pre-defined rather clearly with respect to the research project two. However, new opportunities emerged and were taken advantage of. The realization of such opportunities benefited greatly from the previous cooperation between the MA researcher and the key company representatives.

Interplay Between Episteme, Techne, and Phronesis

The IVR process outlined in this chapter began essentially with the recognition of the research gap that is episteme (see Figure 7.1). The earlier cooperation between the MA researchers and the company representatives and, especially, designing the tool for steering and controlling R&D projects had significantly focus on techne, i.e., building accounting prototypes (Wouters and Roijmans 2011; Laine et al. 2016a), which enabled learning from the issue at hand through the engaged discussions with the managers.

The more detailed research agenda, with a focus on supporting NSD within servitization with accounting control enactment, was again clearly formulated from a theoretical perspective (episteme), despite the active role of Fastems in planning the research project two and hiring the most suitable capabilities to the multidisciplinary research team involved. Earlier work in the techne domain by the MA researchers enabled narrower and thus to-the-point recognition of the research focus. In practice, however, the workshops also featured a techne dimension, particularly conducting current status analysis with new financial reporting ideas on service business, and using R&D tools for supporting NSD activities.

Although the workshops and the discussions facilitated and witnessed by the MA researchers during the workshops enabled responding to the research gap (episteme), the overall process embeds also societal

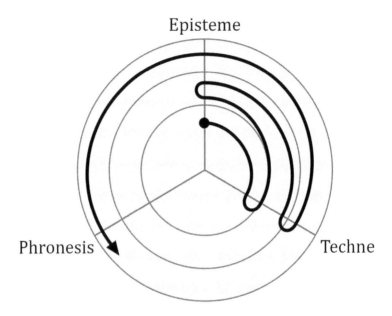

Figure 7.1 The Focus on the Three Intellectual Virtues During the Case.

implications. Understanding better the business potentials of the new (technology-enabled) service businesses responds to the timely challenge in Finnish machinery manufacturing, searching for growth in the export business. Although the societal aspects were discussed only to a limited extent during the project, a starting point of the wider research program was societally extremely important. The subproject on profitability-driven service business renewal has its focus on supporting particular avenues in companies to serve this wider purpose. Moreover, the overall research work undertaken by the multidisciplinary team within this case has potential in recognizing and overcoming several barriers in servitization and new service development within it.

References

Brignall, S., 1997. A contingent rationale for cost system design in services. *Management Accounting Research*, 8(3), 325–346.

Burchell, S., Clubb, C., Hopwood, A., Hughes, J. and Nahapiet, J., 1980. The roles of accounting in organizations and society. *Accounting, Organizations and Society*, 5(1), pp. 5–27.

Gebauer, H., Fleisch, E. and Friedli, T., 2005. Overcoming the service paradox in manufacturing companies. *European Management Journal*, 23(1), 14–26.

Jorgensen, B. and Messner, M., 2010. Accounting and strategising: A case study from new product development. *Accounting, Organizations and Society*, 35(2), pp. 184–204.

Laine, T., 2009. *Exploring pilot projects of a manufacturer on service R&D to understand service as an accounting object* (Dissertation). Tampere University of Technology, Industrial Management, Tampere, 195 p.

Laine, T., Korhonen, T. and Martinsuo, M. (2016b). Managing program impacts in new product development: An exploratory case study on overcoming uncertainties. *International Journal of Project Management*, 34(4), pp. 717–733.

Laine, T., Korhonen, T., Suomala, P. and Rantamaa, A., 2016a. Boundary subjects and boundary objects in accounting fact construction and communication. *Qualitative Research in Accounting and Management*, 13(3), pp. 303–329.

Laine, T., Paranko, J. and Suomala, P., 2012a. Management accounting roles in supporting servitisation: Implications for decision making at multiple levels. *Managing Service Quality*, 22(3), pp. 212–232.

Laine, T., Paranko, J. and Suomala, P., 2012b. Using a business game concept to enhance servitization: A longitudinal case study. *Managing Service Quality*, 22(5), pp. 428–446.

Lindholm, A., Laine, T. and Suomala, P., 2017. The potential of management accounting and control in global operations—profitability-driven service business development. Accepted for publication in *Journal of Service Theory and Practice*, 27(2), pp. 496–514.

Modell, S., 1996. Management accounting and control in services: Structural and behavioural perspectives. *International Journal of Service Industry Management*, 7(2), pp. 57–80.

Nixon, B., 1998. Research and development performance measurement: A case study. *Management Accounting Research*, 9(3), pp. 329–355.

Oliva, R. and Kallenberg, R., 2003. Managing the transition from products to services. *International Journal of Service Industry Management*, 14(2), pp. 160–172.

Suomala, P. and Lyly-Yrjänäinen, J., 2012. *Management accounting research in practice: Lessons learned from an interventionist approach*. Routledge, New York.

Suomala, P., Lyly-Yrjänäinen, J. and Lukka, K., 2014. Battlefield around interventions: A reflective analysis of conducting interventionist research in management accounting. *Management Accounting Research*, 25(4), pp. 304–314.

Tenucci, A. and Laine, T., 2015. The role of management accounting in servitisation: Exploring the potential role of management accounting in servitising manufacturing companies, where services are increasingly offered alongside physical products. *CIMA Executive Summary Report*, 12(3), pp. 1–12.

Tervala, E., Laine, T., Korhonen, T. and Suomala, P., 2017. The role of financial control in new product development: Empirical insights into project managers' experiences. Early access, 21 December 2016, *Journal of Management Control*, 28(1), pp. 81–106.

Vandermerwe, S. and Rada, J., 1988. Servitization of business: Adding value by adding services. *European Management Journal*, 6, pp. 314–324.

Van de Ven, A. H. and Johnson, P. E., 2006. Knowledge for theory and practice. *Academy of Management Review*, 31(4), pp. 802–821.

Wouters, M. and Roijmans, D., 2011. Using prototypes to induce experimentation and knowledge integration in the development of enabling accounting information. *Contemporary Accounting Research*, 28(2), pp. 708–736.

8 Management Accounting Research Reshaping Industry Practices

This chapter is based on a study designed to construct and evaluate a solution to an important managerial problem in a UK public-sector organization. The problem is significant as it is, arguably, one of the most fundamental issues facing both public and private organizations; it concerns the failure of organizations to plan and implement strategy successfully. It has been widely and consistently claimed that this is a common and serious issue in practice, as it is strategy implementation failure that prevents the majority of organizations from gaining the full potential benefit of the strategies they have devised (Mintzberg 1994; Judson 1995; Kaplan and Norton 1996; Wery 2004; Finkelstein 2005).

Thus, the focus in the case was on solving a practical managerial problem (in the public sector). Technical solutions were required and developed to satisfy organizational needs and, in this case, the organization played an important role in specifying what should be done and how the developed solution should be implemented. From this perspective, the case could be considered as not simply a practice enhancement but a contribution to normative theory for practice. The study was longitudinal in nature, commencing in 2004 and continued until 2011. This was necessary primarily because the solution involved the preparation of information that was part of an annual reporting cycle. The long time scale also allowed for implementation and revision of the solution, its evaluation in action and its progressive modification and improvement over several cycles of planning, reflection, and action.

Introduction to the Case

The study was conducted at The Royal Botanic Garden Edinburgh (RBGE). As well as running gardens for the public, it is a scientific organization with a highly qualified staff conducting education, conservation, collection, research, and consultancy work. The societal importance of RBGE has been heightened by the priority given by government to the avoidance of biodiversity loss and the combating of climate change. It is an 80% government funded body and operates under the financial constraint of an annually decided expenditure budget

In 1986 the RBGE was constituted as a non-departmental public body by The National Heritage (Scotland) Act 1985. This, in effect, meant that RBGE became a Trustee governed body that was accountable to, and largely funded by (it also generated some commercial revenues), the government. In 1988 the government required that such bodies should engage in corporate planning and lodge their corporate plan with them annually. According to the government specifications, the plan should include (1) a situation audit of existing circumstances, (2) broad aims and objectives and how they fitted to national and international priorities for botanical research and development, (3) some challenging but realistic targets, and (4) an explanation of how finances would be generated to fund activities. A Corporate Planning Group of senior staff was established to oversee the creation of the required plans.

However, implementing such corporate planning procedures in a scientific organization such as RGBE was not straightforward. Initially, the required planning documents were focused on the detail of current and past work undertaken at the RBGE. There was no explicit identification of the strategic objectives and expected future work for reaching these objectives. Furthermore, only a small number of senior management was involved in the preparation of the plans. The trustees were provided with copies of the prepared plans but no connection or engagement between the plans and the other staff employed by RBGE had ever been made. Indeed, most staff members were completely unaware of their existence. Moreover, no attempt had been made to identify targets which would represent plan achievement or to track progress in achieving the planned strategies. There was no suitable performance measurement system in place which could support such tracking. As a result, it was difficult to know if decisions, actions, and results were consistent with set strategies and plans. In addition, resource allocation and consumption were merely recorded in terms of the inputs which they represented, i.e., a traditional accounting income statement listing, but on a cash flow rather than an accruals basis. Finally, no information was available on how resources had been distributed across the strategic priorities identified in the plan.

Interventions

Thus, as outlined above, there were serious deficiencies in corporate planning at RBGE and much of the effort was cosmetic in nature. This was not uncommon in the Scottish public sector, at the time, as this type of planning was in its infancy.

The challenge of addressing the issue of strategic corporate planning at RBGE became the responsibility of one of the researchers following his appointment as Director of Corporate Services at RBGE in 2000. Thus, the research team comprised the Director of Corporate Services of RBGE and two academics from the University of Edinburgh. The Director was a professionally qualified management accountant and had the responsibility for implementing and reporting to the Board on organizational strategy. The two academic researchers, on the other hand, specialized respectively in strategy and management accounting and both were professionally qualified accountants. The team had good access to the organization, familiarity with its operation and circumstances, and a knowledge base from academia and practice that related directly to the identified problem and its solution. The Director's position and responsibility for strategy provided the authority and the means to implement the constructed solution and assess it in action. In this case, the intervention was practical in its orientation; there was no intention to develop, test, or use academic theories as explanations. Any theoretical contribution was at a level of prescriptive theory for practice. The focus was on producing a successful practical outcome addressing the development of a sound approach to strategic planning which generated relevant information for setting the strategy, allocating resources to facilitate the strategy once set, and to review the outcome to assess whether strategic objectives had been achieved.

To address the managerial problem at hand, the research team worked in close collaboration for about seven years. The long time frame was necessary primarily because the solution involved the preparation of information that was part of an annual reporting cycle. The long timescale also allowed for implementation and revision of the solution, its evaluation in action, and its progressive modification and improvement over several cycles of planning, reflection, and action. Over the period, a range of evidence was gathered to define and substantiate the problem, to construct a solution to it, to implement the solution and evaluate it in action, and then modify it over several iterations. The development work in the field can be divided into five research interventions:

- Analysis of the problem
- Development of modified balanced scorecard
- Linking the developed scorecard to the government objectives
- Creating a strategic objective costing system
- Gathering feedback about the solution.

First, data gathered from a variety of sources was used to gain an understanding of the problem and identify why it had arisen. These sources comprised correspondence between the government and RBGE, minutes of RBGE Board meetings, the various corporate plans that had been prepared by RBGE, and interviews with RBGE staff who had been involved in the early planning process. There was an acceptance by RBGE staff that corporate planning was needed and the extensive documentary records and interviews showed that considerable time and effort had been expended on drafting and redrafting the annual planning documents by those tasked with its preparation. The comment of Regius Keeper (1988–90) reflects the staff acceptance of the government requirement:

> "I thought it reasonable for DAFS, as the funding body, to expect some documentation to explain how public funds were to be spent by RBGE."

The plan was, however, viewed by staff as an unattractive task that was an unavoidable necessity to obtain funding rather than an exercise that could have inherent utility for the RBGE and the government. The staff participating in the construction of the annual strategic plan had no business background (indeed for several years the librarian had responsibility for producing the plan) or corporate planning experience. They had no real conception of what was expected of them in producing a corporate plan. The plans that they produced had several shortcomings. Much of their content (e.g., 38 pages of the 52-page 1989 plan) was simply rich description of the work in which the staff had been and were currently engaged. It was 1995 before a mission statement was introduced, yet it was changed substantially without explanation in the 1999 plan. In the 1991 plan, some KPIs were published but no rationale was given for them and they were not related to the organization's objectives or strategy. No benchmarks or targets were incorporated in their listings. Some of the plan preparers even claimed that its use by government was simply unknown or, indeed, nonexistent. One, for example, commented as follows:

> ". . . I believe that the plan, once submitted, would be filed and put to no further use by government."

Plans produced were shown to the Board of Trustees and lodged with government as required. However, they were not distributed to staff of RBGE. Consequently, there was no communication of corporate objectives and plans internally. However, there was quite general recognition that such a planning process provided some managerial benefits. It provided a good résumé of all the things that RBGE actually did and aided understanding of the complexities of the operation of the organization. There was also recognition that it invoked consideration of spending decisions at a very aggregate level only and provided a justification for obtaining government funding.

The extensive work required to construct the corporate planning document served to be a source of frustration for the staff involved as they struggled with a lack of guidance from government on what was required and their own lack of expertise. Consequently, the whole planning effort at RBGE became a source of frustration to the staff involved and the activity was demoralizing rather than motivating for them as the following comment of a senior scientist illustrates:

> "In my view the corporate plan was a newly imposed requirement by DAFS but was of no benefit to RBGE."

In summary, the problem consisted of the need to devise an overarching vision and strategy for RBGE and to find a way of using it as a basis for constructing a forward-looking set of objectives together with the exposition of the planned actions needed to achieve them. However, formulating a proper strategic plan was only part of the problem. Its implementation had to be considered as well. To become effective, it had to be communicated and used within RBGE rather than being simply a document of record used solely to meet a government requirement. In addition, to enhance the internal utility of the corporate plan, there was a need to ensure it could be used to assess the management of RBGE in relation to the decisions taken in respect of planned objectives and the organization's performance in relation to achieving those objectives. The plan had to be incorporated as a significant element of the RBGE governance. Finally, there also remained the challenge of making the plan relevant and useful for its recipient, the government.

After analyzing the problem at hand, the next step (i.e., second intervention) was to find a way to devise and install a system that would allow RBGE to articulate a strategy reflecting their future intentions in a form that could be documented clearly and communicated through the organization. A search of possibilities for achieving these aims resulted in a shortlist of three possibilities being seriously reviewed by the Director of Corporate Services. These were all well-established methods of developing and implementing strategy and comprised the business excellence model (BEM), the performance prism (PP), and the balanced scorecard (BSC). The BEM had the advantage of providing a capability to take a broad view of the organization's stakeholders when formulating strategy, but it was a very rigid framework not addressing the needs of individualistic organizations; it was felt that RBGE as a scientific organization fell into that category. The PP also had the benefit of adopting a stakeholder-based framework, but available descriptions of it were viewed as complicated and difficult to operationalize. At the time, BSC had become a well-established framework widely used in companies, and the research team considered it as easily comprehensible; it had a copious explanatory literature and numerous illustrative cases were available.

A first design of an organizational BSC was created during a Senior Management Group planning conference in 2004. The perspectives used were different from those of a conventional BSC and reflected the scientific management's antipathy to business terminology. For example, the traditional four perspectives of BSC were replaced with Audiences, Governance, Internal Processes, and Staff/Infrastructure/Finance, as shown in Figure 8.1.

The logic of its initial design lay in RBGE being a labor intensive and intellectual-capital rich organization where staff development would enhance internal process performance and managerial governance improvement. Over the next five years the BSC was implemented and its design was further developed. Objectives statements were developed for each perspective as a basis for agreeing to performance measures for them. The BSC was

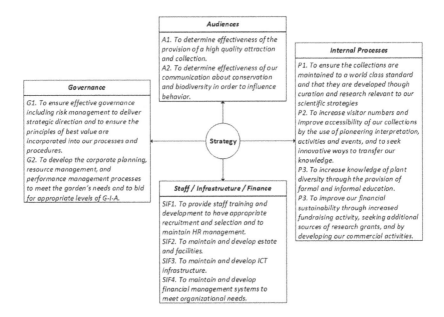

Figure 8.1 The BCS Adapted for the Case Organization.

used to create a strategy map, and this manifestation of it proved the most user-friendly way of communicating it to the staff. It became the front-end interface for the BSC system. By 2008 the BSC was routinely in use and generating monthly reports. Software had been chosen and was installed, KPIs for each perspective operated with a red, amber, and green traffic light visual alert, and the BSC had been cascaded down to a divisional level. A drill down facility linked the BSCs together. Finally, a narrative facility was added to allow staff the capability of raising questions on or providing explanations for the performance levels indicated by the BSC.

Third, after the implementation of the BSC, the research team had to ensure that the strategy would be influenced by an explicit knowledge and recognition of the needs of the major stakeholder, i.e., the Scottish Government; the financial support of government was critical to the ability of the RBGE to meet its objectives. This was first formally done in the 2007 Corporate Plan which demonstrated how the RBGE contributed, through the pursuit of its own strategic objectives, to the objectives of government. It involved no metrics and simply evidenced the means by which the organization could argue as to the value that government could accord to its work. This was seen as of direct significance for the RBGE in its annual funding negotiations with government. This development was extended in a modification made to the BSC design in the following year; the Scottish Government's National Stated Outcomes was added as a fifth perspective to the

RBGE's BSC. This was linked directly to the new impacts perspective (which had replaced the previous audience perspective and provided a focus on the outcomes achieved by RBGE in pursuit of its objectives). This emphasized the importance of the government's requirements and provided a mechanic by which they could be internalized at RBGE. A specific table aligning the government objectives and the RBGE was included in the RBGE Corporate Report.

Fourth, traditionally expenditure records at RBGE were gathered under expenditure types (salaries, power cleaning, etc.) and their only attribution was to divisions. Labor costs represented in excess of 70% of total expenditure, and while this could be identified by division, it was known that employees contributed to many activities that were outside of their division. Consequently, a facility was devised to identify the cost of activities undertaken at RBGE and to attribute the cost of these activities to the organization's strategic objectives. This process was titled strategic objective costing. The mechanics adopted were informed by the concepts of activity based costing. Over 100 activities were identified and they represented the core structure of the new costing system. Their costs were identified by installing a weekly time sheet system for staff and a strategic costing coding system for all other types of expenditure. Cost drivers allowed the activity costs to be distributed to the strategic objectives. The result enabled regular reports to be produced for management showing ex-post how resources had been used in RBGE in pursuit of their objectives. Further developments were made to this system by incorporating budgeting into it. This meant that top management could decide ex-ante on how funding was to be distributed across the objectives being pursued and these could later be compared to actuals to provide feedback. Moreover, through the BSC outcome measures (targets and actuals) were available for each objective. Management therefore had access for the first time to information on the funding and the attainment of their objectives.

When the new BSC and the strategic costing system had been implemented, the researchers were gathering feedback about its use. The solution had been operationalized and was routinely capturing data and generating information for staff and management. Consideration of its output became a standard item on the management group's agenda and also at all divisional level meetings. It was available to all staff and was frequently accessed by staff at all levels. It provides a high level strategic governance mechanism for top management and also, through its hierarchy of BSC performance measures, a basis for operational guidance and performance assessment. As was mentioned by Regius Keeper:

> "There is much greater clarity over what staff are doing which allows a more rational process for determining priorities for activities to achieve the strategic objectives. We have to use the scarce resources available to us in the most efficient and effective manner."

However, not only were the managers with administrative responsibilities pleased with the outcome; also the managers with scientific responsibilities appreciated the new management tool. As mentioned by the Director of Horticulture:

> "Having seen the corporate planning process over a period of 30 plus years, although not always as a participant, I can clearly see the benefits of having a framework to assist with ensuring that the organizational activities are properly aligned to the aims of the organization. Since using the BSC I have seen that it is a much more efficient and less bureaucratic process to complete the corporate plan from the days when each of the divisions had to write long documents in support of the corporate plan, which were eventually simply filed and ignored for the remainder of the year. I attribute that to the clear alignment from the corporate scorecards to the divisional scorecards which ensures that any divisional activities are clearly in support of the corporate objectives."

In addition to the people with management responsibilities, staff was pleased with the new governance tool. One former staff member who had been involved in early corporate planning expressed admiration for the new system and he was of the view that had it been available to them many of their difficulties would have been resolved. The change, represented by the solution, was a significant one given the RBGE scientific culture and the sensitivity that lay in the requirement for all staff to account for their work time. However, staff participated strongly in its design. They provided the detail of the strategic objectives that the organization adopted and its constituent divisions were involved in selecting and naming the perspectives for the divisional BSCs. They also suggested the appropriate measures that could be used for each perspective. Their involvement in the BSC creation contributed to their widespread participation in it. Only 3% of staff did not cooperate in providing time sheet data initially. Instances of staff engaging with the system and contributing ideas in response to its outputs became common. Divisions began to follow aims that are linked to corporate and stakeholder objectives rather than following their own agendas. As a matter of fact, instances of staff engaging with the new governance system and contributing ideas in response to its outcomes became common. For example:

- Computer storage was prioritized over the purchase of continuity hardware backup to relieve critical shortages in image storage which had been identified through BSC analysis as hampering progress with research activity
- The purchase of a DNA sequencer was agreed upon to overcome staffing constraints caused by a government recruitment ban
- Science staff prioritized, for a short period, their grant application activities over research to generate funding

- A new enterprise division was established to help overcome the problems of heavy reliance on government funding
- The greater prominence accorded to the general public stakeholder motivated the enhancement of facilities provided for them in recreational and educational aspects of the organization.

In addition to the management and staff, several members of the Board of Trustees (most of whom had extensive business experience) responded very positively about the new information provided to them, and one who occupied senior commercial positions and had other government trusteeships was extremely enthusiastic:

> "I have never heard of any organization that has been able to trace their input costs through to their output activities and match the associated output costs against achievements. This presents us with a fantastic opportunity to decide upon priorities based upon useful information."

Thus, not only was the research team able to identify the key problems in the strategic planning of this scientific organization, they were able to, in collaboration with the organization, develop a governance system found useful by all levels of organizations. This was a major achievement considering the creative work of scientists and their reluctance to face time management and time reporting issues.

Theory Contribution—MA Construct as a Foundation for the Findings

The study was originally positioned as a constructive case study. In constructive research, the construction itself is often argued as a main theory contribution. In this case, the research team provided evidence on the management accepting the solution in regular use, hence fulfilling the weak market test. The weak market test was also supported by the comments of trustees, many of whom possess senior managerial positions in the private sector and, therefore, can be seen to have excellent understanding of such governance processes which the framework developed addresses, though in the context of a public, scientific organization.

However, the study provides a very interesting perspective regarding the discussion on the strong market test. To fulfill the strong market test, the developed construction needs to contribute to the financial success of the organization. As was discussed in Part I, there usually are so many variables that it becomes very difficult for the researchers to argue the role their construction played in the positive development and, in some cases, the construction itself may have provided positive outcomes then erased by changes in some other variables not controllable by the researchers. In this case however, the case organization pointed out that the framework developed by the research team had helped them capture more government funding compared to other similar, scientific organizations. The use of the new information based on the construction as part of the funding negotiations in 2010 was considered beneficial, as the case organization was the only non-departmental public body to receive a funding increase in excess of inflation and to maintain its funding in 2011 when other similarly funded public bodies were receiving substantial cuts to their funding. Regius Keeper, who led the negotiations, acknowledged the role that the new information played in impressing the government on the value of the work done in the case organization and their sound ability to demonstrate how the funding was used for creating value. According to him, the information provided by the new governance framework was a key factor in obtaining these successful outcomes.

This, then, provides some new insights on the market test and its applicability in the public sector. Thus, as shown by the case, in the public sector, public funding provides the main source of 'income' for the organization. In order to increase the flow of 'income' from the funding bodies, organizations should be able to convincingly show how the money channeled to the organization benefits the society, and the governance framework developed in this project helped precisely with that, resulting eventually in a larger share of the available government funding than before. The idea of the strong market test may, therefore, be very useful as a tool for validating new constructs in the public sector. In the business world, cost savings are often quantifiable but the implications of such frameworks on revenue streams not due to various other influencing factors. However, in the public-sector organizations the increase in the revenue stream (i.e. government funding) resulting from the use of a new managerial construct may be easier to argue, as in this case.

However, despite the discussion on the market test above, the research team did not eventually attempt to argue the framework to be the main theory contribution. On the contrary, the key theoretical findings were connected to various elements identified or recognized in the process of developing, implementing, and iterating the proposed framework. In other words, even though the main intervention focused on the development of a new governance framework for the case organization using the ideas of constructivist research approach, the key theory contribution was not argued to be the construct itself but rather the findings related to the building process, implementation, and usability of such tools in the public sector, intellectual-capital intensive organizations. Thus, even though the study was originally positioned as a constructive case, the theory contribution in the end is argued similarly to the IVR process discussed in this book, making the case (as was phrased by Jönsson and Lukka 2007) more action-research-oriented IVR.

The developed framework in this case was based on a combination of the BSC, government objectives for such a scientific organization and cost allocation; the framework was built using theories/literature on all these three areas. However, the main theory contributions were argued in three areas: (1) BSC, (2) strategic objective costing, and (3) MA change research. Let us next briefly discuss how the case provided new, interesting insights in all these three areas. In other words, now the focus is shifted from arguing the developed framework to be the main contribution of the study to the findings providing interesting theoretical insights in these three areas.

First, as outlined in the introduction, it has been strongly claimed that strategy implementation failure is a widespread and fundamental problem for a significant proportion of organizations. The results of the RBGE study, in the main, add to the favorable empirical evidence that exists on the use of the BSC (e.g., DeGeuser et al. 2009; Chen et al. 2006; Hatch et al. 2005) and on the potential for its successful use in a public sector context (Niven 2003). The claims for its value as a versatile strategy tool (Kaplan and Norton 1996) are given support by the RBGE experience with it. Its initial use proved beneficial in the formulation of strategic plans. The process of selecting and labeling the perspectives proved to be an insightful way of deriving strategic objectives. For example, the original 'customer' perspective was renamed 'audiences' and discussion of their definition prompted a strategic analysis of what should be delivered by RBGE. Time and great care were taken in developing the perspectives structure that customized the BSC to the organization's requirements and the benefits of this investment of effort supports the findings of Assiri et al. (2006), who identify this stage as crucial in the creation of a successful BSC.

The BSC also contributed substantially to the communication and implementation of formulated strategy. The strategy map style of presentation of the BSC content proved extremely useful as a means of presenting and explaining the system to staff. The logic underlying the BSC and the interrelationships of its perspectives and measures were made more apparent in this format. Strategic expectations of the entity, its divisions, and departments were all eventually features which demonstrated the cascading possibilities of the BSC. Strong support from top management was a key feature smoothing the implementation, and this is in accord with the findings of Waal and Counet (2009). However, the implementation was not of the top-down nature implied by its creators (Norreklit 2000). The solution was developed slowly in a consultative and participative way. Trial and error were involved and a great investment of time and effort was required. Simply imposing the BSC as an 'off the shelf' tool would not have met with much success in a scientific organization like the RBGE. The solution to problems of this type is not simply one of technique, equally important is process in terms of the technique's introduction, development, and style of use. It was felt by the researchers that this approach encouraged the staff acceptance and use that became evident after implementation.

The attribute of flexibility (Ewing 1996; Butler et al. 1997) proved to be a very important aspect of the RBGE's BSC. The BSC design was based on a perspectives structure, but the perspectives differed from the original. First they were renamed to downplay the commercial origins of the BSC and match the ethos of a scientific, not-for-profit organization. This contributed to staff acceptance of it. Second, five as opposed to four perspectives were used. The inclusion of governance and Scottish Government perspectives made it particularly distinctive and helped to establish the internal value of the BSC. The use of a governance perspective reflected the BEM model with which one of the researchers had previously worked, and this supported the view of Abdel-Kader et al. (2011), who have suggested that the BSC has the capacity to beneficially link to other performance models. Third, it retained the cause/effect feature of the original BSC but with a different and unique logic. Underpinning the RBGE BSC was the assumption that having a good 'governance process' enabled the sound marshaling and use of 'resources' which were essential to fulfill the organization's scientific 'activities' so leading to the achievement of the desired 'impacts' that, in turn, contributed to the Scottish Government's national 'outcomes.' Thus, the BSC was not employed as an instantaneous standard solution; its adoption involved a period of several years of tailoring it to the organization's situation. Several cycles of experience and revision were involved in its evolution. This is the approach advised by Micheli and Manzoni (2010), and it avoided the main implementation problems that researchers have found with the BSC: an absence of staff commitment (Waal and Counet 2009), incorrect identification of measurement variables, and a lack of top-down communication of the scorecard (Schneidermann 1999), and a lack of linkage between measurements (Brignall 2002).

There has been strong advocacy of the relevance of cost information for strategic purposes (Simmonds 1980; Bromwich 1990). The new objectives costing system at RBGE is an example of how this might be attained in a public-sector organization. It gave an indication of how the organization's resources had been deployed (both in terms of budgetary plans and in actuals) in pursuit of the strategic objectives that had been set. In this respect, it can be considered a fundamental contribution to informing management about their strategic decision-making both ex-ante and ex-post.

Second, the development of strategic objective costing met a specific management need and provides another instance of cost allocation, despite its apparent frailties, generating useful information for management. In this instance, it provided a broad proxy measure of how resources had been deployed in relation to the organization's strategic objectives. The strategic objectives of an organization represent a novel cost object and one that is central to strategic management. The allocations done on this basis could be obtained for individuals, departments, and divisions as well as the overall organization. It was a development that complemented the new BSC. Together, these two aspects of the solution enhanced the governance and management of the RBGE by presenting the following information on each strategic objective: the relative share of resources awarded to the objective through the cost budget allocation, the actual resources consumed in pursuit of the objective through the actual cost allocation to it, the expected performance in relation to the objective as indicated by the measurement targets set for it, and the actual performance achieved as shown by the actual performance measures achieved. This package reveals management intent in the use of the organization's resources (as indicated by the allocation of budgeted costs to strategic objectives) and organizational achievement in relation to intentions (as indicated by actual costs incurred allocated to strategic objectives). When BSC performance measures relating to each strategic objective are also introduced, then it is possible to review the extent to which strategic objectives are being attained (both in terms of targeted aspirations for performance in each area and actual performance achieved). Thus, the solution means strategic decision-making is linked to performance and strategy implementation is given a visibility that can facilitate its success.

Third, both in specifying the problem and in creating the solution, the literature on management accounting change proved to be a valuable source of intelligence. It was particularly useful in alerting the researchers to the potential problems that changes of this type could invoke. This was important given the sensitive character of the change which involved the first direct performance measurement of staff units and the collection of data on how staff time was spent. The scope for this type of information to generate dysfunctional consequences has been well established (e.g., Argyris 1952; Ridgeway 1956; Dearden 1969; Armstrong 1987).

Prominent theoretical perspectives on the management accounting change included institutional theory (e.g., Scapens 1994; Brignall and Modell 2001; Burns and Scapens 2001; Burns and Baldvinsdottir 2005), diffusion theory (e.g., Abrahamson 1991; Bjornenak 1997; Malmi 1999; Dugdale and Jones 2002), and systems theory (e.g., Cooper and Zmud 1990; Friedman and Lyne 1999). Together they emphasized the complex nature of management accounting change involving the existence and interplay of a broad range of technical, behavioral, organizational, and environmental factors. They also identified many circumstances that could lead to change rejection and failure and in this sense provided attention directing assistance. Institutional theory highlighted the difficulty of having new management accounting accepted and used in an organization. It cautioned that, when acceptance is absent, the effectiveness of novel management accounting could be compromised by its decoupling from management functioning, i.e., the change does not become integrated through use in the organization. In order to gain effectiveness, the new management accounting introduction has to overcome human resistance to change and become embedded in the organization. This occurs through its acceptance and its use in the organizational routines that management habitually engage in. Although change can be imposed in a coercive manner by top management, this approach raises the danger of decoupling, non-acceptance, and resistance. Successful change is more likely achieved through convincing staff on a normative basis of it being in the best interests of themselves and their organization. Diffusion theory supplemented and reinforced this guidance by emphasizing the possibilities of change being transitory, short lived, and cosmetic rather than being substantial and useful. New management accounting may be mimetic in origin, representing temporary fashions or fads which assume a bandwagon momentum. This type of change does not represent an efficient choice and is unlikely to generate economic benefit for the adopter. An economic logic for change and a fit to the needs of the adopter have to be established to achieve efficient choice change. Systems theory stresses the processual nature of change (initiation, adoption, adaption, acceptance, routinization, and infusion) and consequently the need to view it as an ongoing rather than a discrete event. A range of factors determine the success of change and the influence of these factors may vary at different stages. They comprise individual factors (e.g., attitude to change, education), organizational factors (level of decision-making centralization, informal organization), technological factors (e.g., complexity, existing practice), task characteristics (e.g., uncertainty, variety), and external environment (e.g., dynamism and heterogeneity of external context).

Awareness of this area of research influenced both the design of the solution and the approach adopted in its introduction. Obtaining staff acceptance became a priority of the project because of the warnings inherent in the concepts of decoupling, routinization, and the fad or fashion change diffusion. The factors identified from systems theory helped the researchers conceive of the situation into which the new management accounting was to be installed and stimulated their empathy to factors such as the non-commercial attitudes of the information users, which required the use of non-commercial terminology, the decentralized nature of much decision-making, which necessitated departmental and divisional BSCs, and the varied needs of multiple external stakeholders, which influenced the selection of strategic objectives. Given the sensitivity of the change and the existence of a highly intelligent staff with a scientific (as opposed to a commercial) orientation, the top-down approach to implementation proposed in the early BSC literature was rejected. Instead a slow (several years) and careful participative approach was taken. Many of the following components of this approach were influenced by the guidance found in the management accounting change literature:

- Providing opportunities for all staff to contribute to the BSC structure and content, allowing staff to select non-commercial terminology for the selected perspectives, and using the more easily understood strategy map presentation to communicate and explain the new approach
- Providing educational presentations on the evolving form of the RBGE BSC so that feedback could be obtained and acted upon, emphasizing stakeholder needs as a salient design feature

- Introducing the new reports as specific agenda items at departmental, divisional, and organizational levels
- Requesting that cases made by staff for resourcing incorporate the new information
- Demonstrating the value of the new information in negotiations with the funding body and in the justification for managerial decisions
- Allowing access to the system by all staff and treating the new system as a work in progress by continually reviewing it in terms of its use and effects as well as responding to the reviews by making modifications to it on an ongoing basis.

The result has been a highly customized system reflective of the situation from which it has emerged. This is apparent in terms of nomenclature, type of perspective, number of perspectives, measurements selected, cause and effect reasoning, links to stakeholders, and cost allocation practice. All of the above factors in design, content, and implementation approach were used to help avoid a cosmetic, decoupled change and to embed the new system in the routines of organizational functioning.

Diffusing the Ideas Within the Sector and Beyond

The discussion above focused on the theory contributions of the case. Considering IVR, the most interesting element in this case is the wide interest the framework developed was able to generate. Originally the researchers attempted to use this wide interest as yet one additional tool to verify the framework; managers of botanical gardens and other similar scientific organizations all over the world being interested in the framework developed would serve as yet another level of market test. However, in this book we see that more as evidence of how well-executed and well-positioned research projects can raise global interest among the selected population in which the results would be valid; very seldom interventionist researchers are able to create such wide interest on their work and that would, instead of verification of the framework, serve as a point of access to global data on such governance practices.

As the solution was developed, steps were taken to have it disseminated to as wide an audience as possible. There are approximately 1600 botanic gardens in the world and they would provide the most obvious outlet for a more general use of the new BSC. As a result, several descriptive publications have been produced for a practitioner audience, ensuring exposure to well over 300,000 accountants through CIMA publications as well as managers of botanical gardens through publication in *Journal of Botanical Garden Horticulture*. The reaction to this exposure has been a positive interest from accountants, consultants, and botanic garden administrators from around the world. In addition to the written publications on the topic, the researchers have made presentations in various professional forums, such as CIMA (Perth, London, Manchester), government agencies, such as Audit Scotland, Scottish Government and Forestry Commission, as well as consulting firms such as Deloitte.

However, what makes the case most interesting is the wide international reach among the botanical gardens. There are about 1600 botanic gardens in the word and the RBGE is usually ranked in the top three. The status in the ranking means it has been able to develop strong links with many other gardens. These established links facilitated the review of the solution by other similar organizations. Visits and presentations were easy to arrange and so feedback and the views of others could be readily obtained. The researchers have given presentations in the following botanical gardens:

- Botanic Gardens in US (Missouri, Chicago, New York, Longwood, and Arnold Arboretum)
- Botanic gardens in China (Kuming Institute of Botany, Chinese Academy of Sciences, and University of International Business and Economics, Beijing)
- Singapore Botanic Garden
- Oman Botanic Garden.

The new BSC has been developed to fit the processes and practices of a botanic garden and, therefore, its specific design characteristics give it the potential for use in this sector, possibly even in its current form. The positive feedback evidence from other botanic gardens given above suggests that this could happen. As was mentioned by one manager form a US-based botanical garden:

> ". . . I personally found our discussion and the materials . . . very interesting. It is my sincerest hope to be able to learn from the work you have done and implement your ideas here in Chicago."

However, differences in organizational and national cultures and different emphasis placed on work specialisms and stakeholders may require the RBGE design to be modified before it can be considered exportable to the botanic gardens of other countries. Exposure of the BSC design through publication and presentation has already elicited interest from other botanic gardens in the Americas, the Middle East, China, and Europe. It is, therefore, likely that it or close variants of it will soon be in use elsewhere, as was evident in an email from a manger of another US-based botanical garden.

> "I'm going to do my best to convey to the rest of the group what you and your people have achieved. I'm very excited about it myself. I've read your Corporate Plan cover to cover already and intend to repeat this several times before passing to my colleagues."

The developed solutions raised interest beyond botanical gardens. For example, the following was a comment from a Director of the Chinese Academy of Sciences:

> "I am very interested in your publication about how you developed the balanced scorecard, a strategic objective costing system and your supporting performance management system. . . . I really hope we can have a chance for co-operation in this research field in the near future."

In addition to the scientific world, the idea of selecting different perspectives from the commercial oriented BSC may also have a wider applicability, particularly in the public sector. For example, where, as in Scotland, the government stakeholder has well specified objectives, it should be possible for other government-funded bodies to link these to their own BSC as the RBGE has done. One of the trustees with considerable experience of working in other parts of the public sector and in the commercial world felt that the new approach had great potential for use in a range of other public-sector organizations:

> "Does Audit Scotland know about this methodology? Do you mind if I invite the Deputy Auditor General for a briefing from you on it? I think this has enormous potential not only for bodies such as ours but also for local authorities."

Finally, it was not only the scientific organizations or other public-sector funded entities that showed interest in the governance solution developed by RBGE. The government reacted positively to the new information that was being reported to them by RBGE. As was mentioned by one of the senior administrators in Scottish Government:

> "It was interesting and beneficial to see the Corporate Plan and the alignment between the RBGE's objectives with those of the Scottish Government's National Outcomes. Indeed, the novel accounting methodology that shows the cost of achieving these objectives is extremely helpful when it comes to understanding the prioritization process undertaken by the RBGE."

The use of strategic objectives as a major cost object is unlikely to be as easily implemented to cover all cost elements in commercial and manufacturing based settings where the service output and product cost objects are dominant and the tracing of production costs to individual strategic objectives would lack validation. In such organizations, there may, however, be possibilities for the association of some types of cost to be analyzed in this way. Some marketing and administrative costs may be more susceptible to association with the strategic objectives of these types of businesses. It is a technique which can potentially provide a strong basis for assessing strategic decision-making, and this attribute is likely to make it an attractive governance mechanism in appropriate circumstances. These are likely to occur in labor intensive, intellectual-capital rich organizations such as the RBGE where most work activity can be readily associated with individual strategic level objectives. There is scope for its use in similar public sector bodies (with appropriate content change) and, as mentioned above, several have been in contact to discuss the RBGE solution.

Finally, in the 2010 CIMA Annual Awards, the solution was highly commended in the Innovation in Business category by leading accounting practitioners. Managerial views of it do suggest that it has improved efficiency at RBGE, and there is evidence that it has been a useful tool in gaining a greater share of government resources at the expense of other organizations (without the intelligence that the RBGE systems provide to negotiators) competing for the same pool of money. Such rewards can also play an important role in diffusing the ideas further within the industry.

Discussion of the Case

This case was based on a seven-year collaboration with a Scottish public-sector organization facing challenges to cope with the new governance practices implemented by the government. When the new governance practices were introduced in the late 1980s, the organization, being mainly a scientific organization, did not have personnel trained for such administrative tasks related to strategic planning, making the preparation process challenging. The new governance policies were followed, though without much motivation and visibility to the use of the reports/plans prepared. Thus, the starting point of the case can be positioned in techne, as shown in Figure 8.2.

In this case, the research team consisted of one insider (senior executive) and two senior academics, one with background in MA and the other on strategic management, both with a long history of working with companies in an interventionist manner. Thus, research literature was harnessed for both solving the organizational problem and positioning the case at the very outset of the project (episteme). The primary focus of this study was to create a successful solution to a pressing practical problem. The existing literature helped in two major ways. First, it provided technical guidance in the form of BSC and ABC ideas that underpinned the performance measurement and strategic objective costing practices that were created. However, these technical practices had to be modified significantly to meet the sectoral and organizational demands, and this was achieved largely through the efforts of the researchers. Second, the literature provided warnings of potential difficulties to be guarded against, e.g., in the implementation of devised strategies and in the challenges to be faced in gaining acceptance for technical accounting change. However, the solution and the process by which it was achieved can provide important guidance for other organizations seeking to achieve similar developments. In this sense, the study can

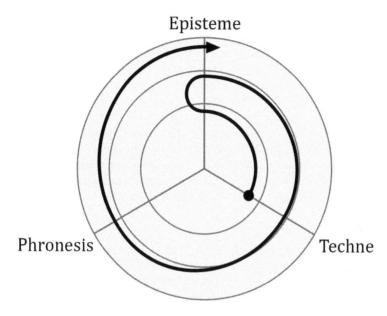

Figure 8.2 Interplay Between the Three Virtues in the Case Study.

be considered to have a normative dimension. In an applied discipline such as accounting there is no reason why normative theory cannot be expressed in technical terms as exemplars of what should be and this case exemplifies this approach.

The key interventions focused on the development of a governance system enabling the organization to fulfill the planning responsibilities set by the government. The BSC framework was modified to fit a scientific organization characterized with knowledge-intensive, specialist work, and the BSC framework was adjusted further to incorporate the government objectives in the governance system developed. Finally, the strategic costing system was developed to see how different strategic areas were resourced in practice in the organization and the connection to the outputs. This work contributes to the expansion of existing technical developments (techne).

After the solution had been developed and implemented, special emphasis was placed on assessing the new ideas by sharing them with the professional community. This was partially due to the embedded constructive approach in the case; the research team was keen on proving that the solution worked and, hence, fulfilled market tests. The strong market test, in particular, is very difficult to achieve. Thus, in this case, as well as validating the solution developed in the organization for which it was created, attention is given to the active diffusion process and the attraction of the solution to others. Following the ideas of interventionist research emphasized in this book, the global-level dialogue within the industry (1600 botanical gardens) and numerous scientific, knowledge-intensive organizations illustrates the societal impact (phronesis) of this case, so far unheard of within the IVR context. As a result, the outstanding practical outcome will provide access to numerous organizations within the 'target population' for more profound studies on strategic governance in knowledge-intensive public-sector organizations.

Consequently, the solution developed in the case study provides potential for intensive in-depth interviews with managers within the 'target population' or data gathering with workshop-type involvement of industry specialists, thanks to the wide publication efforts within the managerial journals. The research team already possesses extensive contacts globally, a very rare asset for the MA researcher. This provides a unique setup for theorizing (episteme). However, reflection of the case already points out some interesting venues for theory contribution, though not yet fully tested.

References

Abdel-Kader, M., Souad, M. and Laitinen, E., 2011. Balanced scorecard development: A review of the literature and directions for future research, in: Abdel-Kader, M. (Ed.), *Review of management accounting research*. Palgrave Macmillan, Hampshire, pp. 214–239.

Abrahamson, E., 1991. Managerial fads and fashions: The diffusion and rejection of innovations. *Academy of Management Review*, 16, pp. 586–612.

Argyris, C., 1952. *The impact of budgets on people*. The Controllership Foundation, New York.

Armstrong, P., 1987. The rise of accounting controls in British capitalist enterprises. *Accounting Organisations and Society*, 5, pp. 415–436.

Assiri, A., Zairi, M. and Eid, R., 2006. How to profit from the balanced scorecard. *Industrial Management and Data Systems*, 106(7), pp. 937–952.

Bjornenak, T., 1997. Diffusion and accounting: The case of ABC in Norway. *Management Accounting Research*, 8(1), pp. 3–17.

Brignall, S., 2002. The unbalanced scorecard: A social and environmental critique. In Neely, A., Walters, A. and Austin, R. (Eds.), *Performance measurement and management: Research and action*. Performance Measurement Association, Boston.

Brignall, S. and Modell, S., 2001. An institutional perspective on performance measurement and management in the 'new public sector'. *Management Accounting Research*, 11(3), pp. 281–306.

Bromwich, M., 1990. The case for strategic management accounting: The role of accounting information for strategy in competitive markets. *Accounting Organisations and Society*, 15(1/2), pp. 27–46.

Burns, J. and Baldvinsdottir, G., 2005. An institutional perspective on accountants' new role-the interplay of contradictions and praxis. *European Accounting Review*, 14(4), pp. 725–757.

Burns, J. and Scapens, R. W., 2001. Conceptualising management accounting change: An institutional framework. *Management Accounting Research*, 11(1), pp. 3–25.

Butler, A., Letza, S., R. and Neale, B., 1997. Linking the balanced scorecard to strategy. *Long Range Planning*, 30(2), pp. 242–253.

Chen, X., Yamauchi, K., Kato, K., Nishimura, A. and Ito, K., 2006. Using the balanced scorecard to measure Chinese and Japanese hospital performance. *International Journal of Healthcare Quality Assurance*, 19(4), pp. 339–350.

Cooper, R. and Zmud, R. W., 1990. Information technology implementation research: A technology diffusion approach. *Management Science*, 36(2), pp. 123–139.

Dearden, J., 1969. The case against ROI control. *Harvard Business Review*, 47(3), pp. 124–135.

De Geuser, F., Mooraj, S. and Oyon, D., 2009. Does the balanced scorecard add value? Empirical evidence on its effect on performance. *European Accounting Review*, 18(1), pp. 93–122.

Dugdale, D. and Jones, C., 2002. The ABC bandwagon and the juggernaut of modernity. *Accounting Organisations and Society*, 27(1/2), pp. 121–163.

Ewing, P., 1996. *Balanced scorecards in use—experiences from ABB/EVITA project.* Stockholm School of Economics, Stockholm.

Finkelstein, S., 2005. When bad things happen to good companies: Strategy failure and flawed executives. *Journal of Business Strategy*, 26(2), pp. 19–28.

Friedman, A. and Lyne, S., 1999. *Success and failure of activity-based techniques.* The Chartered Institute of Management Accountants, London.

Hatch, T., Lawson, R., Stratton, W. and Thornton, R., 2005. Scorecarding in North America part 11; best practices and implementation at Gulf States Corporation. *Cost Management*, 19(5), pp. 39–47.

Jönsson, S. and Lukka, K., 2007. There and back again: Doing IVR in management accounting, in: Chapman, C., Hopwood, A. and Shields, M. (Eds.), *Handbook of management accounting research*, Vol. 1. Elsevier, Amsterdam, pp. 373–397.

Judson, A. S. 1995. *Making strategy happen.* Blackwell, Oxford.

Kaplan, R. S. and Norton, D. P., 1996. *The balanced scorecard: Translating strategy into action.* Harvard Business School Press, Boston.

Malmi, T., 1999. Activity-based costing diffusion across organisations: An exploratory empirical analysis of Finnish firms. *Accounting Organisations and Society*, 24, pp. 649–672.

Micheli, P. and Manzoni, J., 2010. Strategic performance measurement: Benefits limitations and paradoxes. *Long Range Planning*, 43(4), pp. 465–476.

Mintzberg, H., 1994. *The rise and fall of strategic planning.* Free Press, New York.

Niven, P., 2003. *Balanced scorecard step-by-step for government and non-profit agencies.* John Wiley and Sons, Hoboken.

Norreklit, H., 2000. The balance on the balanced scorecard—a critical analysis of some of its assumptions. *Management Accounting Research*, 11(1), pp. 65–88.

Ridgeway, V. F., 1956. Dysfunctional consequences of performance measurements. *Administrative Science Quarterly*, 1(2), pp. 240–247.

Scapens, R. W., 1994. Never mind the gap: Towards an institutional perspective on management accounting practice. *Management Accounting Research*, 5(3/4), pp. 301–321.

Schneidermann, A., 1999. Why balanced scorecards fail. *Journal of Strategic Performance Measurement*, 11(1), pp. 4–11.

Simmonds, K., 1980. *The fundamentals of strategic management accounting.* The Institute of Cost and Management Accountants, London.

Waal, A. and Counet, H., 2009. Lessons learned from performance management systems implementations. *International Journal of Productivity and Performance Management*, 58(4), pp. 367–390.

Wery, R., 2004. Why good strategies fail. *Handbook of Business Strategy*, 5(1), pp. 153–157.

Part III
Lessons Learnt

9 Theory Contributions with Societal Impact— Reflection on the Cases

This book has emphasized the iterative role of the IVR process. Reflections on the five cases presented in this book convey also the idea that the starting point of the IVR process may vary significantly. All three intellectual virtues have been present in all the cases, and every case has had societal impacts embedded to it. Still, only one of the cases was positioned in the phronesis domain in the beginning, while the rest of the cases were initially positioned either in techne or episteme (as conveyed in Figure 9.1).

One driver of Case 1 (Evondos Oy) was responding to the aging of the population (phronesis). In this kind of case, MA could support identifying, assessing, and adopting new approaches and technologies to healthcare. In this particular case, the researchers were involved in designing and testing calculators and visualizations that enabled discussions on the value creation (techne). Addressing the overall big societal question with a tangible tool paved the way towards the following steps in the IVR process.

In Case 2, the starting point was in practice, namely in the evolution of the markets in a particular field (techne). In this iterative process, the theory contribution potential was found after a while, as the operations management perspectives were thoroughly considered with the help of a colleague who familiarized himself with the case. This case highlights the importance of revisiting the pre-understanding of the contribution potential and discussing the case from different perspectives with different experts (see, e.g., Suomala et al. 2014). In addition to outlining and refining the theory contribution, the further steps of the case provide evidence on the possibility that MA research could outline the technology development and research policy within a particular industry. Similarly to Case 2, Case 3 was also initiated with practical development (techne), but in this case, the idea of mockups, and their wider impacts on agile R&D, resonated already at an initial stage with the articulated R&D policy in Finland (phronesis). This was a nice starting point for outlining the versatile theory contribution potential embedded in this approach.

Cases 4–5 were positioned already at a very early stage in the episteme domain, although both of the cases featured technical development at the very beginning. Case 4 presents a continuum where the first research project

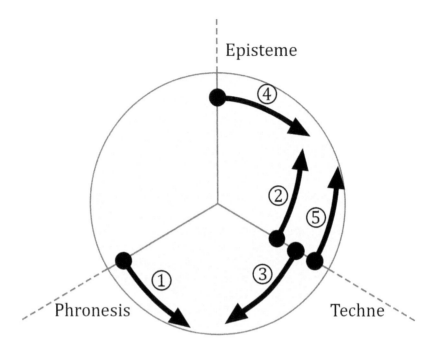

Figure 9.1 Positioning of the Starting Points of the Empirical Cases.

yielded a tool that could be used in the second research project. The second research project addressed the potential role of MA in the timely business phenomenon, i.e., servitization (episteme). Also, Case 5 is based on longitudinal cooperation and development of new kinds of performance measures and governance practices. However, already at the outset of the project, the theoretical challenge of gaining the full potential benefit of the new strategies was articulated (though the starting point was positioned in techne). Interestingly, in both of the cases, the theoretical contribution potential was also linked to the societal impact potential: the IVR process led into solutions that could be utilized in the industry more broadly. Case 5 already provided evidence of this wider utilization.

Regarding the starting point of the case, one should bear in mind that it is highly interpretive where the IVR process begins. Especially in the cases with earlier research projects and long-term cooperation, the IVR process could be outlined in different ways. If the access is already gained in the case, the starting point for the IVR process could be outlining the theoretical contribution potential. This applies to the 'outsider's view' in Case 2 and to the planning phase of the second research project in Case 4.

The discussion above pointed out the various starting points of how the collaboration with the case company can be positioned regarding the episteme, techne, and phronesis as well as the iterative role of these different virtues (as phrased by Flyvjberg 2001) within one research project. The discussion above, however, did not focus on how the access to the case companies had been gained and what role the interventions played in that process. Thus, in this book we continue the idea presented in Suomala and Lyly-Yrjänäinen (2012) regarding the role of the intervention in helping to gain access in interesting organizations and, more importantly, interesting events unfolding within those organizations. Thus, as pointed out in the framework presented in Suomala and Lyly-Yrjänäinen (2012), the intervention does not have to be in the heart of the theory contribution; instead, the intervention can take many roles in the process.

Facilitating the Access to an Organization

In the first case focusing on the medicine dispensing service, characteristic to a startup company, the key resources were overloaded with work, hence making it challenging for the researchers to get 'face time' with them for gaining deeper understanding of how their service works. To overcome the problem, one of the ideas was to participate in the customer training sessions. Though the participation provided an interesting opportunity to observe the execution of the nurse training, from the research process point of view the interesting outcome is synergies for the researcher to get familiar with the case company; the participation in the training session simultaneously worked as a training session for the researcher, without burdening the case company's resources. Thus, when an intervening researcher is familiarizing herself with a new case company, possibilities to find synergies with the existing training and orientation sessions may be worth looking into.

Interestingly, in that same case, the access to the case company was easy; the case company management and the research team leaders found mutual interests easily. In that case, however, the challenges regarding the access were related to the healthcare organizations; MA researchers were placed in the same category with the healthcare researchers and MA researchers had to complete similar evaluations in order to gain the access. Naturally, the evaluations were not designed for an interventionist approach, in which the researcher helps the organization in a development challenge, in order to get access to fruitful empirical data. Even though the 'value proposition' of the researcher in terms of the managerial processes in the healthcare organizations was straightforward (i.e., provide experienced MA professionals to help analyze the impact of the new service for the healthcare organization), the welcome was not as warm as one might expect. Thus, it is very important to find the right person(s) to talk to regarding the access; they have to be the ones directly impacted by the researchers' work or at least in charge of the resources whose work the intervention will support. In the case of City of Joensuu, it was the project manager in the healthcare organization responsible for the technology pilots. As mentioned by her during the first phone call:

> "This seems like an interesting opportunity for us. Personally, I am not very experienced in cost analyses, yet I would have to do them anyway."

Thus, in order to sell the idea of a research intervention (in order to gain access), it is important to recognize whose work the intervening researcher will facilitate. This person will most likely appreciate the idea of a researcher as an expert resource to an organization.

In the second and third cases, the access to the organizations was based on the inventions of the researchers. This, perhaps, is a characteristic more typical of a university of technology; the researchers are attempting to find organizations interested in collaboration in executing some new ideas helping their customers. In both cases, the inventions discussed at the entry phase were based on the long-term collaboration with a key OEM within the industry, known for interest in the development of its supply network. Thus, in Case 2, the active role of the managers in that OEM helped to build the network of companies working on the executing of the new production system for hose assembly kits, resulting in a totally new way of production control. The strong focus on technical development is, perhaps, not very common in MA research, though there should be no reason why not. In the end, cost management holds the greatest impact potential in the early stages of the innovation and development processes. Furthermore, as phrased by the professor experienced in product-centric control from Aalto University School of Engineering:

> "If this is not what the research in a university of technology should be, I have no idea what."

Interestingly, the exposure to the hose assembly manufacturing process resulted in new process needs. Now the close collaboration with the managers in the hose assembly manufacturing company resulted in a situation that they recommended collaboration with their spiral and sleeve supplier (Case 3). Thus, similar to intercompany relationships, managers experienced with the research collaboration were providing references to new potential case companies encouraging collaboration with the research team. Thus, in addition to the tolerance of uncertainties typical of R&D projects, researchers utilizing intervention as a tool for access should actively build a network and use references when looking for access to new companies with interesting contribution potential.

Case 4, as presented in this book, was enabled by a longitudinal research collaboration that took the form of two consecutive research projects. Suomala and Lyly-Yrjänäinen (2012) used the concept research stream for a series of research projects focusing on a same topic with the same or different companies. Remarkably, in Case 4, the previous research project focused on a relatively more mature research topic (R&D control), the results of which were adopted to the new project aiming at exploring a more under-researched topic (controlling new service development within servitization), thus outlining the contribution potential of this project. In practice, many company representatives were involved in both the projects, and the access gained in the first research project could be deepened in the second one. From the perspective of the IVR process, Case 4 takes advantage of a multi-project research team. From the perspective of practically relevant results, and the benefits of the company, the deeper access of the researchers, and the already established ways of collaboration, helped the interventionist researchers to contribute to the practical development, with more to-the-point insights and suggestions.

In Case 5, the primary focus was to create a successful solution to a pressing practical problem in the case organization. The key contact in the organization (Director of Corporate Services) was a qualified management accountant and had the responsibility for implementing and reporting to the board on the organizational strategy. The Director was interested in doing a PhD and a project was set up with the researchers. Thus, unlike in the other cases, the director was considered part of the research team, also participating in writing the conference papers on the case. The director position and the responsibility for the strategy implementation provided the authority and the means to develop the proposed solution as well as implement and assess it. Such arrangements provide excellent opportunities for professional researchers not only to gather secondhand empirical data but also to gain deep access to organizations.

Towards Deeper Access

One of the core elements in gaining access to interesting empirical material embedded in the case under examination is the long-term collaboration that results in mutual trust. This is notable in various different ways.

In Case 1, the trust had to be gained in two domains: the case company and the customer organization. The priority was the latter, and here the active participation in the daily work of the home care nurses played an important role to win the trust of the nurses. The good access to the customer organization and related findings, then, helped to increase trust among the managers in the case company. Access to talk to the customers of the intervened organization tends not to be an easy decision for management; somehow the risks of allowing an outsider access to talk to the customers are considered great. Again, the researchers need to earn this access by demonstrating their credibility as partners in business development. For example, In Case 1, later the researchers have had access to meetings where the project managers work together with the nurses regarding the patient selection, again granting access to new events not so easily opened up for outsiders. In one of the meetings, the researchers took an active role, pointing out the key cost drivers and the logic regarding how patient selection defines the financial benefits of the new technology. When this was done, the project manager seemed shocked about the sharing of the key cost drivers and their relationship regarding the expected payback, yet the nurses appreciated the open attitude. As one of the nurses pointed out:

> "In the end, it is the numbers that our management uses to make decisions on whether this new technology provides us benefits or not."

After that, the nurses changed their mindset, and the reduction in the number of visits became a focus when selecting the patients. Thus, even though the main interest of nurses is the well-being of their patients, they understand the organizational realities and are willing to participate in such discussions if given the necessary inputs.

The next interesting phase will be to join meetings when the Evondos sales team is negotiating with the potential customers to investigate the role cost information plays in that phase of the sales process. This is an interesting opportunity to gain access to the decision-making processes of public-sector healthcare decision-makers to study what role financial information plays in the decision-making process and what kind of representations of financial information would be preferred. Involvement there, naturally, requires that the case company management is confident that the researcher will do more good than harm, even though they may sometimes rattle the cage. However, such an opportunity does not come as a free lunch; it has to be earned by showing the management the practical utility of having the researchers around. This, then, enables gathering of interesting data regarding the role financial information plays in the decision-making, hence following more the original research plan.

In Case 2, collaboration was very tight already from the beginning; the ideas imported to the case organizations 'bought' the access. However, it has been interesting to gradually learn more about how the top management, especially in the Italian company, thinks about business development and the entry to the hose assembly business. One particularly interesting area has been the discussion regarding the Lean philosophies built into the production system. Italian management culture, being more hierarchical compared to the Japanese and Scandinavian management cultures, has made the company rethink many of the ways in which business can be run.

Interestingly, when the new production system had been developed, the role of the researchers was faded down; it was the Italian team taking the driver's seat in the development of the production system and the country managers were responsible for the customer interface. However, the business has not been expanding the way initially planned. The value-added features enabled by the new production system and the developed service concepts no longer are in the comfort zone of experienced hose assembly sales people; instead of hose assemblies, the company is increasingly selling, for example, shorter lead times, traceability, and quality improvements requiring a new skill set from the management team. The research team has been involved in the development of new service concepts related to the hose assembly business, yet lately been asked to take a more active role in the process of communicating the benefits of the new production system to the OEMs in the key geographical markets. The discussions with the top management in Italy have brought the collaboration to a totally new level; the research team has had access to very interesting social processes within the Italian team and the country managers, necessary for expanding the business as planned but not likely to be shared with an outsider.

Similar to Case 2, the access to Case 3 was based on ideas emerging from the process needs regarding the hose assembly manufacturing and the references of the managers involved in the project. In this case, the researchers were provided rather free hands to proceed with the development of the new product concepts. Once some mockups had been built, they were used as a basis for discussion with the management as well as for the related financial analyses. The process of coming up with the patented solutions took time with the owners already becoming impatient. The manager in charge of the business unit, however, showed increasing commitment to the work done by the researchers. As mentioned by him after about two years of collaboration:

> "Even though we have not been able to come up with a solution that fulfills all our expectations, I am very pleased with the collaboration. Thanks to the knowledge we have been able to create, our sales people are very confident when talking with the production managers of our customers regarding how to spiral hoses and cut sleeves."

Thus, even though the collaboration had not resulted in the concrete outcomes, the manager valued the knowledge created in the project, eventually leading into new ideas on how to solve the problems of customers and how to communicate the benefits, too. Interestingly, the theory contributions were argued already without the final, patented product ideas, hence emphasizing the role of the intervention as a stimulant to interesting theory contributions rather than the intervention as a contribution per se.

Case 4 takes advantage of the long-term collaboration, and thus deep access to the company's development project. Interestingly, the company's earlier experiences on collaboration with researchers from different domains enabled designing a research project that allowed a remarkable access and role to the outside researcher, MA researchers included, in line with the idea of engaged research (Van de Ven and Johnson 2006). Remarkably, the interventions focused on a strategically extremely important area that is new service development, which required a multidisciplinary project featuring MA researchers. Therefore, the company representatives supported the collaboration and communication also across the different research teams during the series of the NSD workshops. The results of the different research teams, as well as company's results on their new services, were openly distributed and reflected upon during the research process. Besides, the research stream will continue in the form of a concluding workshop that summarizes the results attained so far. In this case, the forms of collaboration represent an example of relatively mature engaged research that potentially could open avenues of new, also unexpected research topics and setting in the future.

In Case 5, the long-term collaboration from 2004 to 2011 with the same key stakeholders provided a unique setup for gathering empirical data. Such long-term collaboration often leads to new topics resulting even in new formal research projects. However, in this case the research team was able to invest the seven fiscal years in working on the same managerial construct with the same stakeholders. The key lesson in this case is that devising a solution is not a discrete event; in instead it involves an (often long) process over time. The process may be described as one of trial and error as issues arise and have to be dealt with by the researchers as the development work proceeds. Such long-term collaboration not only deepens the relationship with the key contacts inside the organization but also starts to be reflected more broadly in the organization. For example, in the research papers written on the case, all the interviewees allowed the researchers to use their names openly, not very common in such studies touching, for example, government reporting practices.

Intervention Enabling Theory Contributions

The discussion regarding research interventions, thus far, has focused on the strength of the intervention, started by the weak and strong by Jönsson and Lukka (2007) and later added by the five levels of Suomala and Lyly-Yrjänäinen (2012). In addition, the focal points of the interventions have been discussed with the emphasis on the fact that even in an MA study, the focal point of the intervention does not always have to be in the MA domain. Interventions in many cases are used to facilitate access to interesting MA-related phenomenon and can, therefore, be focused on very versatile management-related areas, though the theory contribution will be positioned in MA (Suomala and Lyly-Yrjänäinen 2012). This section attempts to shed more light on what 'actions' research interventions in practice are and what roles they play in the theorizing process.

Table 9.1 summarizes the period and research interventions of the cases introduced in Part II. In addition, the table also shows the key enablers of both theory contribution and societal impact of each case respectively.

When looking at Case 1, the participation in the daily activities of the home care nurses as well as the training sessions were used for becoming more familiar with the context. However, they were seen as interventions because they were focused on the customer organizations; in a sense the researchers, while familiarizing themselves with the context, were actually involved in the interaction with the key customers, something not very common in IVR case studies in MA. Similarly, the interviews regarding both the expected outcomes of the Evondos service as well as the actual outcomes were activities done on the behalf of the healthcare organization, providing valuable information also for the case company; theoretically speaking the healthcare organization or the case company could have done similar interviews using their own resources. These all are considered interventions because they are things that the case company itself could have done.

Access to ERP data enabled the most important intervention; the researchers got access to the real patient profiles and the impact the service has on the home care organization. This data, however, enabled the theory contribution only indirectly. Initially it was to be used for visualization and narration of cost information to non-accounting specialists. Yet, when the outcomes were discussed with the nurses, the idea for the most important intervention (the Lean experiment with the new anticoagulants) emerged, eventually providing the most important theory contribution of the case. Thus, this case illustrates the role an unexpected event in an IVR project can play in providing a theory contribution; the 'intended' contribution potential (visualization and narration of cost information to non-accounting specialists) was put on hold while the 'emergent' contribution potential was focused on. Thus, the interviews, observations and the action research work on the analysis of the data and the resulting interviews were all merely inputs for the most interesting theory contribution, i.e., use of Lean experiments to gain 'ex-post' cost information to be used for facilitating technology diffusion within a healthcare organization.

In Case 2, the interventions were mainly related to different types of analyses provided for the case company (the newly-established hose assembly manufacturer). However, here the first analyses were prepared before approaching the case company; in some cases researchers need to attract the case companies for collaboration by bringing some interesting ideas to the table. Here it was the one man cell concept developed first proposed to the OEM, then fine-tuned based on the analysis of the hose and fitting consumption and, eventually, presented to the fitting manufacturer. Throughout the process, cost information was linked to the development ideas regarding the hose assembly manufacturing process, making the case a cost

Table 9.1 Overview of the Research Interventions and Their Role in the Five Cases.

	Case 1	Case 2	Case 3	Case 4	Case 5
Company name	Evondos	'Hose Assembly Manufacturer'	'Spiral & Sleeve Manufacturer'	Fastems	RBGE
Time frame	2015–	2011–	2013–	2011–2016	2004–2011
Interventions	— Visiting patients with nurses — Participation in the training sessions — Interviews regarding expected outcomes — Analysis of ERP data — Nurse interviews on actual outcomes — Facilitation of the Lean experiment with an anticoagulation medicine	— Analysis of new hose cutting technology and its cost reduction potential in kit manufacturing — Analysis of OEM's hose and fitting consumption — Design of the one man cell concept for kit manufacturing — Facilitating the demonstration in Italy — Break-even analysis for the new factory	— Brainstorming of new ideas and testing them with mockups — Discovery that most sleeves are short/spiral enabling linear movement — Development of fully-functional mockups — Time studies providing ex-post cost data beforehand — Testing the solutions in customers' production — Patented solution	— Planning the three workshops on NSD management — Co-organizing the workshop on ideas for new services (active participation) — Co-organizing the workshop on selecting appealing new services (active participation) — Co-organizing the workshop on Business Impact Analysis (BIA) of new services (facilitation of the workshop)	— Analysis of the problem — Development of modified balanced scorecard — Linking scorecard to the government objectives — Creating strategic objective costing system — Gathering feedback about the solution
Enabler of theory contribution	Access to and facilitation of an interesting experiment in the	Active facilitation of the development of the new production concept connecting	Involvement in a project taking advantage of fully-functional mockups	Longitudinal research collaboration that enabled the access; designing the second	Longitudinal research collaboration focusing on

healthcare process development.	IT capabilities of the case company with Lean ideology and product-centric control.	in building value propositions in a rather conservative industry.	research project according to the identified contribution potential.	the iteration of the developed management control framework.
Enabler of societal impact	Studying a case directly related to an important contemporary social phenomenon.	Connecting the case to the dialogue on objectives of government-funded research projects.	Identifying the connection to the wider governmental R&D policy development.	Connecting the project to the wider research program on a societally important business phenomenon; providing practical means for timely business development challenge.	Positioning the project outcomes within the industry in general and management of academic expert work in particular.

management study, culminating in the break-even point analysis prepared before the new hose assembly manufacturing company was established.

Here the new ideas regarding the production control provided the key theory contribution. Unlike in Case 1, in this case the theory contribution was 'pulled out' by a specialist in product-centric control, and the theory contribution was based on the systematic analysis of the production control in the shop floor and how product-centric control was combined with visual inventory control based on Lean ideology. The theory contribution was positioned in the digital manufacturing genre. Interestingly, even though the automated hose cutting machines were simply 'saws,' the visual inventory control, resulting in no need for materials planning, enabled the factory to be run as if it consisted of several 3D printers. Thus, the factory concept provided some first insights on how additive manufacturing will affect not only manufacturing but also the control systems around it.

Case 3 has many similarities with Case 2, not only the context. Also in Case 3 the researchers played an important role in the idea generation process. Here, however, the first ideas were emerging from the hose assembly manufacturing processes. The use of mockups in communicating the value potential was tested before the case company was approached. The company, however, was not interested in that particular idea yet proposed two other customer problems to look into with the same approach, i.e., building mockups to be used also for time studies. The case, therefore, enabled the testing of the proposed approach and, therefore, argumentation of the theory contribution with two interesting cases. Thus, in a sense, the case can be seen as a theory testing case, though the theory to be tested was not based on a publication but on another case. This is another interesting opportunity a formal research team with a pool of companies in their back pocket can offer and should be utilized whenever possible. Furthermore, Cases 1–3 can be also seen to form a research stream focusing on the agile experiments in verifying value potential, though that was never argued as a contribution in Case 2 because of the small role it played in that particular case.

In Case 4 (Fastems), the starting point of the second research project was already the identified theory contribution potential. Indeed, the MA researchers interpreted the articulated need for tools and techniques in supporting manufacturing companies in their servitization initiatives (Baines et al. 2009; Laine et al. 2012) as a clear indicator for MA contribution potential in response to this need. The design of the second research project in this case took advantage of the previous research collaboration and the identification of this research gap. Therefore, the detailed execution plan of the second research project and, in particular, the details of the research interventions could be designed according to the plan of fulfilling the identified research gap. The objectives of the case company were in line with this idea, which as such confirms the existence of the contribution potential, with practical relevance embedded.

In Case 5, the initial steps related to techne had a normative dimension in it, with a clear link to CRA. In the process of building the managerial construct, the existing literature was used to provide (1) technical guidance regarding BSC and ABC (though these technical practices had to be modified significantly to meet sectoral and organizational demands) and (2) understanding of potential difficulties to be guarded against when implementing the accounting change. The normative element of the theory contribution was based on the long-term collaboration enabling not only a development and implementation of the construct but possibility to iterate it and analyze its feasibility, hence providing the arguments for a market test. To validate the market test, the functionality of the construct was emphasized, not only within the case organization but the 'botanical garden industry' and scientific organizations in general. The strong market test, in this case, was argued based on RGBE being able to increase their government funding at the expense of other scientific organizations as well as the awards granted by managerial organizations (such as CIMA).

Every empirical case presented in this book included reflections and analyses on the roles of the interventionist researchers involved in the IVR processes. Indeed, it is noteworthy that the emphasis on the three intellectual virtues tends to evolve during the IVR processes and vary from one case to another, and at the same time, also the roles of the researchers realizing the impact potential of the cases vary from one case to another, and essentially, also evolve over time. The five empirical cases suggest that in order to understand the impact of the case with respect to the three intellectual virtues (Lukka and Suomala 2014, in line with the idea of relevance by Rautiainen et al. 2017), one needs to understand the dynamics at a lower level in more detail, including the role of the interventionist researchers as actors (Laine et al. 2016). The interventionist researchers may take several different roles in actively identifying the relevant questions and supporting the response to those questions within the case setting. It is not only a matter of depth of the intervention as such, but active influence of the interventionist researcher makes the difference—both with respect to identifying relevant questions and responding to them. The openness to such dynamics during the IVR process makes a difference, as it potentially enables responding to the 'big questions' that could not have been formulated *a priori*, only based on a research gap analysis.

The roles given to and taken by the interventionist researchers varied a great deal, despite many similarities between the IVR processes of the cases. In this book, the researchers acted within a multidisciplinary research team, and the role of the MA researcher evolved from a comrade to an expert. Besides, the role of intervening researcher can be an integrator and facilitator, serving various development purposes within an organization, a network, an industry—or even the society as a whole. Remarkably, in addition to acknowledging the distinction between *etic* and *emic*, Case 3 presented in this book highlights the need to understand the interplay also within the *emic* level, thus driving innovation process in this particular case.

However, the roles of the MA researchers in this book do not represent an extensive list of potential roles. Instead, these roles and their examination together with the three intellectual virtues embedded in the cases highlight the need for detailed level analyses underlying the impacts and contribution potentials of IVR cases—to truly understand the 'value creation' within IVR processes (as a supplement to Suomala and Lyly-Yrjänäinen 2012).

Though normative theory contributions should be welcomed in MA, the most unique contribution potential of Case 5 lies within dialogue enabled by the new managerial construct within the case organization, the 'botanical garden industry,' and management control in scientific, expert organizations in general at the global level. The case contributes to many streams of literature, such as BSC and ABC as well as how the combinations of these two can add new perspectives on the theories on governance systems and strategy implementation as well as MA change, and the global access to empirics would make it unique. This contribution potential, however, still remains to be fully utilized.

Interventionist MA Research Projects with Societal Implications

This book has portrayed interventionist research as an approach or even more broadly as an 'ethos' of conducting empirical research so that active interaction and providing input to collaborating organizations is accepted as a virtue that can be leveraged for improving the quality of the research outputs and outcomes. The ethos of interventionist research can be summarized in two sentences as follows: "*Let's not restrict the means of understanding complex phenomena to those that require keeping distance to the primary objects of inquiry*" or "*Let's genuinely join forces between researchers and those being studied.*"

Through active interventionist interaction, the researchers can not only build solid and sound access to organizations, but also try to make sure that whatever data will be collected, its validity and reliability is at a high level. Consequently, we have put forward an argument that by adopting the ethos of IVR, it is possible to conduct interesting and meaningful research with a substantial impact on society. However, this is not to say that the sole subscription of IVR as an empirical research approach makes this all happen, but there are several issues and sub-questions that have to be resolved carefully for reaching good results both with respect to results and impacts:

- Selecting viable partners
- Carefully designing access strategy
- Acknowledging interfaces and connection both with respect to theory and practice

- Putting up a competent team
- Investing in management of empirical research process
- Active communication of results
- Building engagement both during and after the empirical process.

When looking at the societal implications of the five cases, the first case provided the societal implications without much effort, perhaps too conveniently. Thus, the lesson to learn regarding theory contribution with societal impact is to choose partners working on 'big questions.' Introducing robots and automation to home care is an important topic in developed countries with aging populations, and MA perspectives can provide interesting venues for societal debate. In general, finding cases focusing on contemporary disruptions impacting not only the industry practices but also the society more in general provides very interesting opportunities for MA researchers to contribute in the spirit of 'asking big questions,' as portrayed by Flyvbjerg (2001).

MA, in general, can be harnessed to investigate almost any phenomenon with many such interfaces having potential for theory contribution. However, simply connecting MA to aging populations and challenges in home care will not automatically result in wide societal implications; such a research setup has a risk of remaining in such a level of abstraction not raising interest outside MA academia. Nevertheless, when the big frame story (aging population) is connected to a smaller frame story (a service provider with an interesting robot solution), the research setup has become much more concrete and, therefore, provides potential for wider interest. The research setup, despite the societally relevant content, still has interesting potential for theory contribution and practical relevance to the participating organizations, hence making these three virtues not mutually exclusive. IVR has been considered a resource intensive way of doing research, especially when considering the workload needed for a publication (Jönsson and Lukka 2007); this case shows some ways how being receptive to the interesting events in the case may result in providing interesting outcomes in all the Aristotelian virtues without significant workload. Again, in this case the intervention was seen as an enabler of access to such an interesting event; if attempting to argue a framework developed by the researchers as a theory contribution, the workload and time frame most likely would have been different.

In Case 2, the societal implication was positioned more in the area of government research policy. As was pointed out by Scapens in his final editorial (2014), public sector funding agencies are likely to increasingly ask for practical or societal utility of research results. Even the projects funded by Finnish Funding Agency for Technology and Innovation (TEKES) are budgeted funding for diffusion of the research results within the industry and society; this funding does not mean scientific conferences and publications but rather pragmatic ways of impacting industry practices and society in more general. Various government agencies, for example, are concerned about the competitiveness of the nation, and research should at best provide tools for contributing to such discussions. What also makes this case interesting is the link to the additive manufacturing and the requirements it sets on the production control. In the end, production management theories have been designed mainly for subtractive manufacturing and assembly processes.

The theory contribution in Case 3 was based on how to use Lean experiments for verifying value propositions already at the early stages of the product development process. However, in addition to the theory contribution, it also contributed to the interest of Finnish Government and Finnish Funding Agency for Innovation (TEKES) to increasingly use such Lean processes in R&D, also outside the software and 'creative' industries. The machine construction industry and hydraulics industry within it have been rather conservative industries, and the successful implementation of such experimental culture provides a nice benchmarking point for many other fields. Furthermore, the MA perspective has provided a novel argument how the governmental research policy benefits the companies; such Lean experiments can play an important role not only in concept testing and customer feedback but linking the cost implications of customer benefits to the development process at the early stages.

In Case 4, the societal impact is related to the wider industrial phenomenon of servitization. By supporting companies aiming at greater international service businesses, the research both directly and indirectly affects the competitiveness of the machinery manufacturing industry in Finland. Direct impacts of the case are channeled through the MA subproject, the wider research program, and the network of the companies involved in the research activities at hand. Indirectly, as the theoretical and societal impacts of the case are intertwined, the theoretical contributions on the design and use of tools and techniques, e.g., means of MA, that would support servitization could affect the evolution of the industry in a broader sense. At the same time, however, Case 4 shows that practical development on accounting and control for R&D, and new service development drives theoretical development on the topic. Such practical development is also a prerequisite for remarkable societal impacts. This is in line with the observations in Cases 2–3, where new ideas and innovations remarkably drive the IVR process and its versatile implications.

The constructivist approach in Case 5 makes the societal impact somewhat different from the other cases. The construction itself (though modified to meet the needs of each organization) can add value to the governance systems in various botanical gardens around the globe, 1600 to be more precise. As a matter of fact, very few constructs developed in MA research projects have been provided such explicit potential for industry impact; at the same time it also provides some estimate regarding generalizability of the research results, even though that is not required in a case study. The other approach regarding the societal impact is the potential the construct has on governance practices (systems) in labor-intensive and intellectual-capital rich (scientific) expert organizations. This now resembles the contextual generalization and, unfortunately, giving such an explicit number no longer is possible.

Nevertheless, linking this case back to the final editorial of Scapens (2014), such governance tools may be seen more in the future in various government-funded scientific organizations, hence providing potential for wider societal implications. Thus, when the government spends money funding similar bodies, it and the society wish to know if the money is well spent, i.e., does it contribute to the achievements the government has set as well as the expectations of the society. By explicitly linking spending and performance to the government objective, other public-sector organizations may be able to provide justification for their public funding.

Based on the five cases presented in this book, we encourage connecting the IVR processes to the timely big questions in the society, at least to some extent. Answering such a big question could be a major driver of the case, as in Case 1, the implications to responding to the big question may emerge during the iterative IVR process (Cases 2–3), or the potential societal impact potential may go largely hand-in-hand with the articulated theory contribution potential (Cases 4–5). Our suggestion is, however, not to highlight the wider societal impact of IVR research at the cost of a detailed understanding of practice and feasible practical solutions (techne). Instead, as shown in Case 3 among others, deep understanding about the different *emic* viewpoints may lead to a position of a forerunner regarding a new kind of innovation process with remarkable societal impacts.

The concluding chapter of this book outlines the next generation of interventionist research, with an emphasis on responding to the big questions, through the engagement and commitment of actors with intentions and capabilities. Altogether, regarding societal impact of the interventionist MA research, we argue that practical innovations may have even greater impact on the society, if their (potential) implications to the big questions are continuously examined and critically assessed.

References

Baines, T., Lightfoot, H., Benedettini, O. and Kay, J., 2009. The servitization of manufacturing: A review of the literature and reflection on future challenges. *Journal of Technology Management*, 20(5), pp. 547–567.

Flyvbjerg, B., 2001. *Making social science matter: Why social inquiry fails and how it can succeed again.* Cambridge University Press, Cambridge.

Jönsson, S. and Lukka, K., 2007. There and back again: Doing IVR in management accounting, in: Chapman, C., Hopwood, A. and Shields, M. (Eds.), *Handbook of management accounting research*, Vol. 1. Elsevier, Amsterdam, pp. 373–397.

Laine, T., Korhonen, T., Suomala, P. and Rantamaa, A., 2016. Boundary subjects and boundary objects in accounting fact construction and communication. *Qualitative Research in Accounting and Management*, 13(3), pp. 303–329.

Laine, T., Paranko, J. and Suomala, P., 2012. Management accounting roles in supporting servitisation: Implications for decision making at multiple levels. *Managing Service Quality*, 22(3), pp. 212–232.

Lukka, K. and Suomala, P., (2014). Relevant interventionist research: Balancing three intellectual virtues. *Accounting and Business Research*, 44(2), pp. 1–17.

Rautiainen, A., Sippola, K. and Mättö, T. 2017. Perspectives on relevance: The relevance test in the constructive research approach. *Management Accounting Research*, 34, pp. 19–29.

Scapens, R., 2014. My final editorial. *Management Accounting Review*, 24(4), pp. 245–250.

Suomala, P. and Lyly-Yrjänäinen, J., 2012. *Management accounting research in practice: Lessons learned from an interventionist approach.* Routledge, New York.

Suomala, P., Lyly-Yrjänäinen, J. and Lukka, K., 2014. Battlefield around interventions: A reflective analysis of conducting interventionist research in management accounting. *Management Accounting Research*, 25(4), pp. 304–314.

Van de Ven, A. H. and Johnson, P. E., 2006. Knowledge for theory and practice. *Academy of Management Review*, 31(4), pp. 802–821.

10 Towards the Next Generation of Interventionist Research

A lot has happened and much learning has taken place over the years of practicing interventionist research in Management Accounting and in many other disciplines. Even though interventionist research is still not entirely mainstream as an approach or as a scientific 'ethos,' it's growing recognition and appreciation is clearly visible. It seems that more and more researchers are willing to subscribe to the idea that particularly in social sciences, empirical investigation does not have to be restricted to pure observation. Instead, there are situations and contexts within which a more active role of researcher is a legitimate and justified one.

Particularly in situations where a complex network of actors calls for systematic information production, coordinated and neutral external facilitation, critical analysis, fresh innovation power, or multidisciplinary expertise, interventionist research can be a powerful vehicle of advancing practice and society. As it comes to the dominant paradigms of the scientific community, this means willingness to emphasize more the researchers' role as actors instead of observers and analyzers—even though the latter ones are unquestionably part of scientific inquiry also in the future.

Thus, interventionist research could be considered as an approach with dual aims: one is to improve the validity and relevance of empirical research—and related scientific outputs such as publications—by introducing better connections between science and practice. Another is related to direct and powerful facilitation of change. The interventionist researcher is interested in helping to make the change—improvement to the state-of-the-art—to happen together with real-life organizations and other social actors.

This brings us to a discussion of values. Action is inherently a value-loaded activity. Either consciously or unconsciously, action always mobilizes a set of values. This is to say that an IVR researcher as an actor puts forward some values (at the cost of other 'competing' values) and thus interventionist research can never be entirely value-free activity. Although it can be debated whether any kind of research can actually be value-free—a mere selection of a research question is a sort of value statement—the connectedness with values is an unavoidable fact in interventionist research.

Our stance towards this issue is somewhat pragmatic: as values are inherently a part of interventionist endeavors, it means that there is no point to deny this and instead interventionist researchers should be as explicit as possible with the values that they deal with and subscribe to through their research. It also means that ethical considerations and critical reflections on the values that drive the research should be an elemental part of reporting interventionist research. This would also enable meaningful and balanced dialogue between pieces of work that represent competing or complementing set of values. Overall, in our view, the future of interventionist research could be much more explicit in its discussion of underpinning values.

The value dimension of IVR is not only an ethical question per se, but it is also directly related to the main theme of this book: the impact, and particularly the societal impact, of research. The better we are able to relate our scientific findings to the values that are perceived worth pursuing (or worth avoiding), the better the chances to actually connect the scientific work to the development of society—making a societal impact. The development of society is clearly not a mere fact-based linear process, but it is a value-based one. In that process, the facts produced by research can certainly play a part, but in our view it is far more likely to happen if the facts are understood and even tested in an appropriate value-based frame—in a real-life organization, network, or ecosystem that really deals with the same issues and questions as the research process does.

In this sense interventionist research is a proud step forward from the scientific worldview where a piece of research ends in a good publication (in a lucky case). Impactful interventionist research does not end in a publication (even if it is likely to produce those as well) but in a resolution of a both theoretically and societally intriguing dilemma. Or perhaps it is more accurate to say that we are hoping to be able to build a future world where research does not really end at something but goes on continuously in an intensive dialogue between companies, other social actors, and researchers.

In this world, the success of research is not measured by the number of answered research questions in publications but by the intensity and the quality of engagement between social actors during the process of seeking answers to meaningful and widely challenging social dilemmas. In this world, interventionist research is a powerful approach.

Index

For Product Safety Concerns and Information please contact our EU
representative GPSR@taylorandfrancis.com
Taylor & Francis Verlag GmbH, Kaufingerstraße 24, 80331 München, Germany

www.ingramcontent.com/pod-product-compliance
Ingram Content Group UK Ltd.
Pitfield, Milton Keynes, MK11 3LW, UK
UKHW020944180425
457613UK00019B/508